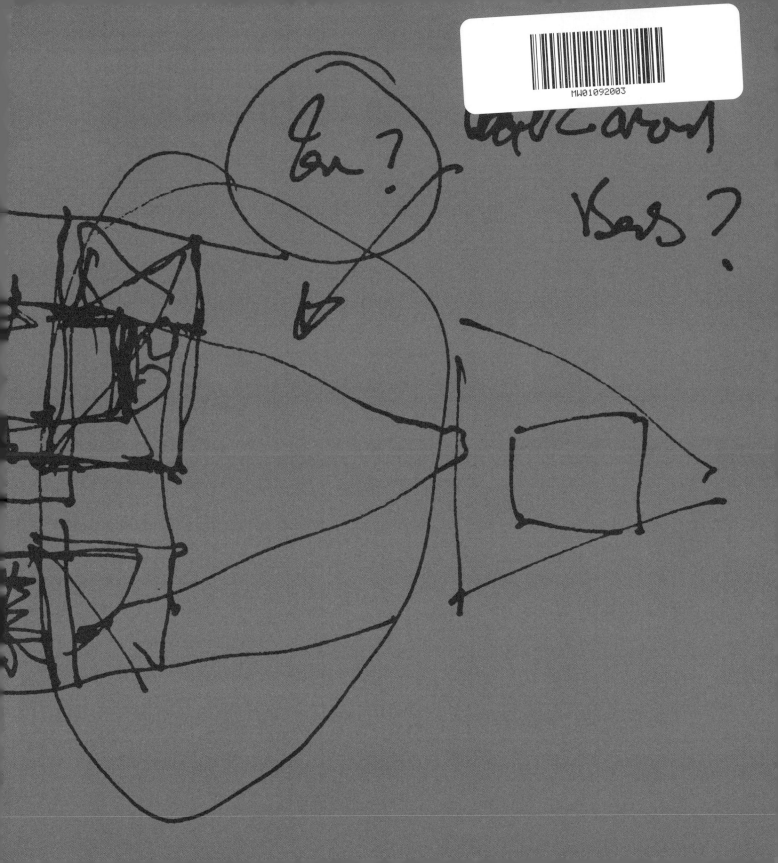

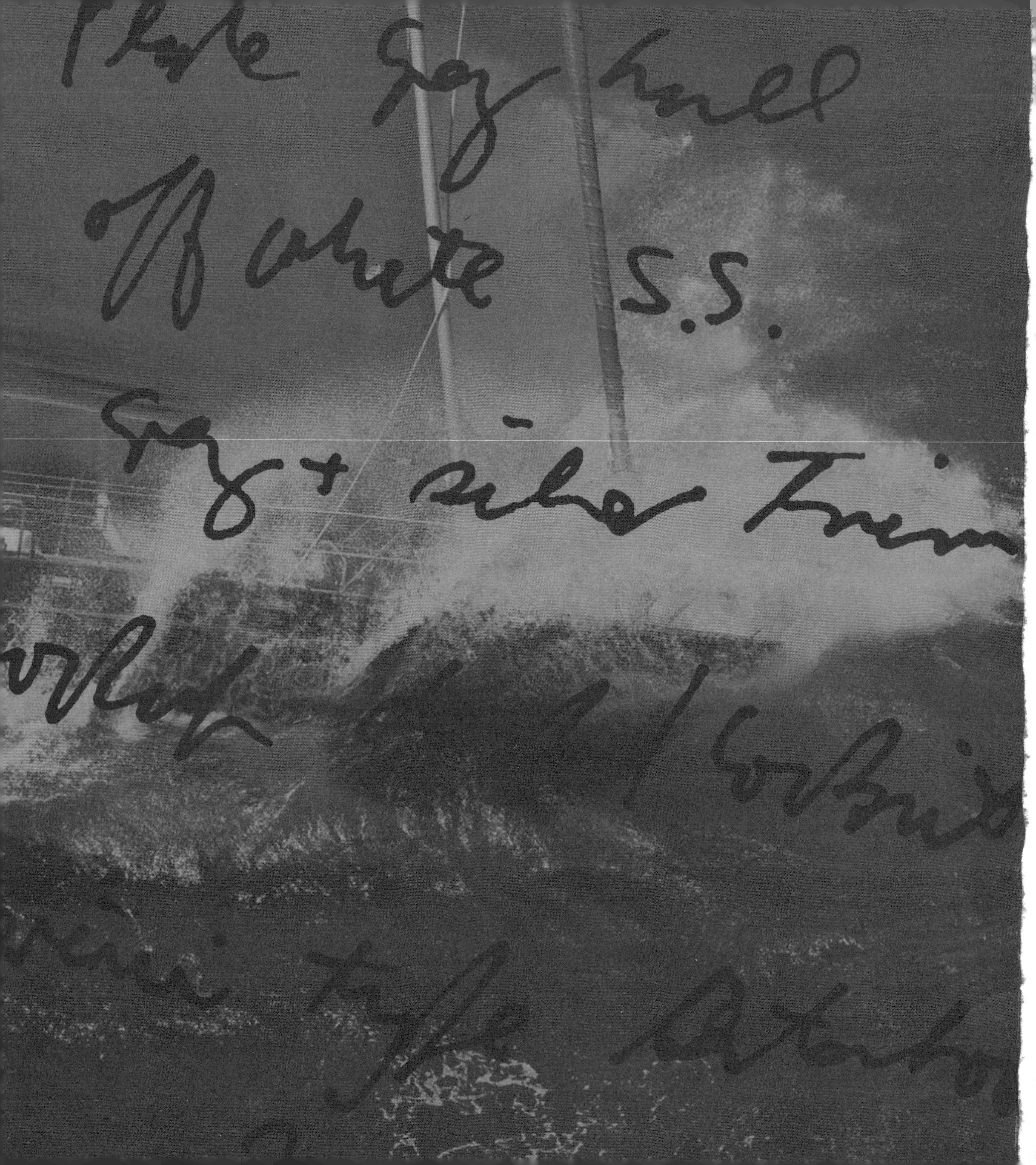

of white S.S.
grey + silver

All The Oceans

a memoir

All The

RON HOLLAND *designing by the seat of my pants*

Oceans

To my mentors, Sterling Hayden, Milton Miller,
Bears Kaufman, and for the next two generations.
My daughters, Kelly, Benna, Aisli and Nicola.
My grandchildren, Kiki, Lila, Chayten, Ariya and Saoirse.
The big lesson, just say yes!

She was a joy to sail

RUPERT MURDOCH

ALTHOUGH SOME PEOPLE MIGHT THINK I GREW UP with printing ink in my veins, which I did, there was also salt water. I learned my sailing as a boy and, as I grew older, I graduated to bigger yachts as most dinghy sailors do and ventured offshore. In 1964 my crew and I sailed my 54-foot (16-meter) ketch *Ilina* to second place across the line in the often wild Sydney to Hobart race. There's a black and white photograph of me and a happy-looking crew aboard *Ilina* after we had tied up at Constitution Dock in Hobart. To this day I'm proud of our performance. I did not race Sydney to Hobart again until 1995 when I stepped aboard Larry Ellison's maxi yacht *Sayonara* and promptly lost a fingertip to a flying rope. Many people think of sailing as a leisurely activity with endless sunbathing and cocktails on deck, but big yachts are extremely powerful and you've got to know what you're doing. Even experienced yachtsmen can run into trouble.

Some of my family inherited my love of sailing. My son Lachlan first raced the Sydney to Hobart on a yacht called *Karakoram* in 1997 and followed that up by joining Ellison aboard *Sayonara* in 2000 in a particularly rough year. I've never lost my love for

sail-powered rather than motor-powered boats and I've been lucky enough to own a succession of memorable yachts even though I've never really had the time to spend as long on them as I would have liked.

My first association with Ron Holland came with my purchase in 2006 of the beautiful *Rosehearty*, a 184-foot (56-meter) yacht that he had designed for the Perini Navi yard in Italy. My second Perini-built yacht, she was made of aluminium (my previous one was steel) and could fly off the wind, especially for such a big yacht. I named her after the village on the Moray Firth coast of Scotland in Aberdeenshire, home of the parents of my late father Sir Keith. With classic sheer line, overhangs and a flying bridge, she was an elegant-looking boat. I've always thought a yacht's interior should have a salty look and French designer Christian Liaigre did a wonderful job of combining the traditional with the contemporary. I owned *Rosehearty* for nearly ten years. A proper globe-girdling yacht, *Rosehearty* has a range of 3,600 nautical miles at a speed of 13 knots. My family, guests and I enjoyed many a happy voyage on her. She was a joy to sail.

▲

In 2002, Perini Navi commissioned Ron Holland Design to collaborate with their in-house design team. The goal was to marry Perini yacht styling with the sailing performance that Ron Holland Design was renowned for.

Rosehearty was the third of this series to be built, and over the next eight years seven more of these designs were completed, creating one of the most successful yacht building programs ever launched

Perini Navi committed to building three sailing yachts over 180 feet in length on speculation. It was an unimaginable program when Giancarlo Ragnetti introduced the idea.

of the

Start voyage

PART ONE

Flying Ant *Tempo* and P Class *Scarab* ready for voyaging on Torbay Beach.

Crucible

AS NIGHT CAME ON, the wind gradually dropped away to a whisper and I was becalmed in the middle of the main shipping lane. In the distance I could hear the throbbing of huge propellers, probably those of a freighter approaching down the channel. Fifty yards away a motor yacht chugged past, her lights reflecting on the glassy water. The air was so still I could hear snatches of conversation from on board.

I was getting scared. I was marooned and totally alone in my little sailing dinghy, a couple of miles from shore without any wind to get me home. Named *Tempo*, my dinghy was known as a Flying Ant, but she certainly wasn't flying.

I had set off that morning into the Hauraki Gulf, the sailing playground of my home city, Auckland, on what I imagined was a "voyage." Although I was only eleven years old, I had already been fascinated by stories about Ferdinand Magellan, Captain Cook, Vasco da Gama and other great explorers, and I imagined myself sailing gloriously in their wake – but I hadn't bargained on the morning's sailing conditions disappearing. Now there was a flat calm, and here I was drifting about aimlessly, waiting in vain for a breeze to return before the next freighter came along. I knew all too well that nobody on the bridge of a big ocean-going vessel would see my puny craft in the dark and she would be swamped, or worse, crushed to matchwood without anybody knowing. Nervously, I scanned the distant lights and checked that my life jacket was securely fastened.

Fighting down my fear, I tried to figure out what to do. For the first time in my brief sailing career I was frightened, and I thought of my mother who would be standing at the water's edge, looking out into the black and glassy ocean, worried sick fearing that this time her son had bitten off more than he could chew. I was more worried about Mum than any danger I felt I was in. I started to cry.

But after a time – I don't know how long – I had an idea. I can paddle, I told myself, anything to get out of the middle of this shipping lane. So I leaned over the side and began to stroke the boat towards a distant and dark coastline, steering in the direction of my home beach. After what seemed like hours, my arms aching from the paddling, I was close enough to the shore to pick out individual bays in the gloom. At last, to my relief I saw the Christmas lights that had been erected on the tall Norfolk pines standing on Browns Bay, close to my destination of Torbay. Sore as my arms were, my hopes rose and I redoubled my efforts. Taking care not to run into a couple of treacherous reefs, invisible in the gloom, that could easily rip a hole in my wooden boat, I gradually closed in on land until I could pick out Torbay quite clearly and identify the lights of the houses on the cliffs above it; and down on the beach, another light being waved in the darkness.

It was after midnight when I reached the shore in a state of near exhaustion and collapsed onto the sand. Sure enough, it was my mother who had been shining a flashlight out to sea, and I will never forget the relief on her face when she saw me. I suspect she must have been in tears, but instead of scolding me, as most mothers would, she helped me drag *Tempo* up the beach and lift her onto the trailer before driving me home.

This experience cured me of my long-distance "voyaging," but not for long. Looking back from the perspective of a life afloat, I still have no firm idea why I took to the sea. I just fell in love with it, with its promise of adventure, and I was fascinated with sailing ships.

I was lucky to have grown up in the 1950s in New Zealand. One of my first memories of being on the water came as a passenger on the wooden ferry boats that plied up and down the harbor on a regular timetable, before the Auckland Harbour Bridge was opened and put the ferries out of business, at least for a while. I liked to stand in the bow on the lower deck, getting wet and watching the waves surging past.

My father Philip was a self-taught dental technician, an actor, and a handy part-time trombonist who played on weekends in a band, sometimes with his brothers and brother-in-law. For amateurs, they played pretty good dance music and jazz in an era when you had to make your

own fun. My mother, Gwen, was a busy housewife caring for her two sons, me and my younger brother who was also known as Phil, and helping in Dad's home business making acrylic false teeth, Luxure Tooth Industries. But she had a musical streak too, and I remember her playing a mean four-string ukulele in the ladies' bar of the nearby Albany pub. Dad was on the road a lot and we hardly saw him for a few years. During that time my mother must have had trouble making ends meet, because when she landed a job in a hotel and had to work long hours to support us, Phil and I were put into St. Joseph's Orphanage for Boys, an experience I hated.

Both of my parents were landlubbers who didn't really know the sharp end of a boat from the blunt one, but at the age of six I expressed an interest in being given a dinghy for my seventh birthday present. I still don't really know why I wanted a boat, except perhaps because I saw Mum's father going fishing, or other boys of my age on the beach and out on the water in boats, and it seemed like a good idea to join them. To my surprise both Mum and Dad were in full support and somehow found the money to buy me a dinghy.

But when I was presented with the boat for which I'd been pleading, perversely I was deeply upset. They'd given me a sailing dinghy and I'd wanted a rowing dinghy! Somehow I'd learned that sailing dinghies capsized, and here I was saddled with a P Class, the snub-nosed boat in which most budding young sailors in New Zealand learned to race, but which

When the Auckland Harbour Bridge opened in 1959 I was 12 years old, and my life changed. We stopped using the ferry boats to get to Auckland City, and beyond to Hillsborough Road to visit Nanna and Uncle Bill. I missed the ferry ride across the harbor, but I had replaced it by being "at sea," with winning yacht races off Torbay and Browns Bay and long-distance sailing across the main shipping channel to Rangitoto Island.

The photo of the bridge and Auckland City beyond also shows the *William C. Daldy* under full steam, getting ready for the 2017 Auckland Regatta tugboat races. During the five-year bridge construction period the *William C. Daldy* held station in a gale, with critical bridge parts, for 36 hours. Here she is over 60 years later, still going strong.

My earliest memories (about 4 years of age) are of living with Mum and Nanna as we knew her (our Grandma, Mum's Mother) at 40 Hillsborough Road. Then Philip and I were in St. Joseph's Orphanage for Boys, across Auckland Harbour near Takapuna, before moving to remote Torbay. After leaving Hillsborough Road I started writing back to Nanna with sketches.

looked to me to be dangerously tippy. The P Class had a pocket-handkerchief of a sail, and a tiny shallow cockpit into which you squeezed with hardly any room to spare. Also, as I would soon learn, my boat was made of solid kauri, the native New Zealand wood, so she was quite heavy. She also had an old-fashioned gunter rig – that is, you attached the sail, a cotton one in my case, to a mast that came in two parts, and you hauled the upper part to the top of the bottom one to set the sail. Another thing I would soon learn was that gunter rigs were already outmoded.

My baptism into sailing confirmed my worst fears. Although Dad probably knew as much about sailing as I did – which was nothing – he insisted on taking me to Blockhouse Bay on Auckland's windy west coast rather than the east coast where the winds and waters were kinder. With both of us jammed into the cockpit, and me enveloped in an outsize "Mae West" life jacket, there was hardly room to move, and Dad was far too big to duck under the wooden boom. So whenever we tacked the boom would bang him on the head. It must have hurt, and we floundered around in the cockpit trying to get the boom across while I was terrified we were going to end up in the drink.

Things went from bad to worse and the inevitable happened: we tried to tack once too often and we both got stuck under the boom, the wind caught on the wrong side of the sail, and the boat capsized. I fell out of the cockpit and started thrashing around in freezing, dirty-looking water, yelling for Mum to come and rescue me. In retrospect, this didn't make much sense because I could have floated around the harbor for a week in my huge life jacket without coming to any harm. It was a couple of local fishermen who saved the day. Spotting our predicament, they hauled me out of the water into their (much bigger) dinghy while Dad managed to get my P Class back upright after a bit of a struggle, climbed aboard and followed me and the fishermen back to the beach.

One memory remains vivid in my mind: as we approached the shore and safety, I looked back at the little boat I thought I didn't want, and suddenly wished I had stayed aboard with Dad. I wanted to be back aboard my boat, and I believe that was the start of my lifetime of sailing.

Nevertheless, the incident put me off for the rest of the summer, and instead of learning how to sail what had become my pride and joy, I just pushed and towed the P Class around in knee-deep water with a rope attached to the bow as though she were a toy. My imagination running wild, I convinced myself I was Captain Cook and my boat was the *Endeavour* and I was exploring the New Zealand coast, just like the great navigator had nearly 200 years earlier. By then we'd given my dinghy a name – *Kahu*,

▲

Brother Philip sailing our first yacht *Kahu* off Torbay. Built with a heavy kauri wood hull and setting a cotton mainsail on the old-fashioned gunter rig, *Kahu* was not the latest in racing technology! We learned to sail her setting us firmly on the path of a sailing life, a life on all the oceans.

a native New Zealand bird – the same name my Grandpa had used for his small fishing boat.

My life brightened up after I turned seven. Philip and I were taken out of St. Joseph's after a few months, and the whole family moved to Torbay on the calmer east coast of Auckland. Instead of just towing *Kahu* around in the shallows, I soon began to race her, and to my and probably my parents' surprise, I began to win races. Soon people began to see me as a natural yachtie, which did a lot for my confidence. In their enthusiasm to support me, Mum and Dad allowed me to store *Kahu* in the living room of our small house during the winter, so she would dry out and become lighter for the next racing season. But she was still too slow to be truly competitive and inevitably I wanted a faster boat. My parents dug even deeper – I can't imagine how they found the money on the family's limited income – and they bought another newer and lighter P Class for me while Philip inherited *Kahu*. My second boat was made of lighter plywood, and instead of the gunter rig, she had a more efficient Marconi rig with the latest Terylene mainsail that you hauled straight up to the top of the single mast. I named her *Scarab* after a sailing dinghy featured in the book *Swallows and Amazons* by Arthur Ransome, a tale of kids' adventures in England's Lake District and on the Norfolk Broads that totally entranced me.

By now the whole family had thrown itself into sailing, and on week-day evenings after school and on weekends we spent most of our time down on the beach at the Torbay Boating Club. I look back on those times with very happy memories as well as a sense of gratitude. I lived for those hours on the beach.

When I say club, that's a bit of an exaggeration. In reality the Torbay Boating Club was originally more of a drinking den for fishermen who liked to get together for a few beers in a corrugated iron shed. Later there were no permanent facilities of any kind – no clubhouse, no storage for the boats, no trailer ramp, no starting tower – practically nothing that would normally be associated with a sailing club. On race days we simply pushed our dinghies across an often-busy road, dodging the traffic as we headed to the beach where we would rig up, and register with volunteer officials sitting at tables in a canvas tent. But there were a lot of willing helpers, mostly mums and dads, and one day my father, who had become extremely enthusiastic about the sport and the drinking club, organized a working bee of volunteers to build a concrete ramp – and it's still there today. Some of the men knew a bit about sailing and they gave us tips about how to tack and gybe, how to "tune" the mast and sail for different wind conditions, how to handle our craft in the sometimes wild easterlies

▲

Getting ready to race. My new
Flying Ant, *Tempo* FA4, together
with a P Class and a selection of
bigger racing dinghies, on Waiaki
Beach, Torbay. This is where I lived
during daylight hours between
the ages of 8 and 12 years. Then I
went sailing in deeper waters.

"There's an informal code in sailing, a kind of ethos of fairness which is understood right around the world, and I acquired its rudiments right there on the beach at Torbay under the guidance of Gary Corkin."

that brought big sweeping waves into the bay, and how to wash the salt off our boats and stow them away after a day on the water.

I owe a lot to all of these people, but one man I particularly remember was Gary Corkin. I was in love with his younger sister, Sharon. A stickler for good behavior afloat, he gave his first unofficial sailing clinic at the club in the late 1950s, and would go on to a successful army career in Washington, DC, before returning to New Zealand and developing advanced coaching programs. Back then he gave himself the job of teaching us the written rules of racing, and the unwritten ones of good behavior when on the water. At the time I couldn't see the point in some of this, but Gary insisted that we know the rules, and much later in my sailing life I learned how right he was. There's an informal code in sailing, a kind of ethos of fairness which is understood right around the world, and I acquired its rudiments right there on the beach at Torbay under the guidance of Gary Corkin.

If the definition of a club is a community of people engaged in a worthwhile project, then Torbay Sailing Club, as it became, was exactly that in the full sense of the term. All the work was done by volunteers, mothers and other helpers who used to spend Fridays toiling at the oven, baking cakes and scones for the kids when they came ashore famished. I can still remember that keen sense of hunger brought on by the salt air. The enthusiasm became infectious, and soon busy people thought nothing of giving up half their weekends to help a bunch of kids go out on the water. With each passing year my father devoted more and more time to the club, and became so proud of its evolution that he took 8mm movies of all this activity on the beach. Like the concrete ramp that's still in use, occasionally they're still showing Dad's amateur film productions at the club today.

I didn't know it at the time, but the Torbay Boating Club was turning into the crucible of my lifelong career in sailboats, and it happened in a number of unexpected ways. At the suggestion of Dad who would become the club's first life member, a lanky red-bearded man often volunteered to help organize classes and races for Kids' Sailing, as it was known. He was a boat designer and builder by the name of John Spencer, who worked out of a small shed in Browns Bay nearby. He lived with his wife Anne right on the beach with a couple of small kids, the perfect location for a home as far as I was concerned. As my interest in sailing developed I used to haunt John Spencer's boat shed, usually dropping in after school and chatting with him and the people, some of them his clients, who often gathered there for an after-work beer and a chitchat about yachts. John, as I came to know him, loved to talk, and it was almost always about boats. I lapped up every single word. And there were lots of them!

If the adults were too busy to talk to us kids, there was always a pile of British and American boating magazines that we could read, and I devoured these too. Sometimes I was told to "Get busy" and given a broom to sweep the wood shavings off the dirt floor, a job that made me feel part of it all.

By this time I had outgrown my lightweight P Class. At a mere seven feet, not much longer than a bathtub, the design was unsuited to sailing downwind because it was too short and beamy to sit up on the waves and plane – that is, to skim fast over the surface of the water – as the newer designs could do. Also, with just the one sail, the P Class wasn't as interesting as a boat that had a mainsail and a jib and a spinnaker, like the Flying Ant, the dinghy John was designing and that I now coveted.

Way ahead of his time, John Spencer had designed the Ant as a stepping-stone from the P Class to the all-out racing dinghies like the Cherub (another of his designs), the unrestricted 12-footers and the R Class – probably the most advanced racing dinghies in the world at that time. He had drawn up the plans with me and some of my friends from Torbay in mind. I enjoyed the feeling of being involved in the design process. I became the proud owner of the second Flying Ant ever launched, naming her *Tempo* after my growing interest in music and playing the drums. My older cousin Kevin Holland jumped at the chance to crew with me. After the P Class, she was a thrill a minute.

▲

The cartoon shows various Torbay sailing kids, including the Holland brothers and Mark Bethwaite. Mark soon moved with his family to Australia where he kept winning races, twice representing Australia at the Olympic Games. The Bethwaite family continues to have a real influence on performance dinghy sailing: Mark's younger brother Julian, too young to race with us at Torbay, designed a current Olympic class, the 49er skiff-type racing dinghy.

And I suppose that's exactly what I was looking for – thrills – and sometimes racing dinghies just didn't give me enough of them. When the easterly gales blew directly onto Torbay Beach and brought the big breaking waves with them, I and three mates liked to jump aboard a newer, bigger sailing dinghy called an OK. The first of its kind in New Zealand, this high-performance, Danish-designed dinghy was a junior version of the Olympic Finn-class dinghy. The property of the Kendalls, another local boating family, she was intended to be sailed by just one fully-grown person. She had a single unstayed wooden mast that bent like a straw in the wind, and with four aboard we reckoned we had equal odds of taking on even the strongest winds.

Getting off the beach was the trickiest bit because the waves pounded straight into the little bay, tossing the moored boats around so violently that it was not unusual for one or two to drag their moorings and run aground, leaving them high and dry when the tide turned. But after a few abortive attempts we developed a slick routine.

Three of us would push the dinghy out into breaking waves, trying to hold her steady enough for the fourth to hop aboard and lower the centerboard and rudder, and then grab hold of the tiller. When the pushers were up to their waists in the breaking waves, somebody would yell "go!" and we'd all scramble aboard. One of the crew would grab the mainsheet, and that was the signal for all of us to lean out against the wind as far as we dared, to prevent the dinghy tipping over. If we got through the first breaker or two without being swamped, we were on our way. Then we'd steer a course past the yachts swinging wildly on their moorings and battle out past the Sugarloaf, the dumpy little island located just off the cliffs, and into the deeper waters of the bay.

Our destination was a reef about a mile off Browns Bay. When we got there we'd tack, a tricky maneuver to pull off in wild conditions. The key was for everybody to duck under the boom simultaneously, but without getting in each other's way. If the timing wasn't perfect, we'd be upside down and swimming in a second. But if we were successful, we'd jump on the windward deck again and head back for the beach, crashing and planing through the wave crests, screaming with excitement and fear, spray flying into our faces.

Throughout all these escapades I never remember my mother trying to stop us. Her advice was always the same: "Wear your lifejacket, Ronnie, and be careful."

So, after I'd recovered from my experience of being marooned in the middle of the main shipping lane – and it didn't take long – I returned to

▶

I was lucky to be born in Auckland. Protected waters, islands, beaches and boats everywhere. From my earliest recollection I was always fascinated with maps. I loved looking at the topographical representation of the land and sea. Still do.

Here I show my earliest overnight passages. I'm trying to keep up with Captain Cook!

MAP LEGEND
—— *Aloha*
—— *Happy Daze*
—— *Haze*
—— *Tempo*

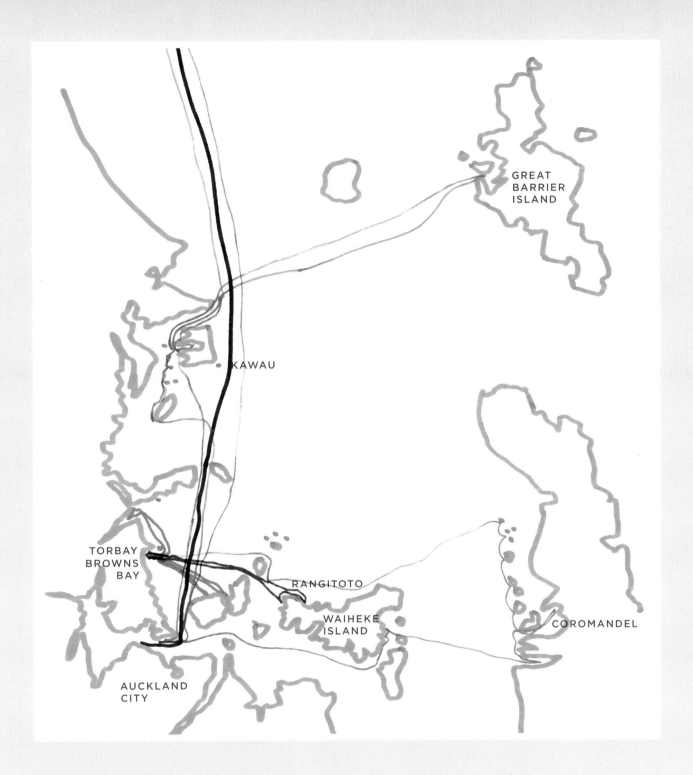

GREAT
BARRIER
ISLAND

KAWAU

TORBAY
BROWNS
BAY

RANGITOTO

WAIHEKE
ISLAND

COROMANDEL

AUCKLAND
CITY

"So after a short but eventful dinghy racing career of five years in total, in the summer of 1958 I found myself sailing around the Gulf aboard *Haze*, the clouds of sail that made her a handful in a blow."

cruising my Flying Ant, including attempting a few more of my "voyages" right across the channel to Rangitoto Island, a dormant volcano and a famous Auckland landmark.

I think I must have been restless in nature because I even began to tire of *Tempo*.

Kevin and I had a lot of success racing her, but the sparkling blue waters and the islands of the Hauraki Gulf now beckoned. I wanted to do some proper voyaging, so at the age of 13 I shipped aboard an 18-footer called *Haze* and went cruising for the first time to some of the islands of the Gulf.

Owned by Brian Holgate, a local panel-beater and automobile painter, *Haze* was a Mullet Boat design, one of a class that had originated from flat-bottomed fishing boats that had lifting centerboards, so they were able to sail in shallow waters. I had seen *Haze* moored up Torbay Creek and she was the biggest boat there, which for some reason attracted me to her. I got to know Brian, and in exchange for helping paint *Haze* in the winter months he signed me up for my first overnight cruise, all the way to Waiheke, an island that wasn't visible from Torbay. I suppose that was an attraction too, the freedom to sail out of sight.

After this first cruise I was hooked. When I told my parents that I was, in effect, turning my back on the Torbay Boating Club, instead of telling me how ungrateful I was after all the work they'd put in, they just said, "Well Ron, we understand that you need to go exploring." I wonder how many parents would react like that today? Somehow the *New Zealand Herald*, the national newspaper, got wind of this 13-year-old adventurer, and a reporter came to interview me around this time for a story that bore the headline, quoting my mother, "The Sea is His Life." Looking back, I think my first publicity got it right.

So after a short but eventful dinghy racing career of five years in total, in the summer of 1958 I found myself sailing around the Gulf aboard *Haze*, with the clouds of sail that made her a handful in a blow. Many a time I was sent below to bail like a madman, as *Haze* took on so much water straight over the side that she threatened to "go gurgle", in the sometimes unique language of the Mullety Boys. It wasn't unknown for a racing Mullet Boat to fill up and turn turtle – one skipper painted *SOS* on the bottom of the hull of his boat, partly for a joke and partly just in case.

The Mullet mob were a bit notorious, frowned on by the more staid members of the Auckland yachting fraternity, and we got into a few scrapes, usually when we'd downed too many beers. (Big for my age, I managed to get myself – no problem – into most of the pubs dotted up and down the coast.) The entire fraternity was banned from some anchorages, most infamously for a time from Mansion House Bay, Kawau Island, the historic home of the first Governor of New Zealand and the favorite destination of all local yachties. The ban happened after a number of Mullet Boats arrived after racing from Auckland, their crews tired and hungry but too late to find food ashore, and – I don't quite know how it started – the crews ended up in the hen coop looking for a nice chicken or two to cook for dinner. In no time we were charging around the coop chasing squawking hens, whooping and yelling amid flying feathers, until somebody eventually turned up to see where all the noise was coming from. In short order we got banished back to the boats. It wasn't always the Mullety Boys who caused all the trouble, but we seemed to get the blame. For a kid it was a real eye-opener and I loved it.

When Brian bought a bigger 20-footer, a "keeler" called *Happy Daze,* we started racing on Friday nights into the islands of the Gulf. We'd row out to the yacht (this was before any yacht marinas were built) in a tiny dinghy loaded with our weekend supplies, which mostly consisted of cases of beer, and set off just before dark. Around dawn we'd end up at some beautiful sheltered anchorage, and the crews would get together on the beach for barbecues and beer and singing. After sleeping it off on Saturday night, we'd sail back to Auckland Harbour on Sunday.

Fun as all this was, it wasn't all drinking and carousing. I spent a lot of time on the beach talking with some of Auckland's best yachties, discussing

▲

At 20 feet in length *Happy Daze* was small, but that did not stop us from long distance cruising and racing. Brian and I sailed her one summer from Auckland to Manganui, in Doubtless Bay on New Zealand's far northeast coast.

My first taste of celebrity: a small story, my first in the *New Zealand Herald* after I started sailing further away from home.

Sea is his life

After spending most of this spare time over many months listening to the tales of visiting yachtsmen at St Mary's Bay, 15-year-old Ron Holland, of Torbay, sailed last week for Australia as a member of the crew of Ian Rabbitt's 36ft ketch Aloha.

Ever since he could read, says his mother, Mrs Phil Holland, only one kind of book went into Ron's bookshelves. They were about cruising or passage making in yachts or sailing ships.

Ever since he was old enough to have a hobby, only boats pleased him. He has owned P-class and Flying Ant-class centreboarders, and he has sailed and cruised locally in mullet boats and keelers.

And ever since hs has attended St Paul's College, Richmond Road, the shipyards at Westhaven and St Mary's Bay have been "on the way home".

A recent thrill, says Mrs Holland, was when Ron met and made friends with Kurt Ashford, the Seattle yachtsman who this year sailed single-handed to New Zealand in the little sloop Sea-Wyff — a performance Ron hopes to emulate one day.

While visiting Sea-Wyff Ron lent a hand to re-fit the Aloha, which was moored nearby. Ian Rabbitt, the owner, was impressed and

Ron Holland

offered him a place in the crew, subject to his parents' permission.

"What could I say?" said Mrs Holland. "Adventure in small craft, sailing ships and deepwater cruising is an obsession with him. Nothing else matters.

"In the back of my mind there is always a niggling worry when Ron is in small ship with a lot of ocean beneath it, but I couldn't refuse him. When I hesitated, he just said: " 'Mum, I'm sorry, I can't help it. The sea is my life.' "

designs and rigs and everything else that goes into a good racing yacht. Instead of telling this curious kid to get lost and leave them alone, as might happen in more formal yachting circles, they seemed happy to share their knowledge with me, and even at this distance I can remember a lot of people from whom I learned so much. Perhaps they recognized how interested I was – I don't really know – but I certainly absorbed it all like a sponge.

Soon *Happy Daze* was sailing further and further up and down the east coast of the North Island, racing bigger yachts and exploring bays and inlets every weekend. Sometimes there were just two of us – Brian and me – while on other occasions my cousin and ex-Flying Ant crew, Kevin, would join us as the third crewmember. These were also some of the best years of my life, until once again I became hungry for even bigger adventures.

To my parents' consternation, my schooling had become an irrelevance, a resented interruption to the rest of my life. In the classroom my mind was elsewhere, dreaming of the next cruise, thinking about Captain Cook or *Swallows and Amazons*. By now I was in secondary school, at St. Paul's College in Auckland City, which involved a daily bus ride across the new Auckland Harbour Bridge from where I could look down at the boats moored behind the Westhaven breakwater.

I had no interest whatsoever in academic work and had already failed School Certificate, the all-important nationwide exam that could determine the success or otherwise of your entire working career. Although I had won a lot of races on my own account in the dinghies and was turning into an able crewmember on bigger boats, I had no confidence in myself in the classroom, and it had always been like that. All the way through primary and intermediate school I was regarded as a bit of a dunce because I had difficulty learning to read and write. It didn't help that I saw no sense in arithmetic, especially algebra, or in bookkeeping, both of which were on the curriculum. Although I could see the point in spelling and learning the times tables off by heart, I couldn't master either of these. The only subjects I enjoyed were art and drawing at which I excelled – top of the class in fact – but overall I have to say I was an academic disappointment, to put it mildly.

My mother did all she could to encourage me, and with great personal effort she dragged me to one remedial reading expert after another. Nothing worked until she was directed to a woman called Marie Clay, who, to my mum's relief, was willing to take on this hopeless case. She gave me special reading lessons at the kitchen table of her house overlooking Murrays Bay, with its big windows providing a panoramic view of the Hauraki Gulf, my favorite sailing waters. This was a lot more fun than sitting in the classroom feeling like a failure.

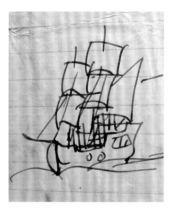

▲

Another example of my earliest drawing and my fascination with square riggers. Still am fascinated! I could never have imagined then that I eventually would have multiple opportunities to sail aboard the US Coast Guard barque *Eagle*.

►

If you love maps and charts this one is special, especially for a New Zealander. Still amazingly accurate, it shows the first circumnavigation of the three principal New Zealand islands. With Joanna, Aisli, Nikki and crew John and Fizz Matla, I sailed my *Golden Opus* into Ship Cove in the Marlborough Sounds where Captain Cook had anchored during his voyages of discovery. This was a special afternoon.

Intuitively Mrs. Clay quickly figured out the key to unlocking my hidden love of learning. Her insight was that I would be happy to read if I were interested enough in the subject, and it didn't take her long to figure out what that subject was. So I took my first few tentative steps in reading by devouring stories about Captain James Cook exploring the Pacific, and about the adventures of other men and women risking their lives by crossing oceans in small cruising yachts. Mrs. Clay realized she had something to build on.

Then she stunned me by producing a massive tome, a naval textbook, as my reading material. You would think that this intimidating volume, which belonged to her husband who happened to be in the Royal New Zealand Navy, would put me off books for life. Far from it; I lapped it up. As long as a book was about ships and boats, I was riveted. So, thanks to my wonderful teacher, I became a "bookworm," albeit without ever mastering spelling. I'm eternally grateful to Marie Clay and I have never forgotten her. Deservedly, she went on to become the first woman on the University of Auckland faculty and is now internationally renowned for her work.

Having discovered reading, I couldn't stop. The only problem was that I wasn't reading the prescribed school texts, because they just didn't seem relevant. Once again, to my parents' frustration, I continued to behave as badly at St. Paul's as I had at Murrays Bay Intermediate School, where I had gained the sorry distinction of collecting the record number of "straps" in a single term – a total of 32. The pain of taking a wallop with a length of hard leather on your hand, held rigidly out sideways to give the teacher a better aim and leverage, just didn't seem to have any effect. All too soon I was back for more, so nothing had changed much by the time I was enrolled at St. Paul's, a more serious establishment, where I was often caned on my bottom with a whippy length of bamboo. This was for a wide variety of misdemeanors, one of which was throwing an empty dustbin at another pupil, just as one of the teaching brothers came around the corner to witness my delinquent behavior. The cane is much more painful than the strap, but yet again the punishment had no discernible result. I continued to dream of sailing, girlfriends and playing drums in a band, something I did most weekends, having inherited my father's talent for music.

Patient and loving, my mother encouraged me in this too. She often took me to concerts in the Auckland Town Hall to hear performances by touring legends, and I fell in love with all kinds of jazz music, especially that of Duke Ellington, Bix Beiderbecke, Dave Brubeck and Louis Armstrong. I was always the youngest kid in the hall. After years of practicing

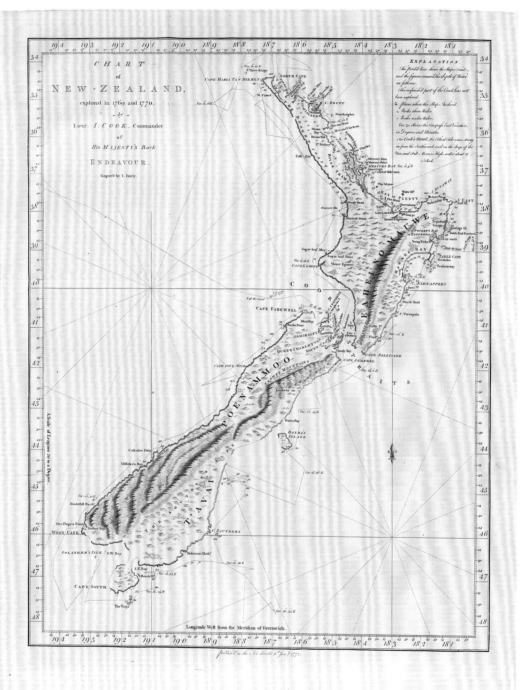

CHART
of
NEW-ZEALAND,
explored in 1769 and 1770,
~ by ~
Lieut: J. COOK, Commander
of
His MAJESTY'S Bark
ENDEAVOUR.

Engrav'd by I. Bayly.

EXPLANATION

Longitude West from the Meridian of Greenwich.

A Scale of Leagues 20 to a Degree.

Published as the Act directs 1.st Jan.y 1772.

"Humiliatingly, I was kept in the same class at St. Paul's two years in a row to face my second attempt at School Certificate. I can remember the embarrassment when my classmates went up a year and I stayed where I was. But it was sailing in some form or another that always rescued me and, smelly and rough as it was, the Westhaven Cement Silo dock became my salvation."

drums on cardboard boxes and tables (I damaged a lot of tables), I finally acquired a proper set of drums, and in my early teens I was doing small gigs in local dance halls with my pianist friend Wayne Bickerstaff. My drumming was heavily influenced by the band The Shadows, but Wayne could play just about anything, and to our surprise we ended up second in a talent concert run by the Auckland Catholic Youth Centre. Although years under the minimum drinking age, we managed to find a few bottles of DB Draught to celebrate the occasion.

I continued to head downhill at a rapid rate, academically speaking. Humiliatingly, I was kept in the same class at St. Paul's two years in a row to face my second attempt at School Certificate. I can remember the embarrassment when my classmates went up a year and I stayed where I was. But it was sailing in some form or another that always rescued me and, smelly and rough as it was, the Westhaven Cement Silo dock became my salvation. As often as I could, I would drop by after school and look for new cruising yacht arrivals from the Pacific Islands, with whose crewmembers I might strike up a conversation about their voyages and their boats. Some of these yachtsmen must have seen me as a bit of a nuisance, but most of them welcomed me and invited me aboard, wide-eyed, getting aboard a foreign yacht to talk about their experiences in oceans I'd only read about.

That's how I met three twenty-something guys who had sailed in from Sydney on a little double-ender called *Carronade*. I'd heard about *Carronade* and Ron Swanson, a Sydney boat designer and builder. Successful on the Australian racing circuit including the Sydney Hobart Race, *Carronade* had sisters that were winning important races. *Carronade* was a little yacht but she was going a long way. The three Aussies were all mates – Andy Wall, Ken Mills and Des Kearns – and they were planning to sail her around Cape Horn as soon as they left New Zealand. I also couldn't help noticing they had no problem getting good-looking girls to help them do chores aboard the yacht.

Cape Horn! I could hardly believe it. For me this was the stuff of dreams, and on several visits to *Carronade* I was able to get to know them well enough to be invited out on a few jaunts around the Waitemata Harbour. On one of these trips, I was told many years later, I had the audacity to suggest a few modifications they could make to improve the performance of the yacht. Apparently, after I'd gone home after one such outing they discussed my willingness to give advice. "Maybe this punk can really sail," one of them said.

I was certain of one thing: this was the life I wanted to live.

Around this time, I heard that the great British cruising yachtsman and author Eric Hiscock and his wife Susan were in port with their yacht *Wanderer III*. One of the favorite books on the shelf in my bedroom (and it still is 58 years later!) was *Voyaging Under Sail*, an account of the Hiscocks' globe-girdling cruises that Mum had given me for Christmas, and I had devoured every word and studied every photo, diagram and yacht design in its pages. Even at the age of 12 I was getting interested in design. The book also contained much technical detail, and I knew parts of it practically off by heart. So when I heard that the couple's yacht was tied up in Auckland Harbour, it was too good an opportunity to miss. I grabbed my copy of the book, caught a bus after school down to Victoria Park, walked to the Westhaven breakwater where most cruising yachts parked after crossing the Pacific, and borrowing a dinghy, rowed out to *Wanderer III*'s moorings to get the great man's autograph.

Although he must have been surprised to see this kid pop up over the side of his yacht, Eric Hiscock received me courteously and gave me an hour of his time while I quizzed him about sailing through the Pacific Islands. He signed my book and I got back into the dinghy and rowed back to shore, a very happy boy.

Perhaps I should blame the influence of Eric Hiscock for what happened next.

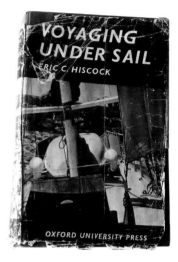

▲

A Christmas gift from Mum: a well-traveled book. For 60 years I have kept it with me, and it's still in my bookcase. 58 years have passed since I rowed out to Eric Hiscock and *Wanderer III* in Westhaven Harbour and asked him to sign it.

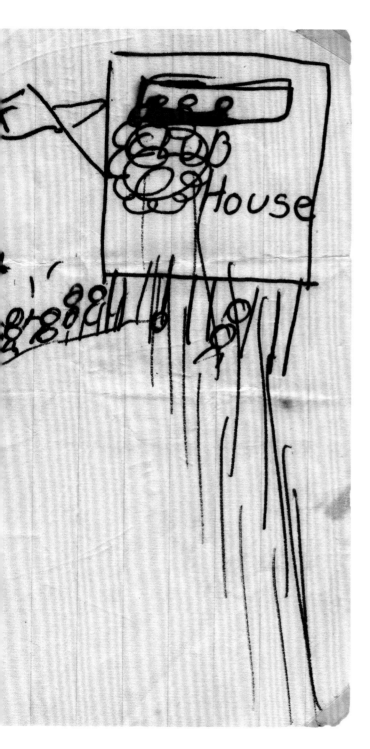

House

I do not remember drawing this (though I did have curly hair). I was drawing boats on everything: school books, school exam papers, even paper tablecloths. I am amazed to see the number of trophies and prize cups – more than I had ever won – but it gave me a good attitude for winning in life!

Aloha's early morning arrival off
the reef, Lord Howe Island 1963.

Offshore

AT THE AGE OF 15, after three years of crewing for Brian on *Haze* and *Happy Daze*, not even the Hauraki Gulf was big enough for my ambitions. I hankered to cross oceans, and one fateful night Dad brought home an American called Curt Ashford, a boatbuilder who had sailed his 36-foot schooner *Sea Wyfe* singlehandedly from Seattle to Auckland via Tahiti. I listened to every single word of his description of the voyage.

Curt immediately took an interest in me and introduced me to Bunny and Fran Rabbits, the owners of a 36-foot ketch which also happened to be tied up at the Viaduct. After I had gotten to know them a little, I had the impertinence to suggest they take me on their planned voyage, which was all the way across the Tasman Sea to Sydney, a distance of over 1,200 nautical miles. To my delight they agreed, and I raced home in great excitement to tell Mum and Dad about it. I'd gone past the stage of asking permission, and anyway school summer holidays were coming up. By now they had seen the inevitable and were resigned to the young adventurer I was turning into.

"What could I say?" my mother later told a reporter from another national newspaper, "Adventure in yachts, sailing ships and ocean cruising is an obsession with him. Nothing else matters." I knew though that deep down she worried and confided to others her fears about her son voyaging up and down the coast with, as she once put it, "a lot of water underneath him."

◄
On my way. *Aloha* anchored on the Northland Coast before sailing west to Lord Howe Island and Australia.

▲
Aloha anchored in the lagoon at Lord Howe Island. After crossing the Tasman Sea for ten days, my first foreign country.

And so with my parents' philosophical acceptance, I set out to cross the Tasman aboard *Aloha*, a 36-foot ketch designed by John G. Alden, the American whose heyday was in the early 1900s.

Aloha was a small yacht and she bounced around a lot when it got rough. After more than a week at sea since the North Cape of New Zealand had disappeared below the horizon, including two days in a full-on storm hanging on a sea anchor drogue to keep us safe, we approached Lord Howe Island, the only harbor lying between New Zealand and Australia.

For centuries this island, which is about six miles long and just over a mile across at its widest part, has served as a reference point for navigators at sea and in the air as they travel between the two countries. We finally spotted Lord Howe's high peaks just before dusk, too late to enter the narrow pass in the coral reef – the world's southernmost reef of its kind – that surrounds the island's west coast, so we reduced sail, slowed down and plowed on steadily towards the island as darkness fell.

I'd done the midnight to 4 AM watch, then gone below and tried to sleep. But tired as I was, I couldn't fall asleep. I lay in the bunk waiting for daylight with an excitement I could hardly contain, as *Aloha* rose and fell in the swells rebounding off the land. When bright sunlight streamed into the cabin I gave up all attempts to sleep, and went on deck to find the rest of the crew already up and gazing at the western coast of the island. I still remember the sight of the mountains, the deep blue sea, the white water breaking on the reef and the cloudless sky, and I stood there staring at the scene for a long time, not saying much. It was enchanting, exciting, thrilling – practically any adjective you can think of.

My first foreign landfall!

I still cherish this memory. It's where it all began, and although I have made many landfalls since then, some with joy, some with relief, but none without emotion, I think of Lord Howe as the landfall moment when I became irredeemably and hopelessly hooked on the oceans.

The rest of the voyage was largely uneventful, and I celebrated my sixteenth birthday in Sydney, popularly known in Auckland as the "Big Smoke." Life had suddenly become hugely exciting, and as a bonus, on my return to Auckland I learned that the voyage had qualified me to become an official member of the Ocean Cruising Division of the Royal Akarana Yacht Club. Not only did this make me at 16 the youngest-ever member, it was quite an accolade because you had to sail over 1,000 miles non-stop to fulfill the requirements.

By then I knew without a shadow of doubt that I had totally outgrown school. Practically all my waking hours were spent sailing, thinking about

▲

Goodbye to *Aloha* in Auckland: at the Cement Silo dock in Westhaven, my family are there to see me off.

L TO R: Nanna Subritsky, brother Philip aged 12, Mum, Dad, and me at 15 years of age.

▲

After the gale we now have good sailing conditions. My watch mate Bob von Bibra and I keep *Aloha* heading west to Lord Howe Island.

sailing, reading about sailing or, increasingly, doodling designs of yachts on school books or stray bits of paper. And when I experienced my first full offshore gale, the die was pretty much cast.

On the basis of my trans-Tasman voyage I was invited to crew on a narrow, double-ended 27-footer called *Elizabeth* in a race around the treacherous east coast of the Coromandel Peninsula to White Island, an active volcano lying a few miles offshore in the Bay of Plenty. As we rounded the island, the smell of sulfur and volcanic ash, borne on the wind, enveloped us as a gale roared in from the northeast. It whipped up the biggest seas I'd ever seen, even bigger than those we'd experienced aboard *Aloha*. Fortunately, *Elizabeth*'s owner Bill Cole was an experienced deep-water yachtsman and he quickly assessed how dangerous the conditions had become. When we saw a yacht called *Roulette* lose her mast at dusk on the second evening, her crumpled rig lying in the sea just to leeward of us, Bill didn't hesitate. He decided to heave to and ride the gale out.

So he sent me and the other less experienced crewmember out on a bucking deck to take down the racing sails, reef the mainsail and set a tiny storm jib. Hanging onto the lifelines for dear life, we managed to set the small jib and sheet it aback to the windward winch, a classic technique designed to keep the bow pointing about 45 degrees off the true wind direction. If we got it right, it meant *Elizabeth* would more or less hold her own in the seas and ride them more easily.

Between the two of us we managed to set up *Elizabeth* to Bill's satisfaction, and with all the equipment battened down we went below and sat it out while the winds howled around us all night. We didn't sleep a wink, and I spent a good part of the night peering through the cabin porthole at foaming phosphorescent crests flying past in the darkness. Even though *Elizabeth* was not making too much leeway, I couldn't help thinking of the jagged rocks of the Coromandel coastline not far to leeward. In the middle of the night we were startled by a loud crash, and we poked our heads out of the cabin to see a second, much bigger yacht, hardly twenty yards away with her entire rig collapsed over the side.

At last, around daybreak, the gale began to abate and Bill decided it was safe enough to set our racing sails again. So we got out on the still-heaving deck, raised the bigger jib and unreefed the mainsail, and continued north along the New Zealand coast to the finish line off the harbor of Mangonui. When we got there, we were astonished to hear that *Elizabeth*, one of only two yachts to finish, had won the race because every single one of the other competitors had been damaged or decided to quit. The other boat to complete the course, a long time after *Elizabeth*, was the largest yacht in the race. I can still remember the pleasure we got from a totally unexpected victory.

Compared with crossing oceans and fighting gales off active volcanoes, the classroom had become a dull place, and not even the threat of failing School Certificate for a second time could motivate me to prepare for the exam. But since it was compulsory, I had to go through the motions and turn up for every paper with great reluctance. By the time I'd reached the final paper, which was my hated subject of bookkeeping, I found I couldn't answer a single question, not one. By then I just didn't care, so I simply scribbled down a few lines, embroidered my paper with a drawing of a racing yacht (in bookkeeping!), excused myself as soon as the rules permitted the examinees to leave, then raced downtown to The Silo dock to see if any new yachts had sailed in from the Pacific.

I was 16 and had no qualifications. All I knew was that I wasn't going back to sit School Certificate for a third time. I'd burned my boats, you might say.

After walking out of school, and, as I'd been warned by my teachers, by doing so consigned myself to a life of low achievement, I was fortunate to be signed on as a boatbuilding apprentice. Keith Atkinson was a specialist in high quality wooden boats who had a small factory around the corner in Browns Bay. A quiet and thoughtful craftsman, Keith agreed to pay me a fiver a week – well, five pounds and sixpence. Even at the age of 16 you couldn't possibly live on these wages, but I was living at home and my parents were giving me additional financial aid. Still, I was pleased to get the employment at the time. In those days an apprenticeship was a serious undertaking for both parties, a five-year contract totaling 10,000 working hours. At the end of that time you were awarded a certificate and could call yourself a Qualified Boat Builder. I suspect my parents were delighted that their low-achieving eldest son had at last made a responsible start to his working life. But I lasted just three years at Atkinson's.

Having started as a gofer – sweeping up the shavings and sawdust, stacking wood and making tea for the real boatbuilders – I learned much about the skills of lofting and building wooden boats of all kinds. I worked on a lot of different boats: a single-skin, carvel-planked, 50-foot fishing boat, a number of 15-foot clinker-built (lapstrake) sailing dinghies, and a couple of 42-foot cold-molded racing yachts from the drawing board of American designers Sparkman & Stephens. One of these 42-footers, *Jupiter*, was a sister yacht to *Clarion of Wight* which had just won the Fastnet Race, and I felt as though I had a role, albeit a small one, in creating one of the most important sailboats in the world.

▲

January 1963: my first overseas yacht club, the Cruising Yacht Club of Australia, Sydney. The *Aloha* crew are given guest memberships during our stay. This was the first of many CYC visits for me.

▲

Keith Atkinson's boatyard in Browns Bay. At 16 years of age I started my boatbuilding apprenticeship, learning to build wooden boats. On the left is a 40-foot single-skin carvel-planked fishing boat ready for caulking. Located behind the fishing boat is the first Sparkman & Stephens yacht we built, the ocean racer *Jupiter*, getting ready to receive cold-molded multi-skin kauri planking.

Jupiter is a sister of the English yacht *Clarion of Wight*, recent winner of the most important ocean race in the world, the Fastnet Race.

On the right is the mold for an Illingworth and Primrose-designed, Top Hat class yacht, another high-profile English racing boat. Hanging in the roof is an Uffa Fox-designed *Flying Fifteen*. Surrounded by important yacht designs, I felt I was working in the center of the yachting universe!

The construction of wooden boats was – and is – an art form, and Keith was a maestro who could build any kind of boat in wood. But while I appreciated being given the job and knew I was learning a lot, my heart just wasn't in it. It took me just one year to realize that I wasn't cut out to be "on the tools," and I recognized that some of the other guys were simply more gifted, especially lead apprentice Kerry Alexander who would go on to become a master craftsman. From my viewpoint, there was another drawback: even fully qualified boatbuilders earned only 25 quid a week, which didn't seem a lot of money to me. I would never own a yacht on these wages.

Although I wasn't the most talented boatbuilding apprentice, I could hold my own when it came to drinking beer, which we did most Friday nights after finishing work. It was a tradition to sink a few bottles of Lion Red, then the beer of choice for yachties and boatbuilders, after putting their tools down. Then we'd head off in our cars to somebody's house to consume a few more. Everybody was more or less expected to join in these sessions, and one Friday the older men issued a challenge to the three apprentices. "Bet you guys can't drink half a dozen bottles each in two hours," he said. "Bet we can!"

So we launched into it. In those days of quart-sized bottles, bigger than those around today, the task soon became tougher than we'd expected. One apprentice fell flat on his face after just a couple of bottles, but Kerry and I battled on, and I can still remember having to force down the last half-bottle. Then, challenge met, we now had to get ourselves home. "I'll drive you," said one of the older boatbuilders who had knocked back his six bottles with no obvious consequences.

Somehow he managed to take us all home, dropping us off one by one, me in such an inebriated state that he just knocked on the door and ran for it. My mother found me leaning against a nearby tree, singing the latest hit songs but unable to stand without her help. I practically fell inside. Typical Mum, she was more worried than mad, and she put me to bed where I spent most of the weekend feeling sorry for myself.

Attitudes towards drinking and driving were different, far less strict in those days, to put it mildly.

As with most New Zealand businesses, and especially firms like Atkinson's, the biggest session of the year came before Christmas when we shut down for the three week summer holidays. These were the notorious "knock-off" drinks, usually provided by the management, and everybody enthusiastically took part. One particular year, after a few too many Lion Reds, we wondered what we'd do next – after all, the night was young – when boatbuilder Bill suggested, "Let's go to my place for something to eat and a few more beers. It's only ten minutes away." We agreed that was a good idea, and piled into two cars. There was no point in going to the local pub because, these being the days of six-o'clock closing, it would be shut.

I got into my buddy Warren Smith's Ford Prefect, and halfway there, he went round a corner far too fast and the inevitable happened. "Look out!" somebody yelled. "We're capsizing!"

I remember the car rolling as though in slow motion, throwing us on top of each other in a heap in the back seat. A bit shocked but laughing, we climbed up and out through the windows and assessed the damage. No bones broken. "What do we do now?" somebody asked. "Push her back on her wheels, of course." So we gave the damaged car a heave. It crashed back onto its wheels, and we got back in and carried on to Bill's. To our surprise, Bill and the rest of the gang weren't there, so we hung around, wondering whether to knock on the door and introduce ourselves to his wife or wait until he turned up. "Better wait," we decided.

Sure enough, a few minutes later the other car pulled into the driveway. "What kept you?" we asked. "Kerry rolled the bloody car," announced Bill. "Let's go inside and have those beers."

Since it was his house, Bill went first with us following along behind. And just as well because he was met at the kitchen door by his wife, furious that he was not only late for dinner, but had a few inebriated pals in

▲

For the first race from New Zealand to New Caledonia I was aboard the latest S&S design *Satanita,* built by Keith Atkinson (and me).

tow. A formidable lady, she started yelling and throwing plates at him. Ducking for cover, the apprentices beat a hasty retreat.

My main problem at Atkinsons was that I was more interested in design and drawing than in woodwork. I lived for the twice-weekly night classes in boatbuilding at Auckland Technical College that were part of the apprenticeship program. These were the highlight for me, and I might have abandoned the apprenticeship sooner were it not for these classes. Our tutors happened to be boat designers as well as boatbuilders, and we spent a lot of time discussing the things in which I was most interested. I still remember their names – Peter Peal and Allan Wright – and, recognizing my interest in design, they encouraged me. For this I'm deeply grateful.

I got my first commission out of these classes. Fellow apprentice Dave Wilson, who always sat beside me and used to watch me drawing boats, promised me a few dozen bottles of beer if I would design him a 26-foot, fin-keeled sloop that, in typical Kiwi fashion, he wanted to build himself. For somebody taking home a fiver a week this seemed a fair price, especially as I'd won the apprentices' unofficial beer-drinking competitions. "She's got to be quick though," Dave said. This suited me fine. I'd seen too many slow yachts in Auckland Harbour and had no interest in adding to their number.

At least he didn't ask me to design a concrete boat. Extraordinary as it seems now, there was a craze in New Zealand at that time for ferro-cement yachts, and for a few years you would see enthusiastic amateurs hard at work in their backyards with concrete mixers, dreaming of taking these monstrosities cruising into the Pacific. A lot of those suburban boatbuilders quickly ran out of enthusiasm, and the rusting hulks of half-finished yachts sitting on the lawn were a common sight. Of those that actually hit the water, a very few floated well enough, but most soon simply "went gurgle." But whether the boat was made of concrete or some other material, many New Zealanders constructed their own boats. They simply threw up a shed at the back of the house and built it themselves, often to their own design after a quick read-through of one of the classic books on the subject, *Skene's Elements of Yacht Design*.

Although I'd read *Skene's*, I very much had my own ideas. So for Dave I came up with a flat-bottomed, dinghy-like underwater shape, including a scimitar-shaped fin keel that I'd first seen on John Spencer's designs. For the rig I designed a modern masthead configuration: that is, the sails went right to the top of the stick. My main departure from the existing convention in Auckland Harbour was to specify a powerful outsized headsail that overlapped a relatively small mainsail. I knew from my reading of

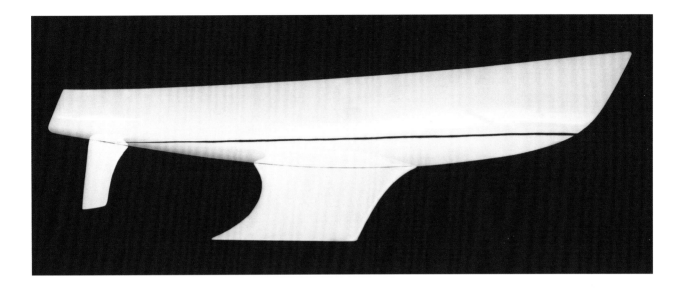

▲

Half-model of *White Rabbit*, my first design. Fellow boatbuilding apprentice Dave Wilson took a chance on me and invited me to design him a 26-foot yacht. She floated and sailed well.

overseas yachting magazines, which I bought with my meager wages, that this was the latest trend in the design of racing sailboats.

But when one of Dave's apprentice mates discovered that I, a mere 18-year-old, was designing a boat for him, Dave got a lecture about how foolish this was. "It won't work," he was told. "Holland isn't a yacht designer." I didn't learn this until years later because Dave thought he ought to keep it to himself, but fortunately the yacht, which he christened *White Rabbit,* was a success. She floated exactly on her lines and met Dave's most optimistic expectations, and to the best of my knowledge is still sailing.

As I got more experienced and better known, one thing began to lead to another. I was being approached to make yachts faster, whether by tuning the rig or making modifications to keels and rudders. I had already been crewing aboard a yacht named *Poseidon*, owned by chiropractor Dr. Milton Miller. Built at Atkinson's, *Poseidon* was one of the local Patiki class of 34-footers, and it was Keith who arranged for me to join the crew.

"I can do better than that," I told Dr. Miller. "I'll bring a mate along as well." So I jumped aboard with Warren, my school chum and fellow-member of the Torbay Boating Club. Milton, as I came to call him, was new to yacht racing and welcomed all the help he could get, but I probably owe more to him than the other way around. He soon became a profound mentor and influence on my life. He was a pioneer in chiropractic, a

profession regarded with deep suspicion by mainstream medicine, but in spite of that he had built up a busy and successful practice in Auckland, and it did not take me long to see why.

The first time Warren and I turned up at Westhaven to crew aboard *Poseidon*, my back was so sore from a rugby injury that I reluctantly told Milton I couldn't go sailing. Taking one look at me, he said, "Come aboard the yacht and I'll have a look at the problem." Somewhat nervously, because I knew nothing about chiropractic, I did as I was told, and down below Milton ordered me to lie down on the settee bunk. A few twists and turns of my legs and back, and the pain instantly disappeared. That really got my attention. As a bonus we won the race, *Poseidon*'s first victory.

For the next two years Warren and I crewed aboard the yacht and I got to know the Miller family, who were Jewish, another new experience for a Catholic boy. As well as my learning what a bar mitzvah was, Milton got me reading different kinds of books (now that I could read properly), mainly American inspirational ones such as Napoleon Hill's best-seller, *Think and Grow Rich*. Under Milton's influence I even signed up for a Dale Carnegie motivational course at what I considered to be great expense.

What I learned from Milton was the importance of studying non-school subjects if I intended to make my way in the world. As I broadened my reading and could converse on more subjects, I began to feel much more confident socially, especially in the rarified milieu of the Royal New Zealand Yacht Squadron, of which Milton was a member. Certainly the "rich guys' club," as we'd always known it, was a big step up from the Torbay Boating Club and the Ponsonby Cruising Club, haven of the Mullet Boys, even if I did miss their camaraderie and sense of mischief.

In sailing as in other things, Milton liked to do things properly. In due course he asked me to improve *Poseidon*'s rating under the international ocean racing rules, which at the time penalized her design compared with yachts of equivalent size. With my encouragement Milton had made it his ambition to race in the Sydney to Hobart classic, and this was the first step. Accordingly, I modified the sail plan by changing the proportion of the mainsail area relative to the headsail, and moved the mast position, which improved our handicap. Next I designed a new rudder that made *Poseidon* easier to steer when she was flying her outsized spinnaker. When that was done, as far as Milton was concerned we were now ready to sail *Poseidon*, a light-displacement harbor racing yacht, across the storm-prone Tasman Sea to take on the Aussies. However, the New Zealand government surveyor, Harry Pope, who was responsible for approving boats to sail offshore, did not agree. Harry put his foot down: "I will

▲

After my first visit to Lord Howe Island aboard *Aloha*, I insisted we stop there when we sailed *Castanet* across the Tasman Sea to race in the Sydney Hobart Race. We beat all our Aussie Carmen Class competitors (the same design as *Castanet*) and then returning to New Zealand won the Trans-Tasman Race. We were the only crew to beat NZ champion *Rainbow II* in any major ocean race.

◄

Poseidon's delivery crew. Saying goodbye to family and friends in Auckland.
L TO R: Dr. Milton Miller, Warren Smith, Gil Littler, Me, Philip Holland. Next stop Lord Howe Island, then on to the start of the Sydney Hobart Race.

The Royal Yacht Club of Tasmania
Club House: Marieville Esplanade
Hobart
28 DEC 1967
19
Honorary Membership
The Flag Officers, Committee and Members invite
Mr R. Holland
to become an Honorary Member during his stay in Hobart.
A. B. NEILSON, Secretary

▲

Royal Yacht Club of Tasmania, 1967. I believed the Sydney Hobart Race was the biggest sailing challenge for any Kiwi yachtie. It wasn't the Fastnet Race but very close! I was in Hobart for the first time aboard *Poseidon;* back the following year with *Castanet*.

not let this harbor sailing yacht leave the New Zealand coast until she's strengthened," he told Milton in no uncertain terms.

So we did what Harry ordered. *Poseidon* was hauled out of the water, and two of the crew, Minky Goodman and Gilbert Littler, also boatbuilders, installed new laminated frames and knees in the hull and cabin, both of which made the yacht much more robust. When the work was completed to Harry's approval, we set sail for Sydney via Lord Howe Island. There were five of us including my brother Phil, who was 16, and I was under strict instructions from my parents to bring him back safely. I was 19.

We knew there was considerable skepticism at the bar of the Royal New Zealand Yacht Squadron about the wisdom of such a young and inexperienced crew sailing what was still essentially a harbor day-racing yacht across to Australia and taking on the notorious Sydney Hobart Race, in which many a boat had been broken by the violent storms of the Bass Strait and the Southern Ocean.

Yet we crossed the Tasman without incident, and *Poseidon*'s youthful crew subsequently performed way above expectations, including our own, in what turned into a wild race. In the later stages, desperately holding onto our big spinnaker across Bass Strait in the dark, we passed one yacht after another and were only overtaken a mile before the finish by the biggest boat in the race, a 65-foot yacht from America named *Nam Sang*. After crossing the line, we tied up in a space in Hobart's Constitution Dock reserved for the first ten yachts to finish. *Poseidon* was by far the smallest of this elite group.

We sailed back to Auckland across the Tasman, extremely proud of what we'd done. Milton had made his point and silenced the skeptics. Phil got home safely, although by plane. And I settled back into the apprenticeship until I was confronted by another turning point in my young life.

A race from Auckland to Fiji was coming up and I was determined not to miss it, especially as Sharon Corkin agreed to meet me in Fiji and sail with me back to New Zealand. Keith had made it clear there would be no more time off for his apprentices to do any offshore racing, so one morning I simply resigned without explaining the main reason. I told my boss that I wasn't cut out to be a boatbuilder, that I wouldn't be coming back, and thanked him for what he'd taught me. Keith didn't disagree that I wasn't his best apprentice, and we parted on good terms: later on I often crewed for him in races around the Hauraki Gulf.

Looking back, I now realize that I learned much more than I thought at the time, and my boatbuilding knowledge would stand me in good stead whenever I walked into a shipyard after starting my design studio. Yet all

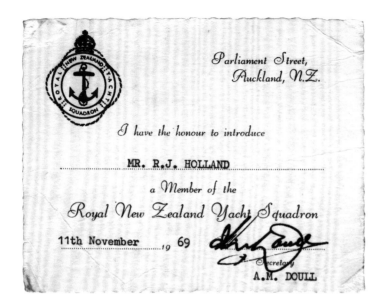

Parliament Street,
Auckland, N.Z.

I have the honour to introduce

MR. R.J. HOLLAND

a Member of the

Royal New Zealand Yacht Squadron

11th November 19 69

Secretary

A.M. DOULL

"FAN TAN"

Royal Suva Yacht Club

The Commodore and Committee
have pleasure in inviting

Mr. R. Holland

to be an Honorary Member

for one month from 28th April '69

Introduced by R.A.Y.C.

Secretary

▲

Royal New Zealand Yacht Squadron
and Royal Suva Yacht Club, 1969.
I had to make a choice: do the
race to Fiji aboard Dick Wheeler's
Fan Tan or stay working at T.K.
Atkinson Boatbuilder in Browns
Bay. I chose Fiji.

I could see ahead of me at the time was years and years of toiling away in a boat shed for a pittance. I was ambitious and restless. I chafed at what I considered to be constricting apprenticeship rules. Also, there wasn't enough time to do the serious ocean sailing I craved. All those overseas sailing magazines had given me wanderlust.

I walked home that day instead of taking the bus as usual, meandering along the beaches lying at the foot of the cliffs, kicking seashells and wondering what I was going to do next. I was also wondering what I was going to tell my mother who had been so proud and pleased that I had finally gotten a steady job.

But, as I was beginning to learn, something always comes up if you follow your star and keep your eyes and ears open and are prepared to say yes. And that was when *Great Hope* turned up. Looking back, it happened because I had put myself in a position to take advantage of such an opportunity if it ever arose – I was free to choose, free to say yes.

I put *Great Hope* through her paces
on San Francisco Bay after arriving
in California in 1969.

Five and a half men

I HAD A PROBLEM. I had to get a 33-foot, harbor-racing yacht named *Spirit* approved for an ocean race from Los Angeles to Tahiti, a distance of over 4,000 miles right across the Pacific. It was at that time the longest ocean race in the world, its course taking the fleet all the way from San Pedro Harbor, around the north of Catalina Island and then directly to Tahiti. After finishing the race, the plan was for me to take over as skipper and to sail on to Australia to compete in the Sydney to Hobart classic. Considering everything it would be quite a voyage.

My problem was that members of the race committee appointed by the California Yacht Club were keeping a close eye on *Spirit*, and with good reason. Her owner, San Francisco-based shipping tycoon George Kiskaddon, was a larger-than-life character who had raced and cruised her over several thousand miles across oceans without worrying too much about the regulations.

When George had commissioned the boat from Sparkman & Stephens nearly ten years earlier, the revered New York design studio thought they were creating a yacht that would be raced around San Francisco Bay on a pleasant afternoon, and no further. That's why *Spirit* had no interior to speak of. But George must have somehow let slip that his intention was to take her ocean racing, because Olin Stephens, already a legend for his winning America's Cup designs among many others, refused to proceed on the grounds that it would be too dangerous to take such a yacht offshore.

He would have no further part in such a foolish venture, and he only relented when a seemingly chastened George promised to confine his new yacht to the waters of San Francisco Bay, as originally envisaged.

In 1960 George had duly taken delivery of his harbor racer with headroom of just four and a half feet. But as soon as she arrived in California he had the cockpit reduced in length, making the sailboat safer for offshore racing, and installed two bunks forward and two quarter berths aft, plus a small plywood chart table and a galley that consisted of a minute alcohol stove without a sink. And, oh yes, a bucket that George, who had a wicked sense of humor, dubbed the "Birch John" after the right-wing John Birch Society which, being a left-winger, he detested. And then he went offshore. As his family would say later, "He must have forgotten what he told Olin Stephens."

Among other adventures he raced *Spirit* across the Pacific to Honolulu, then across the North Atlantic to Copenhagen, which was a particularly bold effort in a small, flush-decked sailboat. In the years since that time *Spirit* won a lot of races, but probably her finest hour was placing first in her class – and remarkably, 20th overall – in the classic Fastnet Race that takes the fleet from Cowes all the way to the Fastnet Rock and then back to Plymouth – an event that would later come to play a big part in my life. When Olin Stephens heard about these voyages he must have been shocked to the core.

But now, to cap it all, George planned to race *Spirit* to Tahiti, and it was up to me to keep the race committee happy. One of their new stipulations was that every yacht in this epic race should be equipped with an engine capable of achieving at least four knots. Yet in all her years of racing *Spirit* had never possessed any form of power other than the wind – and that's exactly how George wanted it.

I had arrived in San Francisco two years earlier, in 1969, on the cargo ship *Saracen* from Auckland. My job at the time was to make sure that a miniature schooner called *Great Hope* reached the city in good shape, and to then take care of her sailing trials on San Francisco Bay. This was all on behalf of the red-bearded Auckland boatbuilder and designer John Spencer, who had taken me under his wing and introduced me to George Kiskaddon during one of his regular business trips to Auckland. Always thinking big, George had initiated the *Great Hope* project as a stepping-stone to a much bigger one.

It happened like this: George very much liked John Spencer's radical light-displacement, plywood racing yachts and wanted him to design and build a 73-foot racing schooner. This was a lot of yacht at the time and

▲

New World, the maxi racing schooner that gave me the opportunity to leave New Zealand for California in 1969, in a photo taken at the start of the 1972 Bermuda Race, one of the toughest ocean race passages I ever made.

◀

Mini schooner *Great Hope* planing across San Francisco Bay. My role was to have her ready for the Kiskaddon family to use anytime, and give feedback to designer builder John Spencer in New Zealand while he was designing and building the schooner *New World*.

▲

Racing from Los Angeles to Tahiti in 1971: 23 days at sea in what was at the time the world's longest ocean race, in the 33-foot flush-decked *Spirit*. Georgie Kiskaddon is on watch and driving, with no land for hundreds of miles. The Birch John stands ready on the after deck.

the maximum permitted length under existing offshore racing rules. But to make sure that John's fearless confidence was justified and the big schooner would sail as designed, both men had agreed that first a one-third-sized prototype would be constructed and put through its paces. That prototype was *Great Hope*, which at 24 feet was probably one of the smallest schooners ever built, and I had been invited to step aboard and helm her in Auckland for her debut outing with the objective of impressing John's American client. The trials went well, and afterwards we all repaired to the yacht club for a few celebratory drinks. Here, to my amazement, George suggested that I accompany *Great Hope* to America aboard a cargo ship and supervise everything from start to finish, including providing feedback to John Spencer. John immediately agreed – after all, this was an important commission for him and he wanted to be sure the little schooner performed well enough to lead to the bigger one.

Naturally I accepted, a "yes" without hesitation, and *Great Hope* was shipped to Long Beach, California, as deck cargo with me in charge. At Long Beach a guy named Warwick Tompkins, whom I learned was nicknamed "Commodore", met me with his Volvo station wagon towing a little trailer on which *Great Hope* would be transported all the way to San Francisco.

I already knew something of Warwick Tompkins. Then in his thirties, he was one of the crew that had just won the Fastnet Race aboard American designer Dick Carter's *Red Rooster*, a daringly original boat that had fired my imagination. I had also read his father's book, *50 South to 50 South*, about how he and his wife had taken their young kids, Commodore and his sister Anne, around Cape Horn on a schooner called *Wander Bird*. When I say I had read the book, that was an understatement. I practically memorized it, scarcely believing that somebody could have more sailing adventures than I had, and at a much earlier age. While I was racing seven-foot dinghies, Commodore was sailing around the world!

I was a wide-eyed 21-year-old on my first visit to America, wondering if I could make a living out of sailing. So naturally Commodore and I talked pretty much non-stop for the entire eight-hour road trip to San Francisco. It turned out that Commodore was one of the first of a new breed of sailing professionals who had sailed aboard practically every kind of yacht, usually as skipper, navigator, or sailing master, and had salt water in his veins. I didn't know it at the time, but this would be the beginning of a lifelong friendship.

After we arrived in the great city, Commodore and I parked *Great Hope* by the St. Francis Yacht Club, donned our "best clobber" in Kiwi parlance, and hit the town. I will never forget my first night in San Francisco.

"For somebody still undecided between a career in sailing, whatever form it might take, or in music, these were heady times. Even better, I would get to know Ramblin' Jack well. ... he was a sailing enthusiast as well as an award-winning musician, and later, when he hit town for a gig, I would take him for a spin on one of George's yachts while we talked of music and our mutual love of square-riggers..."

After meeting Mrs. Kiskaddon – "Please call me Lillian" – and joining her, George and the family of two boys and two girls at a classical concert at the San Francisco Jewish Community Center, we returned for dinner to what was to become my new home, the Kiskaddons' beautiful cedar-tiled house in Divisadero Street, just up the hill from the yacht club. We'd hardly finished dinner when a family acquaintance, folk singer Ramblin' Jack Elliott, turned up with three musician friends including Kris Kristof-ferson, and sat down for an impromptu concert of country music that lasted well into the night. It was the first time I'd heard a song that would become legendary, "Me and Bobby McGee."

For somebody still undecided between a career in sailing, whatever form it might take, or in music, these were heady times. Even better, I would get to know Ramblin' Jack well. Then 37, he was a sailing enthusiast as well as an award-winning musician, and later, when he hit town for a gig, I would take him for a spin on one of George's yachts while we talked of music and our mutual love of square-riggers, a subject about which Jack had an impressive knowledge. That was the beginning of another lifelong friendship.

By then I had become part of Divisadero Street, and I had of course discovered that the Haight-Ashbury district, the world capital of 1960s flower power, was nearby. I spent a lot of time at the Fillmore West rock venue listening to bands like the Grateful Dead, Jefferson Airplane and

SPIRIT *of San Francisco*
SF-1

▶

After saying yes to George Kiskaddon's invitation to accompany *Great Hope* to San Francisco, I was excited to receive this letter confirming that I could join the cargo ship *Saracen* for the passage. Across the Pacific Ocean to California for Christmas, 1969!

SHIPPING CO. LTD.
(Incorporated in England)

P.O. Box 3076
Cables "CRUSHIPCO"
Telephone 34-959

101 QUEEN ST.,
AUCKLAND
NEW ZEALAND

Reference: Ours GSTJ:YMH

Yours

7TH NOVEMBER, 1969

MR. RONALD J. HOLLAND,
7 GRAY CRESCENT,
TORBAY.

DEAR SIR,

"SARACEN" VOY 53 NTH

THIS IS TO INFORM YOU THAT THE MASTER HAS AGREED TO CARRY YOU AS A SUPERNUMERARY BERTHED IN VESSEL'S HOSPITAL FOR WHICH OUR HEAD OFFICE HAVE INDICATED A VICTUALLING FEE OF NZ$200. WE SHALL BE GRATEFUL IF YOU WILL LET US KNOW PROMPTLY WHETHER THE OFFER IS ACCEPTABLE TO YOU.

VESSEL IS PRESENTLY SCHEDULED TO ARRIVE AUCKLAND 13TH NOVEMBER AND TO SAIL FOR HONOLULU 15TH NOVEMBER. IT IS NECESSARY THAT YOU SHOULD HOLD A VALID PASSPORT WITH A VISA FOR ENTRY INTO U.S.A.

YOURS FAITHFULLY,

LOCAL MANAGER

Little Feat, and one night I even got to attend one of Jimi Hendrix's last concerts across the bay at the Berkeley Community Center.

After work George would often look for me at the marina, and we would take *Great Hope* sailing. One evening shortly after I arrived in San Francisco, we were heading out towards the Golden Gate Bridge when an upset-looking George instructed me to "sail close to that ship." How close? I thought to myself, I can get you inches away from it if you want. I had gotten to within a few feet of the big cargo ship when George stood up, yelling, "Turn back, you military industrial capitalists, return those bombs to the dock!" and he threw his half-finished bottle of red wine, smashing it against the ship's side. It was George's personal protest against the war in Vietnam. I was shocked and glad no one on the ship was aware of our attack.

So I put *Great Hope* through her sailing trials, and they went well enough for George to have the confidence to commission the full-sized version, which would be christened *New World*.

As I was getting to know George and the local sailing community I kept hearing about an off-the-wall young yacht designer and boatbuilder called Bill Lee, whose new 30-footer *Magic* was tearing up Monterey Bay. "You've got to go and meet him," said my new crewmates. Bill lived and worked in Santa Cruz, 75 miles south of San Francisco, so I drove out there with a crewmate, making sure to bring the obligatory pack of beer with us. Bill had stuck a sign on the door of his office stipulating beer as the price of entry, though I had also heard that a few joints wouldn't go amiss either.

About ten years older than me, he was a free-thinking spirit who was already being described locally as "The Wizard" for his sometimes radical yachts. Although Santa Cruz was considered by some to be a hotbed of dangerous sailing revolutionaries (and certainly some early yachts launched from there were constructed too lightly), Bill was a mechanical engineer who knew a lot about the stresses and strains to which racing yachts are subjected. After a brief chat and a tour of the boatbuilding shed, he suggested, "Let's go sailing."

Yes, of course! Let's go!

There wasn't much wind but we spent a pleasant couple of hours on the bay aboard *Magic* discussing yacht design. I learned that Bill already knew about John Spencer and his lightweight, downwind flyers, and *Magic* was designed along a similar concept but with more beam. I almost felt as if I were back in John's boat shed in Browns Bay, talking yachts. Then, with the tide falling, it was time to return to harbor.

"This should be fun," said Bill as we approached the sandbar at the entrance. With surfers all around us riding breaking waves, he fearlessly

▲

Ron and Doug talking boats! While we became serious competitors, on occasion we still had time to reflect on our 23 days aboard *Spirit*, racing to Tahiti. We could not have imagined those early yacht design discussions would later lead to the disruptive influence we were going to have on IOR ocean racing design.

▲

I arrived in San Francisco in 1969 and joined the Kiskaddon family on Divisadero Street, just up the road from the St. Francis Yacht Club. George and Lillian Kiskaddon had four children, two girls and two boys. Here I pose with my new "sister" Ruthie Kiskaddon showing off our Irish sweaters. Little did I know that I would spend most of my life in County Cork, Ireland. I was fresh off the cargo ship from Auckland with no idea of what life would manifest. Just keep saying yes, Ron, and see what happens!

steered *Magic* onto the bar. Crash! We hit the bottom. "Godammit!" said Bill. "I thought there was enough water under the keel." But instead of stopping dead, *Magic* popped straight back up and floated across the bar all by herself into calmer waters. "The keel's come off," announced Bill. He didn't seem too worried, but I certainly was. "We're sinking," I said, "Fast!"

Bill dove below, fired up the engine – the water was coming in so quickly there was no possibility of bailing her out – and we headed for the nearest dock as fast as we could. As soon as we got there, we lashed her securely to the mooring bollards just in time – *Magic* was already half full of water – and stepped ashore. Bill seemed unperturbed by the incident, and the next day he dispatched a team to wade out to the bar at low tide, find the keel, which wasn't particularly heavy, and skid it back to shore.

I saw a lot of Commodore while I was working up *Great Hope* and *Spirit*. Together we were also engaged in preparing a brand new 36-foot Sparkman & Stephens design called *White Heather* for a race from San Diego to Acapulco, and we spent many evenings sailing her around San Francisco Bay, often crossing under the mighty Golden Gate Bridge. Commodore was also enthusiastic about a project of his own – a yacht of around 40 feet that would be fast enough to win the Jamaica Race, which he and regular crewmates Skip Allan and Dave Wahle had won the year before, and even made the American Admiral's Cup team for the next edition of the event in August 1971. So we spent a lot of time talking about this imaginary yacht too, and the more we talked the more excited we became. Not wanting to outstay my welcome, I had moved out of the Kiskaddons' basement and began living in Commodore's house in Mill Valley, a city in Marin County north of San Francisco. Inevitably the collaboration became closer still.

Having practically grown up on the water, Commodore had – and still has – an almost instinctive sense of how to get the best out of a yacht. His vision for the 40-footer was based on his study of the Atlantic weather systems. He knew they averaged about nine knots as they moved east, and he surmised that if a yacht could average nine knots it would be able to hook into the lows of these weather systems and ride with them as they marched across the ocean. As Commodore explained, his father had come to the same realization when the family schooner *Wander Bird* set a record, at that time, of sixteen days for an Atlantic crossing: *Wander Bird* had been fortunate to ride the advancing lows.

Imagine a small yacht that could average nine knots! As he would write about my reaction later, I was "amused and excited by the audacity and daring of the idea." I can now see that I was already predisposed to designs

"I was only interested in boats that were better in some way – faster, lighter, whatever – than the ones that were already on the water. I'm sure this was a New Zealand influence that I'd absorbed from John Spencer and other local yacht designers who refused to accept established thinking as gospel."

that challenged convention, and bored by ideas that were run-of-the-mill. I suppose I just couldn't see any point in copying what everybody else was already doing, even if those designs were successful. My motivations were already taking shape: I was only interested in boats that were better in some way – faster, lighter, whatever – than the ones that were already on the water. I'm sure this was a New Zealand influence that I'd absorbed from John Spencer and other local yacht designers who refused to accept established thinking as gospel.

By now I had landed my first job in a yacht design studio, a breakthrough that I owe largely to Commodore, because he introduced me to Gary Mull who already had several successful yachts to his name. I had shown Gary a few designs I'd done back in New Zealand on the basis of my night class courses, and he was good enough to take me on. And so I got my first regular paycheck from a real yacht designer. In truth, as a complete novice I worked very much under Gary's thumb, helping him with the design of a 6-Meter for a challenge between San Francisco's St. Francis Yacht Club and Australia's Royal Prince Alfred Yacht Club, the 6-Meter being a classic boat class that had once been raced in the Olympics. I remember spending a lot of time making the tea, just like when I was a boatbuilding apprentice. Well, you've got to start somewhere.

When Commodore took his dream boat to Gary, explaining that he wanted her designed to a level that would interest people with big enough

"She was to be, in short, a no-compromise downwind ocean racer [with] standing headroom only for the cook and those getting into and out of foul-weather gear below. She also had to be made of wood, and unbreakable, short of hitting something big and heavy. In other words, she was to be audacious and daring."

wallets to turn her into reality, things began to accelerate. Commodore's thinking was already well advanced. "The boat was to be smallish to make her easy to handle with a crew of six, and inexpensive," he would remember. "She was to be 37 feet long, not less than 32 feet on the waterline, narrow, and she was not to weigh more than 12,000 lbs. She was to be sloop-rigged with plenty of sail – as fast a boat as Gary could make her with little regard for rating rules. She was to be, in short, a no-compromise downwind ocean racer [with] standing headroom only for the cook and those getting into and out of foul-weather gear below." She also had to be made of wood, and unbreakable, short of hitting something big and heavy. In other words, she was to be audacious and daring.

At first Gary poured cold water on the proposal. "Can't be done," he declared. Gary was particularly concerned about the narrowness, the light displacement and the big sail area. In other words there wasn't much that he wasn't concerned about. Yet in spite of his misgivings Gary was prevailed upon to "give it a whirl," in Commodore's words, and just one day after being shown an outline he came up with a sketch of the profile of the boat. When Commodore and I looked at it, we could see that Gary had got his head around the boat's philosophy so well that thereafter the lines were hardly changed. So far so good.

Commodore already had two prospective owners in mind, one of whom had long wanted to attempt a full-on ocean racer, while the other had the same ambition, but, being more cautious, preferred to go into the venture with a partner. And then the grand plan ran into trouble. When the concept was explained to them, both prospective owners had such serious misgivings that Commodore dubbed the yet-to-be-built boat HMS *Improbable*. The name was coined during a night race after a discussion with the rest of the crew about how unlikely the project was looking.

But Commodore was not a man to give up. For the next six weeks the three of us played about with the design as Gary gradually overcame his initial doubts. As time went on the exercise became more and more intoxicating because we sensed we had something special that just might shake up ocean racing, even if nobody else shared our enthusiasm. Even better, it could be done on the cheap. Commodore put it neatly: "The three of us developed this design with as much enthusiasm and glee as a bunch of kids building a tree house."

Then our hopes were completely dashed. Unable to shed their concerns, the prospective owners definitively withdrew from the project in what was a heavy blow for Commodore, in fact for all of us. Finally we had what we believed was a fast design but nobody to bankroll it.

While we wondered how to resurrect HMS *Improbable*, it was time to make final preparations for the Tahiti race on *Spirit*.

So here I was in San Francisco Bay trying to figure out how to install the engine that George Kiskaddon didn't want, as well as how to satisfy another awkward stipulation set by the trans-Pacific race committee: there had to be a minimum crew of six, which made sense in bigger yachts, but *Spirit* often raced with as few as four and never more than five. How were we supposed to fit six adults into a 33-footer with just four bunks and no proper headroom? George, whose Marine Chartering Company acted rather controversially in the 1960s, had a suspicion that an ulterior motive lay behind this particular rule; namely, that it was designed to keep *Spirit* out of the race.

George, as I had come to learn, was something of a visionary in business as well as sailing. At the height of the Cold War his was the only Californian company trading with the Soviet merchant fleet; although I knew practically nothing about geopolitics at the time, I could see that George occupied a sensitive position in American commerce, especially when he secured the shipping rights for the American Trust Territories in the Western Pacific, a big business that was controversial because of his Soviet connections. But whether or not the rule makers had an ulterior motive, George's simple, no-engine sailing philosophy – which I admired – certainly posed problems now.

▲

Spirit under full sail on San Francisco Bay. At 33 feet in length, with narrow beam and flush deck (meaning no cabin headroom) this little yacht was designed to sail safely in coastal waters. Yet George Kiskaddon raced her to Hawaii, and across the Atlantic to Denmark. I was aboard *Spirit* from L.A. to Tahiti then across the Pacific to Australia. This was a yacht you could sail anywhere!

There was nothing permitted on the yacht that George didn't consider absolutely necessary. Apart from the absence of a toilet – the rule was "bucket and chuck it" – her technical equipment left a lot to be desired compared with the latest racing yachts. Because *Spirit* did not have the benefit of a radio transmitter, there would be no way of communicating with land if we got into difficulties. In practice, there were no navigation lights because they were battery driven and, without an engine to charge them, the batteries used to run out after a couple of nights. And of course this was long before the days of satellite navigation and mobile phones.

I did, however, have total confidence in the ruggedness of the yacht. *Spirit* was made of one-inch mahogany planking over frames steam-bent from ipol wood, an Asian timber that was said to be as strong as oak but almost impervious to rot, and easy to work. She had been built at the Newton & Sons yard in Junk Bay, Hong Kong, that was managed by Robert Newton and his sons John and Whit. Specializing in custom yachts to the design of the late Nathanael Herreshoff – a hero of mine whose marine museum at Bristol, Rhode Island, I would often visit – and of Sparkman & Stephens and other top-draw designers, they produced boats of exceptionally high quality. Although no caulking or glue had been used between the planks, there were no leaks or weaknesses in *Spirit*.

But not even George Kiskaddon could duck the obligation of installing an engine. The rules were written in black and white and the race committee was adamant. Like all the other entrants, *Spirit* would have to be able to motor at a minimum speed of four knots. So my job was to fit her with an engine, drive shaft and propeller. Under sufferance George had told me in no uncertain terms that the engine should meet the letter of the law and no more. So we looked around for something that would push *Spirit* at the required speed, and found a little lawnmower engine somewhere. Because the engine was air-cooled, this meant we didn't have to make a hole in the bottom of George's beloved boat for the water intake, or in the side for the exhaust.

The day of the test arrived. I had arranged for it to be conducted on the protected waters of Sausalito Harbor, and by sheer good luck it was an unusually calm day. The official, a local boatbuilder named Myron Spaulding, duly turned up and climbed aboard. Myron was a legend on the Sausalito waterfront. Not only was he a trained naval architect, boatbuilder, winning one-design sailor and skipper of the famous Sparkman & Stephens-designed yawl *Dorade*, he was also a concert violinist who regularly performed with the city's symphony orchestra. As owner of the Spaulding Boat Works, Myron had been co-opted by the committee to

"So we looked around for something that would push *Spirit* at the required speed, and found a little lawnmower engine somewhere. Because the engine was air-cooled, this meant we didn't have to make a hole in the bottom of George's beloved boat for the water intake, or in the side for the exhaust."

undertake some of the technical inspections of the local trans-Pacific entries.

I can't remember what Myron said when he saw our pathetic engine but, given George's reputation, he must have wondered if we were trying to put something across the race committee. On his instructions, we started the motor up and slipped it into gear. Off *Spirit* chugged as the crew watched the speedometer with bated breath. Bit by bit, the dial worked its way up to four knots – and stopped there. It made no difference how wide we opened the throttle, she wouldn't go any faster – but as a triumphant George pointed out, we'd met the standard. Myron agreed, and the yacht club had no option but to pass *Spirit*. I still believe that Myron secretly supported George and wanted to do all he could to help us meet the speed requirement. When we'd gotten back to our moorings and I called George with the good news, he said: "The engine will never be used again." And it wasn't.

Next up was the issue of the six-man crew. In all her thousands of miles *Spirit* had never carried more than five crew – a 33-footer just doesn't need six crew, and certainly not the extra weight a sixth man would involve. So we read and re-read the rule book, and to George's delight he spotted a loophole. Nowhere did it stipulate a minimum age. "We'll take Johnny," said George. "They can't object." The youngest of the Kiskaddon family, Johnny was ten years old. He was not particularly impressed to be ap-pointed the crew's sixth member, but I don't think Mrs. Kiskaddon minded too much. She knew her youngest would be in good hands.

"So we read and re-read the rule book, and to George's delight he spotted a loophole. Nowhere did it stipulate a minimum age. 'We'll take Johnny,' said George. 'They can't object.' The youngest of the Kiskaddon family, Johnny was ten years old. He was not particularly impressed to be appointed the crew's sixth member, but I don't think Mrs. Kiskaddon minded too much."

So we raced to Tahiti with a crew of five and a half men. As well as the Kiskaddons – George Senior, 17-year-old George Junior and the reluctant Johnny whose main job was to sweep out the cockpit every morning – the crew was composed of me, aspiring designer and accomplished yachtsman Doug Peterson, who had been ocean racing aboard *Spirit* before, and sailmaker Jim Leach; all crammed into a 33-footer with little headroom, tiny bunks, no toilet and a pathetic gas stove, for 23 days.

And I loved it.

By now I was experienced at racing small yachts – roughly speaking, boats under 40 feet in length – across oceans, and I had developed my own routines. Tired as I was when it came to my watch, I made a point of rolling out of my bunk and staggering up on deck first, still half-asleep, because I wanted to get my hands on the wheel – or in *Spirit*'s case, the tiller – before there was anybody else around to argue. I much preferred the 4 AM watch because it meant I saw the magical sunrises of the oceans, which are so much more spectacular than those you see on land. Sometimes, if conditions were gentle during yacht deliveries or cruising when the pressure wasn't on, and everybody else was still below asleep, I would have the wheel and the entire ocean all to myself. Porpoises would keep me company, leaping up off the waves, sometimes flying above my head and leaving phosphorescent trails behind them. And if I didn't see them coming, I might be hit in the head by a flying fish or even a baby squid.

More than once, I got a squid down the collar of my oilskins. The first time this happens you get a helluva fright.

In the days before instruments came to the aid of the helmsman, steering a yacht at night required a special skill and, without being immodest, I became good at it. It's a matter of touch and feel, sensing the speed of the wind and its direction, and the way the yacht is moving through the waves. I began to notice that whatever yacht I was steering, we would make ground on much bigger boats during the night, and in the morning daylight I would see their crew looking back and wondering where on earth we had come from. But steering in the darkness is also exhausting, and when we were racing I found four-hour watches too long to maintain full concentration on the helm. So when I was in charge later, I made a point of setting up a system of three-hour watches with six hours off, which I believe kept the crew fresher and helped us push the boat faster. But whether it was three- or four-hour watches, I invariably collapsed into my bunk afterwards on the brink of exhaustion and went instantly to sleep, lulled by the motion of the yacht. Even in storms when you could be tossed out of the bunk, I developed a technique of wedging myself in with strategically placed extra pillows and coils of ropes and lashings to hold it all together.

Although I never worried about it at the time, we rarely had radio communications of any kind when sailing across oceans, and of course we had none worth speaking of on *Spirit*. Because of hostile atmospheric conditions, we could sometimes with great difficulty raise a long-range transmission and pick up a weather forecast, but generally we just forgot about civilization as soon as land disappeared over the horizon, and we gladly became lost in our own world of wind and waves. Nor did we have any idea what kind of weather was heading our way until it hit us, and it was only years later that I came to understand how hard it must have been for my parents, worrying about their sons being out there somewhere on the vast ocean.

In those days the food was forgettable. During my crossings of the Tasman Sea, there was nothing but canned stuff on the menu after our meager stores of fresh food ran out or the supplies of ice melted, whichever came first, because we had no refrigeration. For the Tahiti race George moved the quality of the chow up a notch by ordering in a supply of new-fangled, freeze-dried food that had been developed by the Sierra Club for mountaineers. It was quick and easy to prepare – you just mixed hot water with powder – light in weight, easy to store, and it never went bad. Improvement though it was, even freeze-dried food could get tedious. I mean

▲

Ten days to go to the finish line off Tahiti, Georgie on the tiller. Ten year old Johnny is not looking as excited as I was to be racing across the Pacific Ocean.

there's only so much Tuna Neptune that you can handle on a 23-day voyage.

We flogged *Spirit* hard, racing her day and night, and finished a creditable third in class and fifth overall in a 14-yacht fleet, no mean achievement given her size. George felt vindicated, and he was probably delighted he'd once again got one up on Olin Stephens and the trans-Pacific race committee. But I best remember the Tahiti race for the many hours of conversations I had with Doug Peterson about our yacht design philosophies while we shared watches, and it quickly became clear that he was thinking the same radical ideas as me. I had already made a start by working for Gary Mull, but I was burning to turn my ideas into my own designs.

After we crossed the finish line in Tahiti, a barefoot Doug, carrying all his worldly possessions in a single brown paper bag, disembarked *Spirit* and went off to board a flight to Los Angeles, and later to Boston, where he would start a job with Dick Carter in Nahant, Massachusetts. I envied him this break.

▲

A youthful crew parking *Spirit* in Tahiti after 23 days at sea. L TO R: Doug Peterson, Jim Leach, Georgie Kiskaddon, and me on the foredeck. George and Johnny are already ashore! I mostly remember only cold showers being available in our cheap hotel.

▶

After 23 days at sea *Spirit* approaches the finish line off beautiful Tahiti in very light wind. Our competitor *Misty* is a bigger yacht and crosses the line just ahead of *Spirit,* but we have managed to keep her behind us for over 20 days and we beat her on handicap corrected time.

Improbable under the Tampa Bay's old Sunshine Skyway Bridge ahead of her racing competitors on her way to Ft. Lauderdale.

Improbable though it may seem

BEFORE *SPIRIT* HAD SET SAIL FOR TAHITI, the *Improbable* project had been saved by a San Francisco property developer named Dave Allen. He liked and trusted Commodore with good reason: because he had a reputation for winning. Dave had just won the Miami-Nassau race, one of the classics of the American sailing season, in a Gary Mull-designed yacht called *Lively Lady,* and having tasted victory he was eager to return to winning mode.

A former fighter pilot in the Pacific during the Second World War, he was also a man of quick decisions, and after taking one look at Gary's design he got out his checkbook. "Let's keep the name but make her five feet longer," he said. Delighted, Commodore readily agreed because he knew this would make *Improbable* even faster, if more expensive. Now that the grand plan had been resurrected we became even more excited than before, if that was possible. We had an owner with the resources to turn into reality the boat that Gary had said couldn't be done, but in which we had all come to believe.

Time was marching on: we were already well into 1970 and we had to get this boat done. It was now that my abortive boatbuilding apprenticeship came in useful, because I suggested that *Improbable* be built at Keith Atkinson's boatyard in Browns Bay.

"Browns Bay? In New Zealand?" was the general reaction.

"Why not?" I replied. I firmly believed that nobody built cold-molded wooden boats better than New Zealanders, and I argued in favor of exporting the project, so to speak. After a bit of persuasion Dave agreed, and when we approached Keith he readily agreed to take on the job – after all, he didn't get a lot of commissions from America. Gary duly sent him the plans, and even before *Spirit* had left San Francisco my former workmates at Browns Bay had gotten down to work, and the lines were lofted in June.

The material of choice which I had specified, was the kauri wood that is native to New Zealand. So valuable was kauri – and still is – that it was protected by law and could not be exported except in finished form, such as a yacht. Blessed with amazingly durable properties, the wood is of medium density, evenly grained, and has "a light, buttery color," as Commodore elegantly put it in *Sail* magazine a few years later. In addition the wood toughens up with age and is practically impervious to rot, as evidenced by the kauri-built yachts still racing in Auckland Harbour more than a hundred years after they were first launched.

Most importantly, a properly built kauri boat met our stipulation that *Improbable* must be light but unbreakable. In technical terms, her skin was to be finished an inch thick with two quarter-inch diagonal plies and a half-inch ply fore and aft on the outside. This would be coated with a light layer of fiberglass and resin. Instead of conventional frames typically employed with wooden boats to preserve the integrity of the hull against the stresses that come with ocean racing, she would have longitudinal stringers, which was how New Zealand boatbuilders traditionally constructed their lightweight racing yachts.

Gary and Keith had cleverly come up with the idea of spreading the keel loads through an elaborate and sturdy series of galvanized floors that would bear the weight and torque of the keel. In turn, the pressures imposed on the hull by the keel and mast would be distributed through tapered and laminated kauri floors, buttressed by the galvanized fabrications. For extra strength Gary also designed lightweight aluminum frames around the mast, to spread the forces applied to the hull and deck by the rigging. These frames were bolted to the wooden hull structure. An ocean racer has to be strong in every direction, and the boat's longitudinal rigidity, as Commodore explained in *Sail*, "is further enhanced by careful joining of the interior woodwork throughout her length, to port and starboard stringers which lead [at] the ends into a pair of very considerable wooden truss braces." In other words, she was designed to be bulletproof. All three of us had done a lot of ocean racing and we understood how important overall stiffness and structural integrity were in a full-on racing yacht.

But by the time *Spirit* had crossed the finish line at Tahiti, the project had run into trouble once again. The Atkinson yard was over-committed, and

construction had fallen well behind schedule. The only way to speed things up was for me to get myself to Auckland and see what I could do – but I also had to take *Spirit* to Sydney.

After arriving in Tahiti, everybody relaxed for a few days before George took his family cruising for a couple of weeks. This was my chance to fly to Auckland and check on *Improbable*. After the Kiskaddons and the rest of the crew returned to America, I was due to take over *Spirit* in American Samoa. At 23 years of age I was keenly aware of the responsibility. The plan was to visit other Pacific islands and Auckland while delivering the yacht to Sydney for the Hobart Race. There were just four of us: myself and

▲

Improbable under construction at Keith Atkinson's boatyard in Browns Bay, Auckland. San Francisco yacht designer Gary Mull asked me to check on building progress after I arrived aboard *Spirit* in New Zealand on our way to the Sydney Hobart Race.

"'Look, you can see the bottom,' somebody said. The bottom! If you can see the bottom of the sea on the windward side of a Pacific reef, you're in trouble because the boat is sailing straight onto it. I rushed up on deck. 'Spinnaker down!' I yelled. Startled, the crew took one look at me, and sensing the danger, were galvanized into action and dropped the sail in seconds."

17-year-old George Kiskaddon, my 22-year-old girlfriend Kathy from Santa Cruz, and 26-year-old Russ, a member of the winning trans-Pacific crew aboard a boat called *Widgeon*, designed and built by Charlie Morgan in Florida.

Heading westward through these island-studded waters, I had at my disposal just a sextant and a clock, pretty much exactly what Captain Cook had used more than 200 years earlier. Keeping a constant eye on both of them, in favorable weather I took *Spirit* out of Pago Pago, the territorial capital of American Samoa, and headed for the Fiji Islands. Along the way we stopped in Apia, the biggest city in Samoa, where we paid our respects to the grave of Robert Louis Stevenson before continuing towards Fiji. It was between Samoa and Fiji that we would cross the International Date Line, something for which I wasn't prepared. Nobody had mentioned the International Date Line in my admittedly rudimentary navigation lessons. I remember thinking, What do I do now?

Should I flip forward a couple of pages in the navigation tables to get onto Fiji time, or should I stick with today's date? I didn't have a clue, and nobody else in the crew did either. Complicating the dilemma the weather had turned overcast, so I couldn't get a good sun sight with the sextant to establish a reliable position. Basically I had to guess, by something known as dead reckoning. With so many reefs scattered over the Pacific, the term struck me as all too accurate.

These are dangerous waters. Fiji is surrounded to the east by the infamous Lau Group, also known as the Eastern Archipelago – about 60 islands edged by jagged coral reefs that can trap a boat in seconds and rip the bottom out of her hull. We can get wrecked here, I thought. I wasn't being unduly pessimistic: many a Pacific Ocean voyager has come to grief on the Lau Group.

To my relief, just before nightfall during our third evening we spotted the lighthouse that marks the archipelago, pretty much exactly where my dead reckoning had put it. I didn't know whether this was due to good luck or good management, but we were safe for the time being and I was able to relax a little. Because it's impossible to negotiate the archipelago at night, we reduced sail and waited for daylight. Once among the reefs, the only way to navigate is with your eyes. Charts are no help at such close quarters.

When there was sufficient light to see beneath the surface of the water, we set off towards this dangerous passage, the trickiest by far I had ever navigated. I took the tiller in a sweaty palm. The wind had dropped, and in a burst of confidence I ordered the spinnaker to be set and went below to see whether, despite everything, the charts might shed some light.

I was trying to read them when I heard the crew talking among themselves on deck, just inches above me. "Look, you can see the bottom," somebody said. The bottom! If you can see the bottom of the sea on the windward side of a Pacific reef, you're in trouble because the boat is sailing straight onto it.

I rushed up on deck. "Spinnaker down!" I yelled.

Startled, the crew took one look at me, and sensing the danger, were galvanized into action and dropped the sail in seconds. "Sheet in the main! We've got to get out of here." I pushed the tiller across to turn *Spirit* around and take her back the way we'd just come – that is, to windward. But the wind had fallen so light that we couldn't make any headway. The yacht wasn't clearing the reef. Worse, the current was pushing us backwards. Waves were breaking on the coral, just a few yards off our stern. If *Spirit* slipped back into those waves, I knew we were done for.

"Hurry! Get the jib set." The crew dashed to do the fastest jib set of their lives.

With the foresail up, *Spirit* began to make headway with agonizing slowness, everybody concentrating as though an Olympic gold medal were at stake.

It took minutes to clear the reef, and it seemed as though time stood still. When we were finally safe, I was shaking with fright but trying not

▲

Chief Benny paddled us ashore one at a time, and in the bush took us to where a tree trunk lay on the ground. It was obvious that he was making a canoe.

to show it. It took hours before I could breathe easily. I knew that *Spirit* could have broken up on the reef and her crew drowned. I didn't see how anybody could have survived on that coral. Even now I find myself dreaming about that morning and waking up with a start, knowing that I had all those lives in my hands, including George Kiskaddon's eldest boy.

Once we'd gotten over our scare we continued to sail *Spirit* among jagged coral reefs with total confidence in our ability to maneuver around them. Multi-colored, they extended as far as the eye could see, and we zigzagged among them all morning until we came across an especially beautiful island named on the chart as Vanua Balavu. Although we were supposed to clear customs and immigration in the Fijian capital of Suva before stepping on dry land, I just had to go ashore and have a look.

We tacked *Spirit* through a gap in the reef surrounding the island, and sailed into an enchanted bay with steep-sided cliffs from which hung dense vegetation. The trees were so thick with foliage that they fell straight into the sea. Birds sang all around us as we anchored *Spirit* off a golden sandy beach.

Now what? We didn't have a dinghy or any other way of getting ashore. "We could swim," somebody suggested. "How about sharks?" somebody else asked. "Are there any down there?" I wanted to know. "Bound to be," came the answer. "Probably lots of them." All of a sudden nobody was keen to risk swimming the 50 yards or so to shore, but we still eyed the beach. It seemed like an unattainable paradise.

Then to our astonishment a native emerged from the trees in a canoe and paddled alongside. Introducing himself as Chief Benny, he invited us in good English to come ashore. "We can't," I apologized. "We've got no way of getting there." Clearly disappointed, Chief Benny said goodbye and paddled back to his enchanted island. Frustrated, we returned below.

When we woke up next morning, it was to the sound of an axe striking wood in the thick stands of trees behind the beach, and we wondered what was going on. A little later, Chief Benny paddled alongside again and invited us ashore once more.

"I'll take you in my canoe," he said. "You can meet the family this time." We looked at it doubtfully. Basically, a hollowed-out tree, it looked decidedly unstable. But curiosity overcoming our fear, we allowed him to take us ashore, one at a time. Yes, it's tippy alright, I thought. The water was just inches away and, if Chief Benny wasn't worried about sharks, I certainly was.

Before introducing us to his family he took us into the trees and showed us what all the noise had been about. Chief Benny was making a boat for *Spirit*. As he proudly explained, he'd cut down a tree and was turning the

"Over the next two days, with *Spirit* anchored off the beach, we watched as Chief Benny worked on our canoe, banging away half the day with his razor-sharp axe as the pile of chips and shavings got bigger and bigger. It was a revelation to see him at work, shaping the canoe with quick, accurate blows until it was finally done."

log into a canoe. There was a pile of chips and shavings around the log and we could already see where we were supposed to sit. "It's for you," he explained. "You take it with you. And then you can come ashore whenever you want."

Overcome with gratitude, we didn't know quite what to say. I mean, what could we do to thank him? Then we were finally introduced to the family, his wife and two small kids living in a hut made of flax mats. Over the next two days, with *Spirit* anchored off the beach, we watched as Chief Benny worked on our canoe, banging away half the day with his razor-sharp axe as the pile of chips and shavings got bigger and bigger. It was a revelation to see him at work, shaping the canoe with quick, accurate blows until it was finally done. He was a real craftsman, and I took a lot of photographs of him at work. There was a presentation ceremony, coconut water splashed over the bow and a few words spoken in Fijian that we guessed was a kind of blessing. Then Chief Benny gave us a set of paddles and said: "Now you can practice."

It took us several attempts before we could paddle our brand new canoe without capsizing and floundering around in what we'd learned were definitely shark-infested waters, until we were eventually good enough to stay upright.

On the third day we weighed anchor, and waving to Chief Benny and his family gathered on the beach, we tacked back out through the reef and

Chief Benny's canoe

▲

After a short climb from the beach into the bush the *Spirit* crew arrived at the fallen tree to find Chief Benny, axe in hand, standing on the horizontal tree trunk he had cut to the length of the new canoe.

▲

On our next visit, a few hours later, Benny had axed the tree trunk to the external shape of the new canoe. Chips of wood were flying in all directions.

▲

The next morning the canoe was upright and hollowed out to accommodate its crew. With a few final deft slices with the axe it was ready to go. We all helped slide it through the bush to the beach, anxious to test *Spirit*'s new "tender." No launching until baptism, insisted the chief.

Chief Benny performing the baptism of our new tender. In the Fiji Islands coconut milk replaces champagne. When the tide came in the canoe floated off the coral sand and we had fun trying to stay upright, learning how to paddle our new dinghy.

We spent as much time swimming as paddling, relying on Benny's assurance, "No sharks at my beach."

▶

Georgie with Chief Benny's canoe. With our custom-made canoe lashed across the deck we sailed *Spirit* more than 1,300 miles from the Fiji Islands to New Zealand. In Auckland I donated the canoe, together with my photographic report of Chief Benny's creation process, to the Auckland War Memorial Museum where it was displayed for several years.

set a course for Suva. I was sad to leave, but at least we had a memory to take with us – and something tangible in the form of our canoe, lashed across the foredeck with its ends sticking out each side. We transported it all the way to New Zealand, and when we came ashore there I approached the Auckland War Memorial Museum, famous for its collections of South Pacific artifacts, and asked if I could donate the canoe, complete with my transparencies recording its creation. To my pleasure they readily agreed, so Chief Benny's canoe ended up as Exhibit A. For all I know, it might still be there. Shortly afterwards, we set sail for Sydney with an uncluttered foredeck.

After we docked at Sydney, I had to fly straight back to Auckland to meet Commodore who arrived from San Francisco not long afterwards. We rolled up our sleeves and worked long hours with Keith's boatbuilders leading right up to Christmas, installing winches, cleats, compasses, ports, electronics and all the other vital bits of equipment that an ocean racer needs. We hoped to have *Improbable* in the water before Dave arrived, but toil as we did, she wasn't anywhere near finished when he turned up after a long flight from San Francisco. Without complaint, the man paying the bills worked alongside everybody else, in what was turning into a race against time if *Improbable* were to make the SORC and America's Admiral's Cup trials. Unfortunately, Dave had to return to America before the boat was launched. Commodore and I were also up against a tight schedule be-cause we were taking part in the Sydney to Hobart deep-water classic, due to start December 26. By now we were working practically day and night.

Finally, *Improbable* was ready to be floated. With time running out, she was put in the water and motored a short way across the harbor to the ferry wharf at Birkenhead where the mast was stepped, winches installed and lenticular, aerofoil-shaped rigging fitted, the latter being a first in New Zealand. As a finishing touch, and much to the amusement of Dave's boatbuilders, she was equipped with a hand-made cowbell which Gary had specified to comply with U.S. Coast Guard regulations that require the ringing of a bell every three minutes when sailing in fog.

The very evening before we had to fly out to Australia, everything was more or less ready. We broke the brand-new sails out of their bags, looked at the harbor where a steady breeze had been blowing all day, and saw that the wind had dropped to a zephyr, hopeless conditions in which to baptize a racing yacht. Dejected and exhausted, we were about to put the untested sails back in their bag when Commodore said, "Let's go!"

Unable to resist the temptation, we ventured out into the harbor with-out a proper tiller – we'd jury-rigged a length of two-by-four – and lacking a forward lower shroud – yes, the one that helps keep the mast upright, not to mention a few other important bits and pieces. It was dusk and we had no lights, but we got away with it. For twenty glorious minutes we sailed our dream ocean racer to windward. "I think she's a flyer," declared Commodore with a tired smile. And in truth we estimated in the absence of proper instruments that we were getting better than six knots with seven knots of true – that is, real – wind. As Commodore would say later, "So little wind and so much speed."

We docked around midnight after our impromptu excursion, found a place to eat and then returned to the boat to prepare her for the obligatory official measurement before she was shipped to America to take her place in the SORC. Utterly exhausted, we slept a few hours, waking up too late to make it to the airport – or so we thought. I forget who it was but somebody produced a little Morris Minor, bundled us into it and, with the minutes ticking by, somehow got onto the tow of a fire engine that had been called out on a mission. Siren blaring, the firemen unknowingly led us at high speed most of the way to Auckland Airport, just in time for us to jump aboard our flights to Sydney.

In the months-long drama of getting *Improbable* into the water we'd hardly given a thought to the Sydney to Hobart, a race that regularly tested boats and crews to the limit, and with which I'd had a love affair since I was a kid.

I had now competed twice in the classic, first in *Poseidon*, and fired by enthusiasm, a year later in a 30-footer called *Castanet*. On *Spirit,* this would be my first as skipper. After performing creditably in the Tahiti Race we had high hopes, but for the first time I didn't make it to the finish line. After an auspicious start – *Spirit* was first yacht over the start line in Sydney Harbour – we lost our rudder in strong winds as we entered the notorious Bass Strait, so we had to jury-rig a sweep to limp to a safe haven at Eden where other yachts had also taken refuge. This was quite a feat of seamanship by the young crew, the oldest being me, but we made it. At least I was comforted with the thought that while we had been racing *Spirit* to the limit as George would have wanted, *Improbable* was being shipped to Charleston, South Carolina, on a voyage of 20 days. Or rather, I hoped she was.

▶

The Pacific Ocean: I plot *Spirit*'s trans-Pacific voyage and our eventually aborted Sydney Hobart Race. A voyage under my command at 22 years of age.

MAP LEGEND
— *Spirit* trans-Pacific voyage

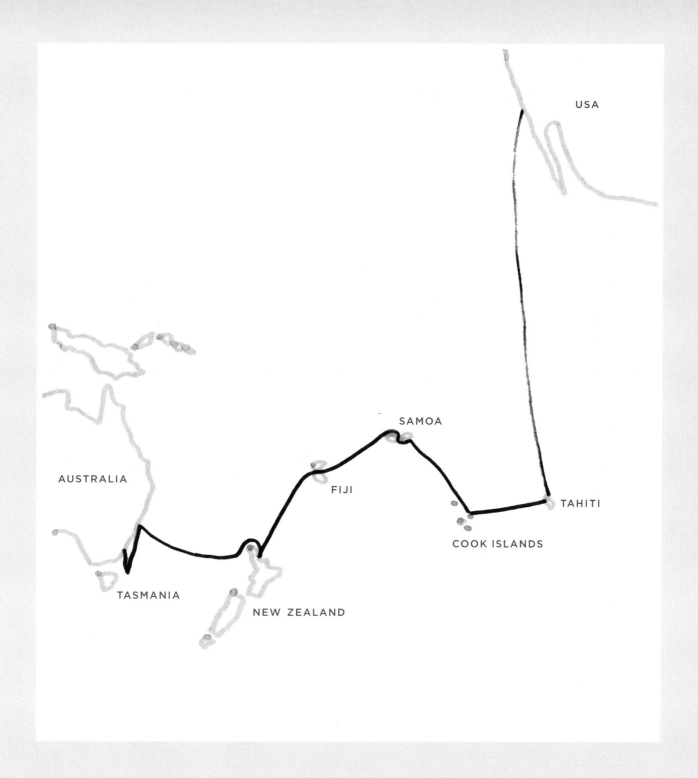

USA

SAMOA

FIJI

AUSTRALIA

TAHITI

COOK ISLANDS

TASMANIA

NEW ZEALAND

The *Improbable* crew climb to
the citadel near Cap Haitien on
the north coast of Haiti before
returning to Florida.

Even more improbable

WHEN WE FLEW OUT OF AUCKLAND, we knew the timetable was tight. If the freighter had a good run from Auckland, from where she was due to depart on Christmas Eve for the Panama Canal, we reasoned *Improbable* would be craned off the freighter in Charleston and onto a truck, then transported to St. Petersburg with just enough time to make the opening race of the Southern Ocean Racing Conference series where we hoped she would show her paces. Generally known as the SORC, or "The Circuit," it was the biggest and most competitive offshore racing event in America at the time.

That would give us a bit of time to bed down all the deck gear and work her up into racing shape. But she first had to be rigged, or rather re-rigged, because the mast had of course been taken down in Auckland after her all-too-brief shakedown sail. Then she had to be re-commissioned and entered in the SORC series. It was a wafer-thin timetable if we were to try *Improbable* out in the SORC and make her shipshape for the Jamaica Race, which was our main goal. We were worried that, if the freighter was delayed by hostile weather or some other event, all our work would be in vain. In what was becoming routine for this project, our worries were justified.

The freighter, the *Cape Breton*, had not sailed from New Zealand until January 10, which meant we were now certain to miss the opening salvo of the SORC. But it was only the first race, we consoled ourselves, and there would still be time to get the boat ready for the following races if there were no further delays.

So I flew from Sydney to Charleston to link up with Dave Allen and make sure there were no further slip-ups. Hardly had the *Cape Breton* docked at Charleston than Dave and I pulled up in a rental car to see our dream boat hoisted off the cargo ship's deck and loaded onto a semi-trailer for trucking to St. Petersburg. Just to make sure she arrived safe and sound, we followed the truck all the way through Georgia and northern Florida to Clearwater, a distance of about 450 miles, watching the hull like mother hens.

With a bare two and a half days left before the second race of the SORC series, the longest one from St. Petersburg to Fort Lauderdale, we all arrived together – the boat, Dave and I – to find an impatient crew waiting.

A good organizer, Dave had hired the Courtney Ross boatyard that thrived on crazy schedules, and its workmen pulled out all the stops. For the next 60 hours they did all they could to help get *Improbable* into the water in time. They gave us the key to their storerooms, their men and the crew worked practically day and night, and somehow we got it done in the kind of all-out, unstinting effort that is so often typical of yacht racing.

The boat was re-rigged, the last few deck fittings were bolted down, sheets were run, and shrouds tensioned in a controlled panic. With about two hours to spare before the starting gun, *Improbable* slipped into the water and we motored out for the obligatory safety inspection by the race committee, while we made last-minute checks and adjustments, including fixing a stripped thread on one of the lower shrouds.

A stripped thread may not sound like much but the shroud helps to hold the mast up, and it was particularly important because of our special aerofoil rigging. Desperately we worked at the problem as the clock ticked down. With ten minutes to go, as we maneuvered around the starting line we more or less fixed the shroud and, in the nick of time, re-tensioned the rigging. We then checked every single one of our sails to see if we'd forgotten something. Incredibly, the entire wardrobe went up and was sheeted home without a hitch, accompanied by a cheer from the entire crew.

What a relief! Exhausted though we were after the furious construction schedule in New Zealand, the rigors and disappointment of the Sydney Hobart Race, the rushed drive to St. Petersburg, and the two and a half days of re-rigging the boat and all the hundreds of other details necessary to prepare a racing yacht, we were elated to make the starting line. As Commodore would remember, "Her construction phase was finally completed, improbable as it may have seemed."

"It took just a couple of hours after the firing of the starting gun for *Improbable* to answer the burning question. Was she fast? As we slid along the western side of Tampa Bay and under the Sunshine Skyway bridge in a light breeze, we looked at each other. Yes, she was."

It took just a couple of hours after the firing of the starting gun for *Improbable* to answer the burning question. Was she fast? As we slid along the western side of Tampa Bay and under the Sunshine Skyway bridge in a light breeze, we looked at each other. Yes, she was.

As soon as we set our big red spinnaker we had the answer, as most of the fleet slowly disappeared astern including much bigger, higher-rating yachts.

The rest of the race proved something of an anticlimax, because after a few hours a cold front blew in from the north and *Improbable* was hard on the wind most of the way to Fort Lauderdale, far from her best point of sailing. Thereafter the rest of the SORC didn't tell us much either, because the wind was on the nose for nearly all the races, a total of 120 hours in our case. Our dream boat performed only moderately well on corrected time, finishing third in her class and twelfth overall out of 60 yachts.

But these weren't her ideal conditions so we were pleased, and we had noticed something interesting: *Improbable* had proven faster than all the other 40-footers, even though we'd spent half the race making repairs and learning how to sail her. She would be dangerous when the wind freed up and blew from aft of abeam, which was what she'd been designed for.

So two weeks later we lined up for the classic Jamaica Race – 500 miles from Miami to Montego Bay – with high hopes. In the intervening days we'd worked hard and were reasonably sure nothing else would break.

OVERLEAF: Dave Allen and the green stripe guys kept on winning. *Imp* was the only yacht to be selected to race for the USA in both the 1977 and 1979 Admiral's Cups.

▲

Improbable winning the Jamaica Race to Montego Bay was a huge success for me. This result encouraged Dave Allen to ask me to sail *Improbable* to England for the Admiral's Cup. My first transatlantic voyage and my first Fastnet Race.

Known as the "Mobay", the race takes yachts all the way around the Bahamas in crystal clear waters, then through the Windward Passage with its typically big seas off the east end of Cuba, and thereafter to the north coast of Jamaica. A flat-out drag race, it's a favorite event because of the warm days and nights, generally pleasant conditions and fast sailing. Having blown away the cobwebs in the SORC, we crossed the starting line in a confident mood. We just needed the wind to cooperate. And it did.

For the entire race *Improbable* was off the wind, either reaching or running with the spinnaker set, in what turned into a revelation. Again and again, while we whooped and hollered on deck she would surf under spinnaker, overtaking breaking waves at more than 20 knots without revealing the slightest strain or any hint of broaching. We didn't know exactly how fast *Improbable* was going because the speedometer only measured up to 20 knots, an exceptional speed for a 41-footer in the 1970s. Yet time and again we kept on running the speedometer up to the max. We joked that we should have bought one that could record 30 knots.

She was not only fast but a delight to sail.

As an impressed Commodore wrote: "*Improbable* ate this up, giving her crew a ride so gentle that we often felt we were loafing along."

We crossed the finish line at Montego Bay in fifth place, three days and 20 hours after the start. Not fifth in our class, but fifth overall. That is, fifth boat-for-boat in the entire fleet. In just her second outing *Improbable* was headed only by much bigger boats such as *Windward Passage* (a much-garlanded maxi yacht named after that famous part of the course); another maxi, *Ondine*; Ted Turner's converted America's Cup yacht *American Eagle*; and *Sorcery*, a brand-new yacht from Canada.

To put this into perspective *Windward Passage* was about 30 feet longer than *Improbable* while *Sorcery,* immediately ahead of us, was nearly 20 feet longer. We'd had these boats within our sight the entire race. Even more promising, the elements had not provided the strong winds in which we suspected *Improbable* would really excel, so we knew there was more to come from her.

We made port in the middle of the night and tied up at the same pontoon as *Windward Passage*, whose crew were noisily celebrating a record time for line honors, first across the finish line. After a snatched hour or two of sleep, around first light we set up an awning over the cockpit, and were tucking into a celebration tropical breakfast when *Windward Passage*'s crew staggered past us heading for the clubhouse. It was only then that they put two and two together: their fabled boat must have been thrashed on corrected time, which is the prize that matters. Commodore reckons this was one of the most satisfying moments of his entire life, watching comprehension dawn on the faces of the boys from the West Coast.

When the last boat had crossed the line, the officials finished their calculations and, taking handicaps into account, declared *Improbable* the overall victor by the whopping margin of an hour. Now, after months of working against the clock, it was our turn to celebrate.

A few sore heads later, the rest of the crew returned home to California, leaving me in charge of the boat. I lived aboard her in Jamaica for over a month until Dave and some of his large family returned to Montego Bay on vacation. As I sat around over dinner with his family, the discussion came up. What next?

Dave knew he had a thoroughbred in *Improbable*, but we'd missed the American Admiral's Cup trials because of all the delays, so we could not represent his country in England. Dave didn't want to leave things there, so he broached the idea of taking her to England anyway and racing her as a private entry in the Fastnet Race, something the rules permit.

"I'm super keen on this," I told Dave, but I had another suggestion: "I might be able to arrange for *Improbable* to represent New Zealand in the Admiral's Cup." After all, I was a Kiwi, I could be named as the skipper, and the boat had been built in New Zealand.

The whole idea intrigued Dave who loved an adventure, so he quickly agreed and contacted the rest of the crew. "Yes," they said in so many words, "Let's go!"

All I had to do was get in touch with my club in Auckland, the Royal New Zealand Yacht Squadron, and see if it would agree to make the arrangements. To my great pleasure and relief the reply came back in the affirmative.

Next stop? Cowes, Isle of Wight, England.

The not-so-friendly reception
during my first visit to Cuba.

Incident in Cuba

BEFORE CAMPAIGNING *Improbable* in the first ever New Zealand Admiral's Cup team, we'd decided to modify her so she would gain a more favorable handicap under the new International Offshore Rule (IOR). We had learned that, designed as she was for the downhill Jamaica Race, *Improbable* would not be competitive in the more variable winds we could expect in England, and she needed a few tweaks if she were to perform at her best. So Gary had gotten out the IOR rulebook and decided that she needed a broader beam, among other changes to her hull shape. Although *Improbable* would always be too narrow and too light to compete with the latest IOR-biased designs from Sparkman & Stephens and fast-rising star Dick Carter, Gary was sure her rating could be improved with a few judicious alterations. When Gary had completed the design work, Dave instructed me to sail the yacht from Jamaica to England – right across the Atlantic – and arrange to have the work done there. "OK," I said, while secretly asking myself, Doesn't anyone realize I'm only 24?

The assignment seemed like a lot more responsibility than anything I'd undertaken so far, but I guessed Dave thought that if I could get George Kiskaddon's *Spirit* from Tahiti to Australia without screwing up, then I could surely manage a voyage across the Atlantic to England, via Bermuda.

For the crossing I recruited a few experienced sailing buddies to join me. There was no shortage of willing helpers, and after stocking up on provisions, we set out from Kingston, Jamaica, and headed east against the prevailing

▲

While sailing *Improbable* across the Atlantic, a couple of times, I couldn't have imagined that one day I'd be working with master yacht designer Jon Bannenberg. Nautor Swan agent Sten Rasmussen invited Jon to join me in designing a large sailing yacht for his client, German publisher Franz Burda.

This new yacht was to be built in Finland by Nautor Swan. At 102 feet in length, this was at that time the biggest Swan ever built. Here I'm working with Jon at the Nautor factory in Finland to detail the yacht's unique exterior styling.

wind, skirting the south Jamaican coast and heading towards the Virgin Islands. From there I planned to follow the old course of the Spanish Main by riding the Gulf Stream to Bermuda before taking the great circle course across the North Atlantic, then into the English Channel. It was much the same course as the square-rigged ships followed in the old days.

After beating into the strong easterly trade winds of the Caribbean, with *Improbable* crashing uncomfortably up and down in rough seas, I was on deck at dawn of the second day as we were cruising off the south coast of Haiti, when I happened to look up and noticed that the leeward rigging – the stays and shrouds – were flapping around in the breeze.

This isn't right, I thought, and looked aloft to see what was wrong. To my horror the lower spreader, a vital component in keeping the mast upright, had come adrift and broken clean off. The entire mast could collapse at any minute. "Quick, sails down!" I bawled. The crew scrambled onto the deck and dropped the sails in double-quick time. "What now?" I asked. Here we were, just two days out and we'd already run into trouble.

Masts of racing yachts are flimsy affairs that are subjected to a lot of punishment, but I hadn't expected the rig to fail under delivery mode. After a brief discussion, we realized we had only one option: head for the nearest port, which happened to be Port-au-Prince, capital of Haiti. We started up the engine and motored for a whole 20 hours into the port, intending to find a boatyard or engineering shop to fix the spreader and reinforce the other three spreaders, so we could continue with confidence on our way to England.

But we had barely tied up when we realized that we'd come to the wrong place at the wrong time. We'd docked on the very day that François "Papa Doc" Duvalier, the voodoo-loving dictator, had died after 14 brutal years in power, and everything was shut by public order. A cannon was firing every two minutes as a mark of respect, and the army was at full alert. Papa Doc, with his murderous secret police, the Tontons Macoutes (meaning "bogeymen"), had been a violent leader responsible, I later learned, for killing 30,000-60,000 Haitians whom he suspected of plotting to undermine him. It transpired that the Tontons Macoutes regularly dispatched the dictator's opponents by firing squad, or by torture such as immersing them in baths of sulfuric acid, while Papa Doc, a doctor by training, watched the grisly spectacle through spy holes in the cells.

But we had no other choice, and as we stepped ashore we could see that white people weren't welcome. All of a sudden I felt very white. Nor did it take long to find out that there was no possibility of getting the mast fixed in this chaotic, poverty-stricken country. We needed to scram

▲

We were never happy just "cruising along," we were always racing against any yacht we knew was in our waters. *Improbable* responded and we arrived at our destinations days before our "cruising in company" friends. Bengt and Ron at the tiller, sailing "improbably fast."

out of there. But it took us two days to get a message through to Dave in San Francisco, who ordered us to abandon the original plan of getting the modifications done in England because time was running out, all over again. Everything to do with *Improbable* seemed to end up in delays.

"We'll get the rigging fixed and the modifications done here in America," he said. "I'll organize Bob Derecktor's yard in Florida."

After hastily making temporary repairs to the spreader, we gladly departed Port-au-Prince and sailed to the country's north coast, where we briefly ventured ashore at Cap Haitien and ascended to the top of a 3,000-foot-high mountain with its precipitous drops, to see the Citadelle Laferrière. While this was a fascinating visit, I've never been back to Haiti and I have no intention of doing so.

Derecktor's yard in Ft. Lauderdale took *Improbable* in hand and ably carried out the big job of the modifications in double-quick time, so we could make a second attempt to cross the Atlantic. For once everything went reasonably smoothly, at least until we reached the English Channel. After three days we were in Bermuda, then after another 16 days at sea we raised the Scilly Isles and Land's End pretty much as expected. I still remember the sense of history that came over me: I was now in the waters of Drake, Nelson, the Spanish Armada and the tea clippers returning from India and Ceylon.

But where was the Eddystone lighthouse? About twelve miles sou'sou'west of Plymouth, we should have sighted it hours ago, at around midday. To see where we were, I took a sextant reading at noon. Whoops! *Improbable* was closer to the French coast than the English one, a mistake which I put down to the wild tidal movements in these waters. I'd miscalculated the power of the currents and tides, and we had almost sailed right past Plymouth. So we turned around, set a spinnaker and returned the way we'd come, arriving just as darkness was falling. It was my first transatlantic crossing.

With her improved rating, *Improbable* was a significantly more formidable competitor than she would otherwise have been. Although the winds in the early races weren't to our liking, *Improbable* finally got the conditions she needed in the Fastnet Race across the Irish Sea. On the way back to England, flying along under spinnaker in a strong westerly wind, she passed every yacht in sight. And after the Fastnet, when we won the Plymouth to La Rochelle race to wrap up *Improbable*'s European campaign, Dave was more than pleased. Despite the delays in construction, his ownership of *Improbable* had brought him more than he'd hoped, and he stepped off the boat to return to San Francisco in a happy frame of mind.

In the meantime I prepared to sail *Improbable* back across the Atlantic with a new crew that included a young woman named Laurel Carlin. Daughter of a family I had come to know in Florida during the SORC races, Laurel was an accomplished yachtswoman. A Miami girl, she had started sailing as a kid and knew a lot about boats. I'd met her when *Improbable* was undergoing her modifications at Derecktor's, and I invited her to join my crew for the Atlantic crossing delivery to England and back to the United States. To my surprise she promptly accepted, and I had grown to value her company on the way out.

On the way back, the Atlantic was once again kind to us, and soon enough we found ourselves following the trade winds back to the Caribbean, skirting the southern coasts of the Dominican Republic and Haiti en route to Florida via Jamaica. This time when we'd stopped off in Jamaica I had been warned about sailing too close to Cuba. Fidel Castro was said to be paranoid about foreign surveillance, especially by American vessels of any kind. I'd taken the warnings to heart and fully intended to heed them.

But one day we found ourselves sailing lazily along Cuba's exotic southern coastline, and I forgot about the warnings. Well, I didn't exactly forget. If we were to avoid Cuban territorial waters, it would involve a 90-degree change in course and many more miles of sailing, which seemed a bit silly. Anyway, I reasoned, how could the Cuban navy possibly be worried about a little red racing yacht? What harm could we possibly do? So I made a decision to continue ambling along the coastline and save us a lot of time. As the crew sunned themselves on deck, we were about half a mile off a beach near the western end of Cuba, and I was congratulating myself on a good decision. Laurel had the binoculars out and was training them on a beach we were passing. "Lots of people running around there," she said. "Looks like soldiers going on parade." "Really, soldiers on parade?" I grabbed the binoculars and took a look for myself.

"Let's get out of here!" I yelled. We did a 90-degree turn, steering *Improbable* due south and away from the beach. "Let's get her into deeper water."

"Now the soldiers are running towards the beach," Laurel continued her commentary. "They're all on the wharf. They're getting into a fishing boat. The boat's coming at us fast. Look, the soldiers are waving at us!" "Waving at us?" I took the glasses from her again. "Let me see."

Bloody hell! A boat, packed to the gunwales with soldiers, had cleared the harbor and was heading our way, plowing up a big bow wave. "That's no fishing boat," I shouted. "It's a gunboat! Start the engine!" I was hoping we could outrun the Cuban navy. As the engine kicked into life, I handed back the binoculars to Laurel and went below. "Can't we get the boat to go

▲

The Cuban army commandante explaining to Ragga and me that Fidel also came to Cuba in a small boat, and that is why he had to arrest the crew of *Improbable*. At least, I think that is what he was saying. Bengt had the courage to shoot a couple of photos after *Improbable* was boarded. Looking at these photos over 40 years later, two things stand out in my mind: first, how young the Cuban soldiers look, and second, where are all the guns that were so prominent when they boarded us? I guess after they spent all afternoon with us they realized it was not going to be necessary to have guns at the ready.

"That's odd, I thought. Firecrackers? Then I heard more of them. Crack, crack, crack. I grabbed back the glasses. Real live bullets were ricocheting off the water between *Improbable* and the gunboat. Dangerously close. More soldiers crowded around the bow were taking aim. 'Dive for cover!' I yelled as another fusillade of bullets tore up the water."

faster?" I pleaded. No, we couldn't and, anyway, it was too late. The gunboat was almost on us, youthful soldiers brandishing their weapons in a highly threatening manner that I didn't like one little bit. Suddenly, I heard firecrackers going off somewhere.

That's odd, I thought. Firecrackers? Then I heard more of them. Crack, crack, crack.

I grabbed back the glasses. Real live bullets were ricocheting off the water between *Improbable* and the gunboat. Dangerously close. More soldiers crowded around the bow were taking aim. "Dive for cover!" I yelled as another fusillade of bullets tore up the water.

The five of us hurled ourselves down below onto the cabin floor in a desperate attempt to take shelter, huddling for protection around the engine as it thumped away in a futile attempt to get *Improbable* into open water. There was more shooting. I had a sickening feeling that I'd just made the biggest mistake of my life, and we might die because of it.

Crash! Without anybody at the controls, *Improbable* rounded up into the wind, and the gunboat hit us, shaking the yacht from stem to stern. Within seconds we heard heavy boots thumping along the deck above us, and I remember thinking, God, what am I going to tell Dave? I'm going to lose his yacht.

Nervously we got to our feet and emerged from the cabin one by one, with our hands up. There were about a dozen soldiers on board, all teenagers apart from their commander who looked to be around 30 years old, armed to the teeth with machine guns, pistols and big ferocious-looking knives. To a man they looked eager for a fight. Trying to stay calm, I approached the commander to express my apologies and concern, but he spoke no English, and it soon transpired that none of them did.

Fortunately, Miami girl Laurel came to the rescue with some Spanish. Translating for me, she said hopefully to the commander, "What harm can we do? We're a little racing yacht."

"Che Guevara and Fidel Castro arrived here in a small boat like this," he growled, as his soldiers continued to look as if they wanted our blood. Mostly by sign language the commander indicated that we would be taken ashore, where I knew anything could happen. I'd heard of yachtsmen being imprisoned for months on end in Cuba for no good reason.

They threw us a line from the gunboat, and following their instructions, we tied it on. At high speed the gunboat towed us towards the shore, and despite me yelling a warning about the depth of our keel, *Improbable* ran straight aground on a sandbank. At this stage I was starting to get mad, and I berated the Commander for needlessly putting our yacht at risk. Somehow this distracted him and, stepping off *Improbable,* he ordered the gunboat to take him back to the wharf where he presumably intended to ask his superiors for instructions.

Now we had a dozen trigger-happy soldiers on board, with nowhere to go. Thinking quickly, Laurel went below and came up with a *Playboy* magazine, a perfect example of the western decadence that President Castro professed to despise. As it happened, I only had it aboard because of an interview that the eccentric business mogul and ace yachtsman Ted Turner had given to the magazine, but the kid soldiers loved it and passed it around with a few grins. All of a sudden Laurel was no longer a decadent, imperialist American but a real *chica*, and the boys began to get on with her famously.

After an interminable two hours, the slowly incoming tide floated *Improbable* clear of the sandbar. The commander returned and stepped back aboard. *"Pueden irse,"* he said. He gestured, you can go. I still don't know why he let us off. On the very same day, I learned later, French sailing legend Eric Tabarly was hauled off his Pen Duick as he tried to slip past the north coast of Cuba en route to race the SORC and was cooped up in jail for several days.

We'd been lucky.

▲

The soldiers leave *Improbable* with "American education" after absorbing Laurel's *Playboy* magazine gift. Thank you Hef.

Eygthene's first English landfall, the White Cliffs of Dover, after crossing the English Channel from Dunkirk.

On a shoestring

AFTER I HAD SPENT A FURTHER SEASON looking after *Improbable* during another SORC series in Florida, Dave Allen invited me to come back to San Francisco. I saw myself as a yacht designer rather than a boat navigator. A member of the fraternity of guys, and a couple of girls, whose job it was to deliver the yachts to the next race and keep the yachts shipshape between races on behalf of the owners. We had our own coat of arms – a mop crossed with a winch handle – and were proud of it. In fact I still am, and a select group of aging BNs remains in touch around the world.

I was still doing plenty of sailing. George Kiskaddon had taken delivery of *New World* in Auckland and sent her over to Newport, Rhode Island, for the 1972 Bermuda Race. The start of the race was delayed a couple of days to allow a gale to move off the race track, but after we started the gale returned and it was a very rough, windy race. How windy? "Blowing dogs off chains," or as the Aussies say, "Blowing Poms out of pubs." A wind speed of 84 knots, hurricane strength, was recorded on one of the competing yachts. We survived, but that was a race to remember.

But I was still burning to turn my design ideas into reality with my own boat. And so, after a lot of thought, I turned Dave down. I knew I'd miss him and his family, whom I'd gotten to know so well, and San Francisco, especially the Haight-Ashbury district. But Laurel and I had decided to settle into life on land, more accurately in St. Petersburg, Florida, and it was wonderful to have our first home after living aboard small boats for so long.

▶

In 1972 I encouraged friends at St Petersburg Yacht Club to create a Quarter Ton regatta, the first of its type in the USA. A good fleet of new yachts arrived on the start line. *Eygthene* won, and my yacht design career was off to a good start. Next, the Quarter Ton Cup in England.

Terra firma at last.

We were now married. We'd tied the knot before sailing *Improbable* back to Florida, in the village of Kenmore in the Scottish Highlands from where Laurel's family had once emigrated, and I had gone looking for my first land-based job in the United States since Gary Mull had taken me on.

Charlie Morgan, founder and chief executive of Morgan Yacht Corporation in Largo, Florida, had hired me as a loftsman. I had met Charlie during the SORC and I had hoped to get work in his design office, but there weren't any spare places – Charlie did a lot of the design work himself – but I did get a job lofting, and I felt this was a good start.

The job of a loftsman was to create a full-size drawing of the design on the loft floor against which the actual boat was constructed, the frames for the hull being shaped around these lines. I had been taught the skill as an apprentice at the Atkinson boatyard, and although I didn't like it nearly as much as working on design, it had taught me many useful things about developing the shape of boats. But even then lofting was a dying skill and practitioners were in short supply, so it got me in Charlie Morgan's door.

Morgan Yachts was a busy place, busier than it needed to be, because Charlie was a perfectionist. He didn't hesitate to change the details of a design even if the boat was already partly built. This meant that we would have to do another full-size loft all over again. Charlie was relentless in his pursuit of excellence: only the best-designed boat was good enough. So in spite of re-lofting designs again and again, I did enjoy the work. And in my leisure hours I was doing a lot of sailing at the invitation of members of the St. Petersburg Yacht Club.

Established in 1909, "St. Pete" was one of the older yacht clubs in the United States and one of the most famous. Located on Downtown Street, smack in the middle of the St. Petersburg waterfront, its noble architecture and pillared balconies were a far cry from the Torbay Boating Club's rudimentary premises, which consisted basically of a shed and a tent. St. Pete was primarily a social club but they also had a good racing organization. The club had been founded with the stated mission "to encourage and support yachting," and I was enjoying life there all the more because, as a veteran ocean racer at the tender age of 25, I was in demand as a crew. I spent most weekends racing around the magnificent Tampa Bay and Gulf of Mexico aboard a variety of yachts. But I still wasn't satisfied. I hungered to get my own designs out there. It wasn't for want of trying: I had shown a concept for a 30-footer to Charlie but he wasn't impressed. So I put my thinking cap on again and came up with another idea, this time for a smaller design, a Quarter-Tonner. And I planned to build her myself.

At that time the Quarter-Tonners were the wild things of ocean racing. I had first come across them a year earlier in France after *Improbable* had won the race from Plymouth to La Rochelle. Salt-caked but victorious, we motored through the imposing castle entrance into the historic harbor, and there they were: parked on the stone quay was a fleet of the most original-looking designs I had ever seen. I was bowled over and couldn't wait to have a look around, tired as I was from a couple of sleepless nights spent navigating our way around the rocky coast of Brittany. These boats represented everything I dreamed of as a designer – experimental, daring, radical, and a bit scary. Small and fragile-looking as they were, Quarter-Tonners were nevertheless classified as genuine ocean racers. Would I want to race offshore in one of these? I asked myself as I wandered around the imposing port guarded at the entrance by great stone fortresses. Yes, I decided, I definitely would.

The more I saw of the Quarter-Tonners, the more enthralled I became. Even the boats' irreverent and untraditional names, such as *Sing Sing* and *Dollar*, appealed to me. The Quarter-Tonners struck a chord in particular because of what I'd seen growing up in New Zealand; all those fast, light-displacement boats from the drawing boards of John Spencer, Jim Young, Des Townsend and others. Every boat I'd ever sailed or crewed had been designed or redesigned to be as rapid as possible, something that usually required creative thinking and a willingness to take risks. Even better, because Quarter-Tonners had an IOR rated length of just 18 feet and an overall length of around 24 feet, there wasn't a lot of boat to build. That meant they had the great virtue of being relatively cheap, which was one of the reasons why many of these Quarter-Tonners at La Rochelle were so extreme in design. If the boat turned out to be a dud or a dog, it wasn't the end of the world.

Thus, after my 30-footer got the cold shoulder from Charlie Morgan, I had come to realize that if I was going to design anything at all, it had to be a Quarter-Tonner. There was a problem though. Inexpensive as Quarter-Tonners were, I still didn't have enough money to buy one. Nowhere near enough. The obvious conclusion was that I would have to build her myself with the help of anybody I could persuade to join me in this brave project. I estimated that a Quarter-Tonner of my own design would cost around $6,000 all in, provided we did all the labor and cadged a lot of materials at hefty discounts, or even better – for nothing. As it happened, my entire savings came to $6,000.

At least, I reflected, I didn't have to pay any fees to the designer.

I was lucky to have friends who I hoped would be happy to throw their weight into my own dream project. Commodore was always gung-ho for an adventure, and Laurel's sailmaker brother, Gary Carlin, lived in California but was willing to relocate and help me out. I knew his assistance would be important: Gary could turn his hand to anything. A few of my workmates at Morgan Yachts also seemed willing enough to pitch in if needed.

I also needed help from people who knew nothing about building a yacht. I had come to the conclusion we needed a showcase to create some excitement and interest in the Quarter-Ton class if it were to hit the headlines, and I had an idea. It seemed to me there was little point in building a yacht that simply floated around the Gulf of Mexico on its own, or raced against other differently-rated yachts on some kind of handicap system. Not only would this mean nothing to me, it would do little for my reputation as a designer. I wanted to test my design against boats in the same class, just like in France.

So I drew a deep breath and approached senior members of the yacht club committee with a proposal that they organize an event that would showcase the Quarter-Ton class on Tampa Bay: a level-rating event, a true test of the relative merits of the yachts. Considering I was not even a member of the club – and a New Zealander to boot – I was probably asking a bit much. But to my gratitude, instead of rejecting the idea as just the madcap scheme of a wild-eyed newcomer, the committee embraced the proposal, and they set about the big task of mounting the grandly titled US Quarter-Ton Mid-Winter Series, America's first such championship. As an incentive to potential entrants, one of the yacht club members threw in a tempting prize: the winner would earn the right to represent the USA at the world championship in Weymouth, England.

A time for the event was agreed upon – late 1972.

While all this was happening in the background, I got going with the design and construction of the boat. Laurel was supportive, understanding this would involve me in many a late night. Brother-in-law Gary offered to throw in his labor for nothing, as well as convincing his employer, Levinson Sails, to supply the sail wardrobe for free. Another friend who was keen to join the crew had a spare shed across the bridge at Tampa and invited us to take it over for the duration. All I had to do now was produce a design worthy of all this enthusiasm and support.

And so, working after hours at home, I began to play around with the International Offshore Rule as it applied to Quarter-Tonners, to see how I could extract every bit of advantage. The IOR-set limit of 18 feet maximum rated length was the principal challenge. While my yacht of course had to comply with the same rules applying to other designers, I somehow had to make my design sail faster than the competition in a variety

I decided that the fastest and cheapest way to build *Eygthene* was to build wooden frames and cover them with fore-and-aft stringers. This allowed the fiberglass and end-grain balsa wood hull to be molded within tolerance close to my design.

of conditions. I spent weeks and weeks trying to figure it all out, staying up late night after night. With my modest budget I knew I had only one chance of getting the boat right, because I lacked the funds to make any alterations if she didn't perform straight out of the box. I simply couldn't afford for the boat to turn out to be a "dog", in designers' parlance. But in contradiction I couldn't play safe either, because I knew instinctively that a cautious design would lead to failure in a highly competitive class that rewarded original thinking.

I decided to be bold – well, radical. The boat would have a narrow waterline because this reduces underwater resistance: the more boat there is in the water, the harder it is to push her through it. This is known as drag. I made the boat very narrow on the waterline.

So far so fast, I hoped. However, narrow waterlines come with a sting in the tail. The less boat there is in the water, the more unstable and tippier she becomes, especially in heavy weather. There's little point in designing a light-weather flier that falls over on her ear and sails slowly in a decent breeze. After a lot of thought I got around this dilemma by giving the boat an unusually wide beam at deck level, the idea being that the weight of the crew would provide the stability we needed by sitting out on the side of the yacht. That meant we would have a lot of weight topside to stiffen the boat in a decent breeze. I knew it would be wet out there, but who cared? This was Quarter-Ton racing. So now the boat measured up on my

After the hull was molded we turned it upright and fabricated a plywood deck. I never planned on interior amenities – they would have added weight and cost. We could sleep on the floor!

plans at a slender 6ft 9in on the waterline and a whopping 9ft 8in at the deck. Both of these measurements would soon become talking points on the waterfront.

There were plenty of other problems to solve. Even with all the crew perched on the side of the yacht, I knew the boat would still be tippy – that is, it would heel over at a steep angle in strong winds. (I had already decided on a tall mast and powerful sails.) At steep angles of heel my narrow waterline would turn into a fat one because so much of the wide beam at deck level would be pushed into the water. At that point the drag would increase, and my fast Quarter-Tonner would probably become a slow one. So I drew and re-drew the shape of the hull above the waterline, steadily refining it to prevent this from happening.

I thought about it day and night. Had I missed something obvious? Could I change something and make my yacht go faster? Nor could I prevent the poison of doubt working away at me. Would my radical design turn out to be the dreaded dog? Rather like creating box office successes in movies, there's no magic formula in the creation of a fast yacht designed according to the level rating rules, because the vagaries of wind and sea introduce a high level of uncertainty.

Practicalities aside, my philosophy of yacht design was heavily influenced by Nahant, Massachusetts-based Dick Carter, as well as by New Zealanders such as John Spencer, and another designer I admired, Bob

Stewart. Carter's dinghy-like yachts had taken the world by storm during the 60s mainly by taking risks and being innovative. For instance, his keels were almost like the centerboards of dinghies, exactly what I'd seen at La Rochelle, and even earlier back in Auckland. He also insisted on spade-like rudders that were located independently behind the keel rather than being part of it. One of his original breakthroughs, the 33-foot *Rabbit*, had shocked the purists, but they changed their tune when she won the Fastnet Race on handicap.

As the weeks went on, I became pretty much obsessed by the Quarter-Ton and IOR rule books. For instance, the rules specified a minimum headroom below, the purpose being to make sure the boats were all-rounders with half-decent cabins rather than cramped yachts suitable only for all-out racing. But I wasn't prepared to make any compromises to the rule book if I could possibly help it, so I gave the boat a heavily cambered deck that looked a bit like a blister. The top of the camber was high enough to satisfy the rules, but the sides tapered away into almost nothing and sharply reduced the internal volume. That meant the boat was virtually flush-decked, which gave low windage as well as extra working area on deck for the crew.

It may seem contradictory for somebody hoping to create a fast yacht, but my boat would be relatively heavy. I designed her to weigh in at 4,300 lbs, including 2,200 lbs in lead ballast, all of it in the fin keel. This would give her a substantial displacement – the amount of water that would be expelled if she were placed in the sea. But I had concluded that the IOR rule book favored this approach because it entitled her to carry a lot of sail – 270 square feet – which would more than compensate for the weight. Therefore, in theory, she would be more powerful and, I hoped, faster in many different wind conditions.

So it was a matter of giving a bit here, taking a bit there. Even at that early stage I realized that great yacht design is the art of compromise because the weather is never constant: it's always changing in a way that can make a boat that's fast in some conditions, slow in others. Eventually I was satisfied with what I had drawn, and I signed off on my Quarter-Tonner and prepared to launch into the construction phase. I believed she would be quick, but then I didn't know what America's established designers were doing. The announcement of the US Quarter-Ton Mid-Winter Series had aroused a lot of interest.

With the help of the knowledge I had gleaned from sailing with Commodore, I put a lot of thought into the rig and sailing systems. Despite the powerful sails, which were the biggest permitted under the rules without suffering heavy penalties, I wanted a light albeit tall mast, and a long boom. There were a variety of reasons behind this, but the main one was to keep the weight low down in the yacht: the lighter the mast, the lower the boat's center of gravity. Therefore, the less she would heel over, because of the reduced weight up top. A reduced angle of heel would be critical to her success.

I was taking a chance here. The winds in Tampa Bay are usually gentle but not always so. And there was always the risk of a fragile mast collapsing. I weighed the odds as best I could, made up my mind and bought a light aluminum mast used by a much smaller yacht, the Morgan 22, and just hoped I hadn't cut things too fine.

By now, the inaugural US Quarter-Ton Mid-Winter Series was approaching all too fast, and we had just a few weeks to build the boat from scratch, throw on the rig and conduct sailing trials. We had decided to employ a relatively newfangled but promising method of construction based on a glass fiber balsa sandwich. Light and strong, it was composed of resin-impregnated fiber mats packed onto both sides of a balsa core, like a honeycomb. If you did it properly – and there was still a lot of experimentation at the time – this had the big advantage of being not only strong and light but also quick to build. As the days slipped by, speed of construction had become imperative.

Once we started building the boat, Gary and I broke all records. Working nights and weekends, we toiled away in the borrowed shed all the hours that God could spare, sometimes with the help of our boatbuilder friends. First we constructed the hull, then the deck. It seemed as if I crossed the Tampa Bay bridges hundreds of times, driving between home and the shed, my skin crawling with "fiberglass itch."

The opening race was scheduled for December 4, 1972. As the date approached Gary and I practically lived in the shed, scraping and sanding, banging and screwing. It was a case of all hands to the pumps to get the boat done.

She had already been christened. My Quarter-Tonner would be known as *Eygthene*, probably the most unpronounceable name of all time for a yacht. I had never lost my Kiwi accent, which is considered to be nasal by speakers of other forms of English. And I had obsessed so much about the 18-foot IOR limit that my fellow-workers at Morgan Yachts had named the boat for me. If you say "eighteen" the Kiwi way, or so I was told, it sounds like *Eygthene*.

Whatever – it's probably one for the philologists. But the name stuck and *Eygthene* was launched on December 2, shockingly late. Commodore

▲

During the early stages of building *Eygthene* I wanted to be sure the end-grain balsa core material would conform to my carefully-designed hull shape.

▲

Eygthene's first sail. We were ready the evening before the start of the 1972 Quarter-Ton Mid-Winter Series on Tampa Bay, a quiet evening, perfect for our test sail.

I had high hopes for my first racing design.

dropped everything and came over from San Francisco to throw his knowledge into the project. There was no time for sailing trials or other tuning-up processes that are considered essential to develop a yacht's full potential. We just had to hope that the rig had been set up properly, wouldn't fall down, and that everything had been screwed down tight. The final two days leading up to the opening race were a frenzied panic of work on the last-minute details of deck equipment, rigging and mast and sails. By then I'd spent my last dollar of savings. There was nothing left of the $6,000 – and Laurel had thrown in her housekeeping money as well.

The word having got around about the event, entries had poured in from all over America. Some of them looked impressive, especially a new Kirby 24 called *Seaducer*, a name I thought was in the irreverent tradition of Quarter-Tonners.

To our relief the winds proved to be light for the opening race on December 4, exactly the conditions for which *Eygthene* had been designed. We were also worried about how strong the rig was. We weren't anywhere near ready. As we sailed out to the start, we were still screwing on fittings and making final adjustments to the sails and rig. Our hearts were in our mouths – none of us really knew how our radical Quarter-Tonner would perform. With an untested boat by a novice designer, we could hardly be more of an underdog. I'd noticed we never rated a single mention in the pre-regatta write-ups.

We didn't lack confidence though. After all, we were all experienced harbor and ocean racers. Without being immodest, the crew of *Eygthene* knew how to extract the last ounce of speed from any kind of yacht.

In the first race we placed fourth, a fair result considering the circumstances. In the second, we improved to third. That was OK, but we still had a lot of points to make up if *Eygthene* was going to win nomination for the next world champs in Weymouth, England. By the third race we had started to understand our boat, and we crossed the line second.

The days of racing were flying by in a whirlwind of tactical decisions, more last-minute adjustments, post-race discussions and hasty fine-tuning. But with every hour we spent on the water we were learning about *Eygthene*, how to set up the rig and extract the best from her. We could all see she had potential.

It came down to the final overnight race, the longest in the series, carrying extra points. A victory would clinch the title and we'd be on our way to Weymouth at the generous yacht club member's expense. A second place would not do the job because there was no hope of raising the funds to get *Eygthene* – and us – across the Atlantic. The cupboard was bare.

Eygthene under spinnaker, heading for the finish line off St. Petersburg, Florida. If we won the race we were going to England, shipping paid, for the 1973 Quarter-Ton Cup.

We cracked a good start that put us ahead of the fleet as we headed out into the Gulf of Mexico. I looked around. "OK, let's kill these guys," I said. But we didn't.

During the night things hadn't worked out as well as we'd hoped, and approaching the finish line in an early morning haze, *Eygthene* lay third. Not good enough. With the finish line lying a tantalizing four miles or so in the distance, the wind dropped to nothing and the sea turned to a glassy calm. Soon the entire fleet was parked.

All three leading boats were pretty much in line astern, close-hauled on starboard tack but making little headway. The fourth boat was way behind us and posed no threat. Although not quite hopeless, we were in a difficult position. If the wind filled in from the same direction, it would reach the boats ahead of us first and there would be no opportunity for *Eygthene* to improve to first or second. In other words it would be a procession to the line. Then somebody – I don't remember who – spotted a plume of smoke on the northern shore. It was moving in a different direction from the prevailing wind that had died away.

A new breeze!

We decided to take a gamble. We tacked onto port as discreetly and quickly as we could – we didn't want to alert the boats ahead to what we were doing – and headed for the smoke. This meant *Eygthene* was sailing away from the finish line at a 90-degree angle. Our competitors up ahead probably thought we were nuts, but we reasoned there was nothing to lose and everything to gain. Agonizingly slowly, we ghosted along in the remnants of the old breeze. Although we were getting closer to the new wind, every second took us further away from the finish line. It was a race against time.

At last we hit the new breeze, immediately tacked back onto starboard and our sails filled. Within minutes we'd sailed right around the two leading boats, their sails still drooping uselessly. Jubilant, we crossed the line first and started doing the numbers. Because of the extra points given for the long race, we worked out we'd won the regatta by a decent margin.

When we stepped ashore, proud of what we'd achieved on a shoestring budget against a tight schedule, we felt vindicated. Not only had we won the US Quarter-Ton Mid-Winter Series, I hoped I had launched myself as a designer.

All we had to do now was repeat the process on the other side of the Atlantic, but against much stiffer competition – including those radical French designs.

The
years

crazy

A broken mast off the Royal Yacht
Squadron a week before we are
due to race for the 1973 Quarter
Ton Cup.

Laurel to the rescue

AFTER EMPTYING OUR POCKETS while building and racing *Eygthene*, the prize for winning the Mid-Winter Series felt like a Christmas present. A free berth for my yacht meant that, with a bit more saving and scraping, we would be able to fly across to Britain. The venue for the World Championship was the British holiday port of Weymouth.

Jim Pugh, one of my crewmates from the SORC series, was British, and since he was returning home he had already offered to travel on to Dunkirk and supervise the unloading, berthing, rigging and everything else necessary to get *Eygthene* race-ready. That meant I could stay in Tampa and continue working for Charlie Morgan and earn some money while *Eygthene* was en route aboard the freighter. With all this ahead of us, it made the victory celebration at the St. Pete Yacht Club even more enjoyable.

On Monday morning, I turned up at work at Morgan Yachts with a sore head but very proud and excited. I found Charlie in his office, told him we'd won and said, "I'd like to take time off to race in the World Champs in England," expecting him to be delighted and to grant me unpaid leave. "No," he said, "I need you here to continue lofting." Taken aback, I just looked at Charlie for a moment.

When you think back, there are crucial moments in your life when your reaction will take you forwards, sideways or in a different direction altogether. That was one of those moments. My only immediate prospect of earning any money was with Morgan Yachts. I had our living costs to pay, including the rent on our single-bedroom wooden cottage, and I had just enough money put aside for the airfare to England. I didn't want to risk that, or I might be stranded in Tampa Bay while *Eygthene* was in Dunkirk. See ya later, I thought, but I didn't say it. First, hoping to change his mind, I tried to explain to Charlie that racing *Eygthene* in England was the most important thing for me and that I just had to do it. I thought I was pretty convincing – after all, the event would have also provided good publicity for Morgan Yachts – but Charlie didn't budge. "Can't let you," he repeated. "Need you here."

At that point I didn't hesitate, and finally I did say "See ya later."

So I worked out my week's notice, drove out through the gate and never returned.

For the second time in my life I'd left a reliable paying job. I can't remember whether I thanked Charlie or not for hiring me in the first place, but I was probably too annoyed to do so. When I got home and told Laurel about the encounter, she took it philosophically. "I'm not surprised," she said. Most people would probably counsel that I should have stayed where I was and built up some capital before heading off on my own and taking a leap into the unknown, and I knew my friends in Charlie's engineering department thought I was taking a big risk. But I never thought of it as a risk. I suppose I had the confidence of youth.

Now what? Another lesson I've learned is that you must have faith in yourself rather than listen too much to other people. This approach is called self-referral. So I decided to chase design work and build momentum on the success of *Eygthene*, which had aroused considerable interest in the Tampa Bay area and in the yachting press. And that's pretty much how it happened. I worked hard on contacts in the yachting industry, including journalists, and the results began to arrive. In short order I was given a commission for a 26-footer by the family of Oscar Hubert Rogers, a young local sailing ace known universally as "O.H.", who'd been a valuable member of the *Eygthene* crew and had been sufficiently impressed to persuade his family to foot the bill for a new boat.

My design for O.H. was based on the 30-foot Half-Tonner that had failed to impress Charlie. I still had faith in the concept which embodied the knowledge I had built up in New Zealand, from my studies of Dick Carter's daring designs and from my interminable discussions with Doug Peterson over those 23 days and nights on watch on the way to Tahiti aboard *Spirit*. I've got to say that my thinking was also influenced by the Morgan 27-footer that was winning a lot of races around the west coast of Florida. Charlie certainly knew how to design a fast yacht.

"By now I had mounting confidence in my design philosophy. The lines of the hull had to be separated – that is, independent – from the fin keel rather than the two of them being part of a whole, which had long been the design tradition. This was a concept that allowed the keel to work more efficiently, similar in principle to the wing of an aircraft."

My new design was christened *Cherry Bomb*, which was a lethal firecracker, and in the hands of young O.H. and his crew she certainly had a kick. *Cherry Bomb* won so many races around Tampa Bay and the Gulf Coast that people were beginning to think that, just maybe, this 25-year-old Kiwi wannabe knew something about yachts.

Another commission landed on my plate, a 33-footer intended for the inaugural US Three-Quarter Ton Cup in Miami. This event was a big deal, a showcase for the emerging class of professional yachtsmen as well as for designers and builders. By now I had mounting confidence in my design philosophy. The lines of the hull had to be separated – that is, independent – from the fin keel rather than the two of them being part of a whole, which had long been the design tradition. This was a concept that allowed the keel to work more efficiently, similar in principle to the wing of an aircraft. I also believed the spade-type rudder should be moved as far aft as possible because it gave the helmsman much better control. The overall design philosophy was inevitably influenced by the IOR rules because these boats had to race under them, but I also believed it was the right way to go. I never doubted that faster yachts, provided they were constructed with integrity, were safer yachts because they spend less time in bad weather.

The owner of the 33-footer, which was christened *Quest*, invited me to race aboard her and I readily accepted. I was beginning to realize how

▲

I was surprised to see the Daniel Forster photo of my face on the Swiss *Yachting* magazine cover.

important it was to steer my own designs, mainly because I knew how the boat should be sailed. This put me in a better position to help the owner extract the best possible performance out of her. Also, I had already learned that winning yachts were good for business.

Although we were all experienced yachtsmen aboard *Quest*, we weren't a hot crew compared with some of the opposition, which boasted Olympic and America's Cup sailors. Despite this, *Quest* ended up second behind a Ranger 36 designed by none other than my former boss Gary Mull, and crewed by Ranger Yachts' works team including Gary and future America's Cup skipper Tom Blackaller, one of the country's great racing sailors.

While I was booking design commissions, my brother-in-law Gary Carlin was building on the success of *Eygthene* and developing a yacht construction business he called Kiwi Boats. Naturally, the first design off his small assembly line was a cruiser-racer version of *Eygthene* called the Kiwi 24, this time with a bigger cabin. Generally she was more comfortable than the stripped-down prototype. The Kiwi 24 was the first production boat constructed from my design, and I derived a lot of satisfaction from that fact.

So all in all I had some big months behind me when I flew out of Tampa for Denmark in July. Why Denmark? The successful Swedish designer Peter Norlin had invited me to race aboard his latest boat, *Kiss*, in Denmark's Admiral's Cup team. It was an offer I felt I couldn't turn down. Not only was it gratifying to be asked, it showed that the word was getting around. I flew out to Denmark comfortable in the knowledge that *Eygthene* would be put back into racing shape while I was sailing the Admiral's Cup with the Scandinavians.

This time I hoped for a relaxed and measured build-up to the Quarter Ton Cup, with none of the usual screwing and banging and last-minute emergencies as we approached the starting line, not to mention running repairs during the race. There would be shakedown races during Cowes Week, one of the longest-running and biggest annual regattas anywhere, so *Eygthene* could get properly tuned up.

None of the original winning crew would be aboard for Cowes Week because *Eygthene* had been commandeered by an all-woman team. Laurel and her Florida pals, Cathy Phillips and Cherry Perry, plus a Dutch friend Eilsa Green – all good yachties – had decided to take over the yacht for the duration of the regatta. So while I was in Denmark Laurel flew out to check up on *Eygthene*, landing in England and taking a train and ferry to Dunkirk.

That's when things starting to go wrong. We all thought the job of preparing *Eygthene* would be fairly straightforward, but completely unknown to me, no sooner had Laurel arrived, then she ran into one difficulty after another. With about a week to get the job done, which we thought would be plenty of time, she landed right in the deep end.

When Laurel arrived at Dunkirk, she was startled to find the yacht on a trailer parked in a fenced-off compound, instead of sitting snugly in her berth in the marina as planned. She was told that the captain of the freighter had hired a trucking company to get *Eygthene* off his deck, because when loaded aboard she had been positioned over the hatches, and now he couldn't get them open to unload his cargo of phosphate. He couldn't just drop *Eygthene* in the harbor because the vessel was moored at the end of a long jetty with no access for the cranes, so she'd been parked in the compound.

So now it was all up to Laurel to get *Eygthene* in the water. Obviously the first problem was how to get her off the trailer and out of the compound, and Laurel soon discovered there were no cranes with suitable lifting strops for rent. Working from a French dictionary she'd bought along the way, she asked around. The French were polite and helpful, doing their best to understand Laurel's Franglais, but none of the correct strops could be found anywhere. With time slipping by, in desperation she called some Dutch friends in a boatyard at Flanders who assured her that, yes, they could find some lifting strops, plus a stout hook. Although she had little money – we always managed on a shoestring – Laurel rented a car and drove straight to Holland. She threw the strops in the car, then turned around and drove back to Dunkirk to meet her sisters, Lana and Bonnie, who'd come to help in any way they could.

Unsurprisingly, none of them knew how to lift a nearly two-ton boat into the water. So this time Laurel called one of my crewmates from *New World*, San Franciscan boatbuilder Bill Green, who happened to be in Britain for the sailing season. Highly resourceful, Bill immediately enlisted the help of a most unlikely friend named Haar who lived in Holland. Actually a skilled lute player who would later become a physicist, Haar had no real experience in international yacht racing, but he turned out to be bright and resourceful. He arrived to find Laurel violently ill from eating mussels, quickly assessed the situation and took charge.

That very same day he found a crane and oversaw the lowering of *Eygthene* into the water. This made a huge difference because it meant that Laurel could live aboard instead of in a hotel that we couldn't afford. Jim Pugh was the next to turn up, this time from England, and he helped Haar and the girls set up the mast and the rest of the rigging.

As had happened with *Improbable* and so many other yachts with

▲

Switzerland may be landlocked, but that did not stop Ernesto Bertarelli of the Société Nautique de Genève from winning the America's Cup for Switzerland. I have many sailing friends that are members of Swiss yacht clubs.

▲

Being isolated from the sea does not prevent members from creating a yacht club. Gstaad Yacht Club in the Swiss Alps is another great example of an active yacht club located a long way from the ocean.

which I'd been involved, yet again we owed a lot to people who just wanted to pitch in and help. As Laurel would say later, "I couldn't have got the job done without the charity of complete strangers."

Meantime Laurel had been studying a chart of the French coast that she'd bought somewhere. She'd also ordered a chart of the English Channel, but it was late in arriving. When she was more or less happy with the preparation of *Eygthene*, she jumped on a train to Denmark to meet me. We'd hardly had time to say hello before we had to get back on a train to Dunkirk, where Lana and Bonnie were ready and waiting to deliver *Eygthene* to England against an ever-tightening timetable.

By the time we all met at the marina it was getting late in the day. The sun had set and it was growing darker by the minute. *Eygthene* had not left harbor since arriving on the freighter, and we had no idea how her rig would stand up to a decent breeze. Yet time was running out and I was anxious to cross the Channel while the weather and current were favorable.

"I can remember how to get to Cowes and The Solent (on the opposite coast)," I told Laurel, not feeling as confident as I hoped I sounded. "Sure?" she asked. So we untied *Eygthene*, hoisted the sails and set off into the night, armed with only a road map of England to guide our way. The chart of the Channel with its notoriously unpredictable tides never turned up.

It felt a little scary heading into the heavy shipping traffic in the dark in an untested 24-footer, but I reasoned a westerly tide would be with us for the first few hours. We ran watches right through the night, and when I was in my bunk the girls did a good job of following the compass course I had given them. All went well and as daylight broke next morning *Eygthene* was sailing past Brighton Pier on our way to the Solent and the Isle of Wight, all without proper charts or tide books. Laurel was annoyed with my lack of preparation, but at least we'd arrived and the rig was still standing. *Eygthene* would be in one piece for Cowes Week with its hundreds of competing yachts.

The rest of *Eygthene*'s all-woman crew duly turned up, causing quite a stir among the British yachting establishment. Nor did it hurt that they were all extremely attractive. The racing started quietly and the girls soon got the hang of the 24-footer, mostly finishing in the top half of their class.

In certain conditions the Solent can get choppy and it did in the next race. While I watched anxiously from behind the windows of the Royal Corinthian Yacht Club overlooking the racing, the all-female team negotiated the first few legs of the course without any apparent difficulty. But the wind was gusting strongly and the waves were getting bigger. "The girls aren't used to this," I thought.

"'The girls aren't used to this,' I thought. To my horror, on the homeward leg the mast suddenly crumpled. The entire rig collapsed, the top half hanging over the side and the boom and mainsail dragging half in and half out of the water."

To my horror, on the homeward leg the mast suddenly crumpled. The entire rig collapsed, the top half hanging over the side and the boom and mainsail dragging half in and half out of the water.

It's not a terrible sin to lose a mast on a racing yacht. They're necessarily light and flimsy, and are only held up by thin wire rigging. If a shroud breaks or a crewmember is too late winding on the running backstay, that can tip the mast over the side. Also, racing masts take a pounding, being bent and twisted and shaken sometimes for days on end. I'd crewed on yachts that had lost their masts, and in the years ahead I would lose more. In the case of *Eygthene*, she had the same stick we'd used on the Gulf of Mexico where the conditions are generally lighter. Now we'd been caught out.

As I watched anxiously, I just hoped the girls could sort out the mess and get everything – boom, sails and other bits of rigging – back on deck before the hull was damaged. A broken length of metal can punch a hole in the side in a moment. I needn't have worried. With Laurel directing things, they quickly hauled the flotsam aboard, flagged a tow from a small launch crewed by several friendly Englishmen, and were soon heading for the dock.

Here we go again, I thought as they approached land. Another panic to get *Eygthene* shipshape in time.

The Quarter Ton Cup would start the following week and I had to find somebody prepared to repair our mast in double-quick time. At least, I consoled myself, the hull was still intact.

Small Yachts

During the 1990s I designed a range of production yachts between 30 and 36 feet in length for Swedish boatbuilder Rolf Gyhlenius at Omega Yachts. Rolf also commissioned me to design a small one-design racing yacht. Every boat built would be exactly the same, ensuring cost-effective production and very close racing. Fast, fun and affordable were the goals. The 11 Meter One Design was the first design to be registered with the International Yacht Racing Union as a Sportboat, a new category of small racing yachts that was to become a very popular sailboat class. My original design idea, following Rolf's one-design concept, was to design a fast, easy-to-build yacht that looked like a small version of the then-new America's Cup Class of keelboats.

In 1991 Rolf contracted to build two prototypes of my design at Precision Boat Works near Sarasota, Florida. These yachts were intended to be used as full-size test models for optimizing keel, rudder and rig designs. The original, first design performed so well that we decided to put it directly into production. I was excited about this design and decided to own the first of the prototype yachts. With sponsorship from Timberland, I raced my 11 Meter in Cowes before sending her to Ireland and mooring her at the Kinsale Yacht Club marina in County Cork, right in front of our studio.

Fortunately, we found a boatyard and volunteers in Cowes who were prepared to save the day. After a couple of late nights with everybody pitching in, the expert English craftsmen managed to repair the mast, making it stronger in the process. With time running out once again, we installed the mast in record time, re-rigged the boat and set off for Weymouth, which was roughly another day's sailing down the English coast.

The wind was kind and we made port with a few hours to spare, to the relief of the rest of the four-man crew, who were waiting dockside. We tied up, hurried ashore and signed in with the race committee to complete our official entry.

It was a good crew. There was Laurel's Good Samaritan, Bill Green, who'd been the first skipper of George Kiskaddon's *Spirit* and his schooner *New World*. Bill was a huge asset. Although barely into his forties he'd sailed thousands of ocean miles and was already a legend. The local press described him as a "professional" which I suppose he was, except that he certainly wasn't getting paid to race aboard *Eygthene*. Later Bill would settle in England and establish a yacht building business in Lymington, moving later to Southampton, that would become known as Green Marine and would produce many winners. We had another American on board: Dick Nelson was the man who'd loaned us the shed in Tampa in which we'd thrown *Eygthene* together. Dick had also put up the prize of free transport for *Eygthene* to Dunkirk, so Gary and I thought the least we could do was invite him along. Commodore would have liked to come too, but he was too busy racing yachts in the States. He was winning races himself in Florida on *Cherry Bomb*.

After signing in, we wandered along the Weymouth Harbour dockside and looked at the competition moored there. We were impressed, even intimidated. There were 37 entries, nearly twice as many as the previous year, including a hot-looking fleet of French yachts. There was a new design called *Chien Jaune* – Yellow Dog – sailed by the previous winner Laurent Cordelle with the backing of what looked to us like a professional works team.

Cordelle was on fire: *Chien Jaune* had just been named "Boat of the Week" at Cowes. Heavily built and bearded, Cordelle was a star of French yachting: he would soon afterwards go on to train the crew for France's first America's Cup challenge under Baron Bich, the founder of the ballpoint pen and razor brand, and become a stalwart of later America's Cup challenges. Besides the formidable-looking French contingent the British had turned up in numbers determined, so the yachting magazines said, to break the French and Swedish stranglehold on the event. But as we strolled around we could see that everybody who mattered in this free-

"I noticed I was one of maybe three people who designed, owned and skippered their own design. As usual, the class had excelled itself with some daring naval architecture. Gary and I were particularly startled by an English boat called *Black Bottom* that looked like a floating box. 'If she's faster than *Eygthene*, my career in yacht design is all over,' I told Gary."

wheeling class was present and correct. As well as a strong presence from Britain and France, there were representatives from the Netherlands, Sweden, Italy, Finland and Germany.

Listed as a "prototype," *Eygthene* was the only American entry. I noticed I was one of maybe three people who designed, owned and skippered their own design. As usual, the class had excelled itself with some daring naval architecture. Gary and I were particularly startled by an English boat called *Black Bottom* that looked like a floating box. "If she's faster than *Eygthene*, my career in yacht design is all over," I told Gary. Another boxy-looking design was *Quarto*, which I soon learned came from the drawing board of English designer David Thomas, who had moved into Quarter-Tonners from the Olympic Soling class. Another owner, designer and skipper, he had come up with a shape that reflected a similar design philosophy to Sweden's *Robber*, one of the stars of the previous year. Not round-hulled like *Eygthene* and most of the other yachts, *Quarto* had a triple-chine construction and – a big talking point – featured a completely open transom. If you wanted to you could step straight off the cockpit floor into the sea. The idea behind this was to save weight. With her open cockpit running halfway up the boat, she looked like the most uncomfortable yacht imaginable. But then, Gary and I agreed, we weren't there to be comfortable.

In one respect though *Quarto* was like *Eygthene*, with a token cabin that would become known as "blistered". We noticed that David had incorpo-

"By general consent the winners were likely to come from the top boats in the previous year's event. As French yachting magazine *Bateaux* wrote, 'We will certainly find the hottest competitors among those who raced last year,' which of course did not include us. The English journalists expected their own boats to dominate, given that there were 25 of them in the fleet."

rated some fancy ideas including a hatch in the foredeck into which the spinnaker disappeared by pulling a string that ran inside the cabin. There was also a self-furling jib like the Olympic Dragon class: all you had to do was pull another string to furl it or set it. Strictly speaking, the administrators of Quarter Ton racing should have banned open sail hatches because they could be dangerous at sea, but this class was still finding its way and the rules were highly flexible.

Robber was back again, but with a new, lighter keel and higher freeboard. That meant she would sit lighter in the water. I knew *Robber* would be dangerous. She'd been designed by an unknown, just like *Eygthene*, and built in a hurry. I'd learned that if *Robber* hadn't broken a rudder in 1972 she might have beaten Cordelle, and although I didn't know it at the time, some heavy duty science had gone into her modifications. Her keel was the result of research by the Swedish Institute of Technology, which had run a lot of numbers and concluded that 440 lbs could be taken off the appendage without affecting the boat's stability. In the meantime chopping 440 lbs off a keel represented a huge weight savings that would probably make *Robber* a tearaway in the lighter winds, especially under spinnaker. Even so, Gary and I felt she wasn't built strongly enough.

As expected, there was a lot of experimentation with materials. More boats were built with various combinations of the latest synthetics – fiberglass or various mixes of fiberglass and foam, just like *Eygthene*.

And, just as I'd seen at La Rochelle, the names played havoc with yachting tradition. There was the unpronounceable *Shoupiloulouma* from France skippered by a couple of Olympic sailors; *Jonathan Livingstone Seagull* named for the best-selling book by Richard Bach; *Billy Goat Gruff* from Scotland; *Tequila Show* from Germany; another British entry *Golliwoog* (just to be different), and some incomprehensible names like *Partial Eclipse Proctor*. Compared with these *Eygthene* sounded quite ordinary, although I must say I was often asked what it meant and I had to resurrect my strongest Kiwi accent to explain.

By general consent the winners were likely to come from the top boats in the previous year's event. As French yachting magazine *Bateaux* wrote, "We will certainly find the hottest competitors among those who raced last year," which of course did not include us. The British journalists expected their own boats to dominate, given that there were 25 of them in the fleet. "It is most unlikely that the cup won't stay in England," one wrote. "I feel like we're a bunch of amateurs," I told Gary as we worked our way along the lineup. He didn't disagree.

As for *Eygthene*, once again she wasn't properly ready. It's one thing to repair a mast so it won't fall down, another thing to fine-tune it so it synchronizes with the sails in a way that produces maximum speed. We really didn't know how our new stick would work in the conditions in Weymouth, which weren't familiar to us. In addition, the early forecast was for light winds, which we feared might not suit *Eygthene* because we had her set up at 4,400 lbs. She was one of the heaviest yachts in the fleet. The pre-regatta writeups – and there were a lot of them, so fascinated was the sport by the Quarter Ton class – made several references to *Eygthene*'s relative heftiness. They reckoned she needed at least a couple of heavy weather races if she were to worry the favorites. To build our confidence we reminded ourselves that we'd won in Florida in light winds. As we had seen, *Eygthene*'s weight was offset by the large sail area I'd been able to give her under the rules.

It was a tight racing program with five races spread over a week, including a 70-miler and a 150-miler, the two overnight races. As always in level rating regattas, the longer ones would be crucial because they counted for extra points, with the 150-miler being awarded double points.

▲

The Royal Ocean Racing Club in St. James's, London. The centre of UK ocean racing and my London home base.

The 1973 Quarter Ton Cup. After crossing the English Channel, *Eygthene* catching *Chien Jaune* with the finish line ahead.

Yellow dog

AT THE START OF THE OPENING RACE the wind was coming and going – and light. It didn't get above five knots, not the conditions we wanted. But, we told ourselves, in sailing and yacht design you've got to take what the elements hand out. It's always changing.

Although I was young (another thing the yachting press often alluded to), by now I'd been racing boats of all kinds for nearly 15 years and I'd developed a philosophical approach. You never know how competitive you are going to be until a few minutes after the starting gun fires for the opening encounter.

With Gary calling the 10-minute countdown we hit the line just a couple of seconds late, which wasn't too shabby. As I'd often been told at the Torbay Boating Club, better to be a little late than too early, otherwise you have to return and start again, or carry on and risk being penalized. I was on the helm, Gary trimming the sails, Bill advising on tactics and strategy, and Dick waiting for orders. We talked only when necessary. We watched and waited. Were we fast enough?

Very soon it became clear that we were more or less hanging in with the leaders and we were certainly faster than most of the fleet despite the unfavorable conditions.

"Hey, we've got a chance here," I said, much relieved. After all, it would have been a long way to come to discover *Eygthene* couldn't foot it with the best. It still felt to me as though she was practically dragging an anchor

117

in these zephyrs, especially when running before the wind. She wanted to fly but couldn't. As the wind steadily built to over five knots we managed to scrape across the line in twelfth place, two places behind Cordelle in *Chien Jaune* who was obviously also struggling. Ominously, *Robber* won by a street.

Once we'd tied up we discussed how to modify the rig to suit these light conditions, and I decided to rake the mast back a few degrees. I was confident this would improve our speed immediately after the start, a vital part of the race because you've got to get away from the rest of the pack and clear your wind. Feeling a little more confident we went ashore.

The event was being run by the Royal Thames Yacht Club, one of the oldest sailing organizations in Britain with a lot of experience in managing hotly contested championships, and almost immediately the race committee was put to the test. Cordelle had protested another lightweight flyer named *Odd Job*, skippered by English yachting journalist Jack Knights. *Odd Job* had finished way up in the fleet but Cordelle, watching from astern, filed a technical complaint about how *Odd Job*'s sail had been sheeted, claiming it was illegal.

The Frenchman was perfectly entitled to protest on the grounds he felt *Odd Job* had gained an unfair advantage, but the protest committee was all at sea. From what we heard later, Jack Knights mounted such an eloquent defense that the committee decided the matter was one for the highest authority, in the form of the Offshore Racing Council. Since the council's officials weren't available to rule on such short notice, the whole matter got deferred. As far as I was concerned, it was further proof that the class needed a few more rules to make it a fairer playing field. I was pretty sure that could be done without stifling the class's creativity.

The next day as we headed out for what's called an Olympic Course race around a short triangular course, the sea was dead flat and the wind was blowing at around one knot. "It's getting worse," I said. "They won't start us in this wind," Bill pronounced.

But they did. Anxious to maintain the schedule, the officials fired the starting gun just as the wind miraculously picked up. After an indifferent start, we picked off one boat after another and improved to seventh at the finishing line. Not bad against 36 other boats. *Robber* led from start to finish.

Seventh wasn't great, but in a five-race series it's consistency that matters, and we all believed *Eygthene* was still in the hunt. And we were right. After we got ashore we learned the Swedish rocket had been over the line before the starting gun. Result: a five percent penalty. That meant *Robber*'s overall time for the course was increased by that amount, which

▲

Eygthene and *Chien Jaune* battle for the 1973 Quarter Ton Cup in Weymouth Bay, England.

brought her back down the field to fourth. That cheered us up a bit. Nor were we unhappy to see that Cordelle and his works crew were having a rough regatta by their high standards: *Chien Jaune* had finished way behind us in fourteenth place.

The wind picked up a little for the third race two days later. It was blowing east nor'east at around eight knots, which was more to our liking. Once again *Robber* led from start to finish, but *Eygthene*, showing what she was designed for, improved in the closing stages to finish third. Nobody other than *Robber* could touch us on the wind in more breeze, something the yachting press picked up on. *Chien Jaune* had a seesaw race but finished just one place behind us. Cordelle was warming up.

"It looks like *Robber*'s got the speed, guys," I said. "She's the yacht to beat."

"Yes, but there's a good chance she'll break," said Bill. "*Robber*'s just not built strong enough." As a boatbuilder his opinion was usually sound.

As always in these so-called level rating regattas, the longer races would prove decisive. And Cordelle had a great record at longer races, especially overnight ones to the French coast, where he had valuable local knowledge.

The wind was stronger and the seas choppier when the starting gun fired off Weymouth for the 70-miler. These were conditions in which *Eygthene* thrived. All we had to do was manage the contrary swirling tides of the Channel. Our main concern was how to find the all-important turning mark off the Isle of Wight, especially if we had to round it at night. In the days before GPS navigation this would be a true challenge of navigation and seamanship.

As it happened we approached the area in a weak early-morning light with a haze obscuring the horizon. All hands were on deck, straining their eyes to spot the buoy. After racing through the night we had no idea where we lay in the fleet.

"There it is," somebody yelled. We were pretty much bang on. We could see just two boats ahead of us and it took a while to identify them in the poor visibility. To our dismay but not to our surprise, the leading yacht was *Chien Jaune*. Following behind was a British boat whose name we could not decipher.

Eygthene rounded the mark about five minutes in arrears, and setting our spinnaker and trimming the sails to every puff of wind, we set off after our rivals on the long downwind leg to the next navigation mark at the Shambles, one of the most notorious places in the entire Channel. The Shambles is marked by two buoys and we had to sail around the northern one. Described in the charts as the Shambles Bank, it's a ridge that lies off Portland Bill, the promontory that the fleet had to clear before heading

▲

A gift from Captain Alf Inman before I sailed across the Tasman Sea to Lord Howe Island and Sydney at 15 years of age. I also had it with me aboard *Spirit* during our 1970 trans-Pacific crossing six years later.

back to Weymouth. The tides are dangerous, roaring around the Bill at up to ten knots at times and often kicking up vicious seas. Many a yacht has come to grief in what is known as the Portland Race.

We were extremely wary of the area. Of course we'd studied the tide charts we carried with us – if you don't carry tide charts of the Channel, you're wasting your time – but the currents sometimes have a mind of their own. At least we had the opposition in our sights. "We'll have to race like there's an Olympic gold medal at stake," I said.

A few hours later we'd worked our way into second, and in the improving visibility we could see the finish line off Weymouth. "Now let's go for *Chien Jaune*," I urged, although I didn't really believe we could catch Cordelle before the finish. But gradually it became clear that *Eygthene* was hauling in *Chien Jaune*. Cordelle, who was on the helm, started looking over his shoulder.

"Trim like your life depends on it," Bill muttered. "We're closing."

You could have heard a pin drop as we reacted to every gust, constantly easing and tightening the sheets to adjust the sails. Whenever we could, we took *Eygthene* higher on the wind, sailing above the Frenchmen. And then we sailed straight over them. There was nothing that Cordelle could do. On that day *Eygthene* was just too quick.

After we'd crossed the finish line with the customary pats on the back, we wondered where *Robber* was, surprised not to have seen her at all during the race. Later we learned that for the second year in a row she'd lost her rudder and was struggling in under jury-rigged steering. For the Swedes this was a calamity that effectively put them out of the entire regatta.

With *Chien Jaune* closing up on points and *Robber* off the table, the entire dynamics of the regatta had changed. *Eygthene* now led the series, which meant we had to adopt different tactics and be certain to cover the Frenchmen in the 150-miler. But we had other rivals such as David Thomas's *Quarto* which had moved up the rankings. "We've got to keep an eye on her too," said Bill.

And so we came to the final race. Anything can happen in a 150-miler across the Channel – and it did. It all came down to the last few miles.

After a nerve-racking night negotiating the tides and currents on the crossing back from France to the English coast, the leading boats were approaching the finish line around daylight when the wind dropped away almost to nothing. *Eygthene* lay sixth. Through the haze we could identify the yachts ahead of us. Equipped with a new rudder, *Robber* was in front by a good distance but she looked to be stranded on the wrong side of the current. Anyway, she was no longer a contender. *Chien Jaune* lay fourth,

"As we furiously tried to figure out the final points, *Eygthene* crossed sixth. There were 30 boats behind us, but was sixth good enough? Exhausted though we were from a night of wildly varying conditions and fortunes, we hurried to the clubhouse where officials were posting the results on a board in the bar."

which put her several points behind us if she stayed in that position. But we noticed that Cordelle, clever sailor that he was, had placed the yacht on the right side of the current. We couldn't afford to let any other boats go past.

For the next few agonizing hours the first six yachts drifted around the Channel at the mercy of unpredictable currents and fading winds. Powerless to influence things from our sixth position, we could only watch the drama unfold before us. Little by little Cordelle worked his way up the fleet, passing one boat after another. He was sailing, as a competitor would write later, "with nerves of steel." As we watched, he got *Chien Jaune* into second position. Then, just before the finish line, into first.

As we furiously tried to figure out the final points, *Eygthene* crossed sixth. There were 30 boats behind us, but was sixth good enough? Exhausted though we were from a night of wildly varying conditions and fortunes, we hurried to the clubhouse where officials were posting the results on a board in the bar.

Cordelle and his crew had beaten us to the clubhouse, and he came straight up to me. "Congratulations," he said. "Did we win?" I asked. "*Oui,*" he said, "by two points."

Two points! When I looked at the scoreboard, we'd scraped home by 188 points to 186, about as tight as you can get in a five-race regatta. But it was enough. For the first time I truly began to believe that maybe, just

▲

Tired but happy: *Eygthene* winner of the 1973 Quarter Ton Cup ahead of Laurent Cordelle's *Chien Jaune*. Not a big trophy, but to Gary Carlin and me this was a huge event.

maybe, I had a shot at becoming a real yacht designer. Here we were, in the epicenter of the yachting world on England's South Coast, with a boat that had won against the odds. Not only had the entire exercise – the building and racing – been done on a shoestring, we'd come the longest distance of any of the competitors to race in unfamiliar waters.

As a bonus *Eygthene* had demonstrated that in the right hands she could outsail a French works team. The yachting press picked up on the "American yacht" or, as one journalist wrote, the "Half-New Zealand, half-American yacht." Two of Britain's best-known yachting journalists, Jack Knights and Bob Fisher, had raced in the regatta and having seen *Eygthene* close at hand, gave us a generous write-up.

We were young and crazy then. From a much more experienced perspective 40 years later, I look back at that event and think how insane it really was.

Those Quarter-Tonners were little more than dinghies, and here we were, racing them hard in waters that can turn dangerous in minutes. If we'd gotten the severe weather that often occurs in the English Channel, the fleet would probably have been scattered up and down the coast. Lightly built as they were, more than a few of the Quarter-Tonners would probably have broken up and sunk. And then there was the heavy shipping traffic: an oil tanker could crush a Quarter-Tonner like matchwood and the crew on watch wouldn't even know. We'd all gotten away with it, but I was certain there'd be a day of reckoning. The rules had to be tightened up.

After the trophy presentation Laurel and I returned to the boat, wondering what to do next as the rest of the crew went their different ways. Gary and Dick flew back to Tampa Bay, and Bill drove to Lymington where he would later establish his Green Marine boatyard.

We didn't mind the prospect of living aboard *Eygthene* – after all, all of our married life had been spent on a boat – but I was getting to the stage where I needed some stability after years of being on the move. The safe thing might have been to return to St. Petersburg and Tampa Bay where Gary and I were developing a reputation in our different fields. Gary planned to turn his boatbuilding prowess into a bigger business, largely on the back of a string of commissions for Kiwi 24s. I could have joined him but I didn't see myself as a boatbuilder: I had no illusions about my skills. So I donated my apprenticeship tools to Gary. Laurel and I concluded it would be smarter to stay in England and try to turn *Eygthene*'s success into something more permanent.

A few days later we sailed back along the South Coast of England to the marina at Lymington that had been in the hands of the Berthon boatbuilding family since 1877. Making ourselves as comfortable as we could, we settled down for the winter: we certainly couldn't afford to rent accommodation ashore. After years of non-stop racing we would take a break.

At the marina I got to know the owner, David May, who was a Berthon family member. An accomplished racing yachtsman in his own right, he knew everybody in the sport, and we often spent time chatting together. To my surprise we'd only been at Lymington for a few days when people began approaching me to talk about building Kiwi 24s in Britain. Master Marine, a new boatbuilding company in the Channel Islands, put up a proposal. Next a Bournemouth boatbuilder expressed an interest in doing a production version of my 33-footer *Quest*, the one I'd designed for the US Three-Quarter Ton Cup. When these and other people called, David would obligingly wander down the dock and call me to the phone.

One day when I was down below I heard a shout from the dock, "Somebody from Ireland on the phone." I popped my head out to see David. From Ireland? "I don't know anybody in Ireland," I told him. "Definitely from Ireland," he said. Thanking him, I hurried to the office where a man on the other end of the phone identified himself as Johnny McWilliam, a sailmaker from Cork, who was representing a businessman and yachtsman named Hugh Coveney. He explained that they knew about my success in the Quarter-Tonners, and at the One Ton Cup in Italy where I'd just raced with Doug Peterson aboard *Ganbare*. They'd like to talk to me about designing a One-Tonner as the launch of a serious Irish tilt at the Admiral's Cup. "We'll send you and your wife tickets to fly over and talk to us," he said.

Ireland! It didn't sound too promising, but we had nothing else to do. At least we would have a few nights in a nice hotel instead of living aboard a cramped 24-footer. Laurel had never been to Ireland either and she loved to travel. "Sure," I said, "when do you want me?" "Can you come now?" said Johnny. "Alright, on our way," I said. So we took the train from Brockenhurst to Woking, then a bus to Heathrow Airport to spend a few days in Ireland.

I would stay there for more than 40 years.

Golden Apple ahead of the English One Ton Cup fleet off Portsmouth Harbour. The first Irish challenge, 1974.

Golden yachts

HUGH COVENEY AND JOHNNY MCWILLIAM met us at Shannon Airport in County Clare in the west of Ireland. I wasn't told until much later, but their hearts sank when they saw me. Although I have no recollection of my dress at the time, I was apparently wearing cowboy boots, jeans and a shirt emblazoned with an Admiral's Cup logo. My welcoming committee had probably hoped I would be dressed in tightly pressed slacks and a white shirt underneath a silver-buttoned blazer, but I must have acquired my fashion sense from the Haight-Ashbury district rather than from the San Francisco yacht clubs. I'd also been part of the "hippie" crew as we were called on *Improbable*, and had been asked to leave several Florida yacht clubs for offending the dress code. I would soon learn that sailing in Ireland can be quite formal and punctilious, especially at the more upscale clubs.

But all that passed over my head at the time. On the two-hour trip by car to Cork through the Irish countryside, the Irishmen outlined their ambitions. As they talked Laurel and I became more and more interested. Hugh and Johnny Mac, as we would come to know them, had raced the latest Fastnet, enjoyed the experience and returned home with high ambitions. Their immediate goal was to mount an Irish challenge for the One Ton Cup which would be conveniently located in Torquay, England, and they were hoping I would guide them on how to get the very best design for the series.

They wanted to put Ireland on the international sailing map.

Then it was my turn to bring them up to date on my experience and

latest designs, starting with *Eygthene*, and followed by *Cherry Bomb*, *Quest* and the Kiwi 24 production versions. I also told them about all my years of racing and delivery voyages aboard *Spirit* and *Improbable*, about the Sydney Hobart Races, and the Bermuda Race on *New World*, and anything else that seemed useful for them to know. Quite apart from the boats I had already designed, I think they were surprised that a 25-year-old had done so much ocean racing. They were interested to hear about how I had won the Quarter Ton Cup against works teams and about how I'd recently helped my mate Doug Peterson perform impressively during the One Ton Cup in Porto Cervo, Italy, aboard his *Ganbare*, the yacht he'd designed and built with a loan from his grandmother after eventually leaving Dick Carter's office and striking out on his own.

We parked at the Royal Cork, officially the oldest yacht club in the world, and kept on talking boats, this time with the extra company of Hugh's wife Pauline and Johnny's wife Diana. The day turned into a meeting of minds until eventually the Coveneys, handing us the keys to their beautiful house in Cork City as well as to a car, excused themselves to fulfill another engagement elsewhere. I took the opportunity to make an impromptu tour of the yacht club.

I'd been inside my fair share of historic yacht clubs, but the Royal Cork is special. Founded in 1720, it's based at Crosshaven overlooking the Owenboy River, where, history has it, Sir Francis Drake had once sheltered from pursuing Spanish galleons. Bearing the official insignia of a mermaid attached to a golden crown-bearing harp, the club takes its history seriously, as it should. Classic maritime oil paintings depicting the earliest yachting scenes hang above the fireplaces and on the walls.

This is where it all started, I told myself. I could hardly know that I would soon become a member and spend the next four decades in Ireland.

Before we even got back to the Coveneys' house Laurel and I had pretty much decided to stay in Ireland. After all we had nothing else to do and, as Laurel said, "The Coveney house sure beats living on a Quarter-Tonner at a marina with the English winter coming on."

The very next day we bought a house, our first house anywhere. It was quite unintentional.

We'd driven through the enchantingly wild countryside of West Cork on my personal mission to see the Fastnet Rock lighthouse from land. Thereafter we kept on driving until we ended up at Ireland's most southwestern point, the rugged Mizen Head. We stopped at a tiny village called Dunkelly on Dunmanus Bay that boasted just four houses in all, and stretching our legs, we were having a look around when we noticed a For Sale sign

◀

Almost a lost art. Creating yacht designs in the days before CAD required the use of drawing splines, wood or plastic, held in place with lead weights. Here I use weights cast from a mold created by Florida yacht designer Ralph Monroe (1851–1933). I used them for over 40 years.

We were proud of our LP collection, and Butch and I always returned to Cork with the latest releases. We decided one day to make music a bigger part of the creative process, and moved the piano from the house to the studio.

outside one of the cottages. It was constructed in stone. Or rather, what was left of it. The roof had collapsed and a wall was missing. But Laurel took an immediate shine to it. "We could buy this," she said. "Our own place."

As it happened the man sitting on a nearby stone wall turned out to be the owner. Introducing himself as Dinny McCarthy, he was only too happy to engage us in conversation. When we expressed an interest in the property, we engaged in a bit of bargaining, a skill at which the Irish excel. Despite a difficult negotiation, mainly because Dinny had no teeth and a challenging accent, within a few short minutes we found ourselves the owners of a quaint but tumbledown Irish cottage in one of the country's more remote locations.

The price? A £20 deposit paid to Dinny, with the balance to be paid later. To this day I don't think Dinny could believe that he'd sold a decrepit cottage to complete strangers. We paid Dinny cash there and then, shook hands, and without benefit of lawyers or banks the place became ours. The formalities could be handled later. On the way back to Cork City Laurel was already making plans for a major renovation.

I don't know if the Coveneys thought we were crazy when we broke the news that we'd gotten ourselves accommodation in remote West Cork, far from the Royal Cork Yacht Club and all the sailing activity, but at least they could see we'd made a commitment to Ireland.

So the ball started rolling. It was 1973. With me having become an Irish resident, Hugh committed to building a One-Tonner of my design for which Johnny Mac would provide the sails. Laurel and I looked around for a place to rent, as Dunkelly was too far away for daily travel. We ended up with a small corrugated-iron-clad cottage near the beach at Fountainstown, just west of the entrance to Cork Harbour and only a mile from Crosshaven; near enough to the action.

Our next purchase was a car that we bought with the deposit on the design fee that Hugh paid for his new One-Tonner, and I began to commute between Fountainstown and University College Cork. This institution boasted a small Olivetti computer that could run a program that I had bought from the Sparkman & Stephens office in New York and that contained all the IOR rating rules. The One-Tonner had already been christened *Golden Apple*, and every morning I drew several variations of her plans on an old door that I had turned into a drawing table, then re-measured them and drove 40 minutes into the University. Here I fed in the data and checked that I was still complying with the One Ton rating limit.

Much later I would count myself lucky to be launching my design career in the early years of the IOR rule that became the international

Reflecting my lifelong love of music, starting at a young age listening to my father playing trombone with his brothers and friends, I've chosen three albums from my extensive collection to show my diverse interests.

Ramblin' Jack Elliott, who I met in San Francisco in 1969, knows as much about sailing ships as he knows about music.

Guest conductor Edward Heath chose my design for his last *Morning Cloud*, K2468, and for the Black Dyke Mills Band LP cover inscribed with a personal note to me.

Jazz Workshop reflects my father and his brothers playing trombone.

"It was a refreshing and creative era in which to be working because the new rules lifted a lot of the old restrictions that had hampered designers and opened up a lot of new opportunities. But it was also fraught with risk."

standard. Until the late 60s there were two different sets of rules for ocean racing which applied on opposite sides of the Atlantic. The Americans worked under the Cruising Club of America (CCA) rules, while the British and much of the rest of the world, including New Zealand, embraced the Royal Ocean Racing Club (RORC) rules. The effective result of having two conflicting measurement regimes was that the handicap given to a yacht measured under the CCA rule pretty much rendered it uncompetitive against a boat carrying an RORC rating, and vice versa.

Unfortunately, this had been happening at a time when international ocean racing competition was growing in the form of the Admiral's Cup and other events such as the Southern Cross Cup in Australia. Adding even more weight to the need for reform was the development of level-rating events such as the various "Ton" cups, like the one *Eygthene* had won.

After much debate the Americans and British agreed on a new international system of measuring and handicapping yachts that was designed to harmonize racing, regardless of where the yacht came from. Headed by Olin Stephens, who was hugely influential in the reforms, the process took three years but the IOR rule eventually emerged, meaning competing yachts could be more accurately handicapped one against the other. Basically the idea is to make the racing more even by providing for yachts of different shapes and sizes. A 40-footer could beat a 60-footer on handicap under the system known as corrected time.

Here in Cork I was operating under IOR Mark III, the latest version of the rule. It was a refreshing and creative era in which to be working because the new rules lifted a lot of the old restrictions that had hampered designers and opened up a lot of new opportunities.

But it was also fraught with risk. In their desire to level the playing field as much as possible, the measurement rules were based on a range of specific elements that attempted to encompass the basic overall principles of a yacht and her potential sailing performance. Among other factors these covered effective sailing length, beam, displacement, keel depth and sail area. And of these, a particularly important element was the measurement of the yacht's stability – that is, her resistance to heeling in strong winds. But there were several other critical elements, all of which a designer had to take into account, because once they were all thrown together the resulting number was the yacht's all-important rating from which her handicap was calculated.

Inevitably all of us designers were trying to trick the rule by creating a yacht that sailed faster than her actual rated performance would suggest. So where was the danger? Well, you could try too hard. By tricking the rule to gain a favorable rating but possibly at the expense of genuine performance, perhaps because of a distorted hull shape for example, your design might earn a good handicap but end up dead in the water.

The plans for *Golden Apple* were signed off in early 1974, and building was to start as soon as possible at the South Coast Boatyard owned and managed by Barry Burke. George Bushe and his son Killian were the principal boatbuilders. They were friends of Hugh's and experts in constructing cold-molded wooden boats, just like the Atkinson yard. I'd quickly come to realize that Johnny Mac, an engineer by training and an aerobatic pilot, was an expert sailmaker, and he'd gotten down to work on *Golden Apple*'s wardrobe using the latest sailcloth materials.

I handed the responsibility for the design and manufacture of the mast and boom to Lars Bergstrom. Lars was a Florida-based Swede whom I'd gotten to know through his sailing friend and colleague Ragnar Hakansson, who had joined *Improbable* for the return trip to Florida from the 1971 Admiral's Cup. Lars and "Ragga" were skilled yachties and boatbuilders who could turn their hands to practically anything. Highly resourceful and inventive, Lars was also a pilot who used to play around with the design and construction of gliders in his spare time. He was always coming up with interesting new ideas and concepts.

Apart from the rig this was to be very much an Irish affair. One of a long-established Cork merchants' family, Hugh Coveney was a chartered

▲

I was lucky to collaborate with Swedish pioneers Lars Bergstrom and Sven-Olov Ridder. *Golden Apple* was the first One Tonner to use their B&R Rig, and no doubt this contributed to her windward speed during the 1974 One Ton Cup. Lars, based in Sarasota, Florida, influenced Kiwi Boats' lightweight "space frame" construction used during the design and building of *Imp*. Sven was designing advanced rigging systems and winged keels at the Swedish Institute of Technology way before *Australia II* made winged keels famous during the America's Cup.

Oldest yacht club in the world, Royal Cork Yacht Club, located in Crosshaven, just across the river from our home and design studio.

quantity surveyor by training. Not yet 40 at the time, he'd only recently started sailing and had fallen in love with it. Most importantly, Hugh was a natural administrator.

Then the project nearly sank almost before it started.

In 1973 Ireland was hit by one of its periodic economic crises, and Hugh was having second thoughts about what the local business community might see as a wasteful exercise during such a tough time. The weeks went by, and still no decision. With the first race of the One Ton Cup due to start on July 17, time was running out and we didn't have a boat.

Eventually Johnny Mac and I decided to twist Hugh's arm. Late one night we turned up at his house to discuss it all but, not surprisingly, found the entire place in darkness. Hugh and Pauline clearly had gone to bed. I'm not sure whose idea it was, but we decided the only thing to do was wake them up by the time-honored method of throwing gravel at what we assumed was their bedroom window. Eventually Hugh poked his head out of the window wondering what was going on and, a bit startled, agreed to come downstairs for an impromptu meeting.

About an hour later Johnny Mac and I came away still unsure as to whether or not Hugh would make the commitment. From my viewpoint the cancellation of the project would put my design life on hold. After all, Laurel and I had come to Ireland for the express purpose of helping launch Ireland's assault on the international level-rating scene. If Hugh were to back out – and I understood his dilemma – Ireland might be the wrong place to launch an international career in yacht design. To put it mildly, Laurel and I were on tenterhooks, especially as we'd both come to love Ireland in the short time we'd been there. Also, we had acquired some real estate of our own, even if it was a cottage without a wall in one of the country's most remote places.

To our relief, a few days later Hugh gave the go-ahead and the *Golden Apple* project was back on the table.

With time running out once again, *Golden Apple* was built in a hurry and launched, a lovely-looking hull finished in varnished teak planking that Hugh had stipulated. She floated to her lines, and under sail felt beautifully balanced and fast. An Irishman to his fingertips, Hugh named her after the last memorable lines of a much-quoted poem by W.B. Yeats, "The Song of the Wandering Aengus":

> *Though I am old with wandering*
> *Through hollow lands and hilly lands,*
> *I will find out where she has gone*

▲

Beautifully built by George and
Killian Bushe at South Coast Boatyard in County Cork, Ireland,
Golden Apple arrived in England in
1974 and started winning races.

The British, who were in a One Ton level-rating frenzy, had suggested that Hugh come over and compete in their own One Ton trials at Gosport on England's South Coast. The invitation came through Peter Nicholson, scion of a legendary English boatbuilding family whose father-in-law owned an estate near Crosshaven in County Cork. With our encouragement Hugh jumped at the chance, and when we got there we found no fewer than 20 yachts, most of them newly built. They'd all turned up in the hope of being selected for Britain's team.

Nobody gave *Golden Apple* much of a chance, so little being known about Ireland's place in the level-rating world. To be truthful, Ireland really didn't have a place; not that this worried us because we believed – well, hoped – that the yacht would be quick. We certainly had a handy crew.

Our secret weapon was helmsman and tactician Harry Cudmore, another son of County Cork. A member of a family that owned a chain of grocery stores, Harry was famous for spending as much time as possible on the water and as little time as he could in the family business. He had won selection for Ireland to the Olympic Games. Although he had a quick brain for tactical decisions, Harry was highly excitable behind the helm and easily the most volatile yachtie I'd ever sailed with. If things didn't happen fast enough or as he expected, he would start yelling and shouting. In close racing this could work out well because it intimidated other crews within earshot into giving us a wide berth, but in the early days it could lead to tensions on board. In his day, however, Harry was one of the best tactical skippers in the world: later, he would become the first non-American to win the Congressional Cup match racing series. He was the natural choice to call the shots.

Golden Apple had been sailed across to Gosport a few days earlier by some of Hugh's sailing friends, and had been through the obligatory measurements and other checks. The arrangements called for four of the crew to take the ferry from Cork to Wales, then to drive to the South Coast while Johnny Mac flew Hugh and me over in his light aircraft. This was a fabric-covered, single-engined Beagle Airedale in which you felt a bit like a pioneer aviator with the wind whistling past outside the fabric skin. Hugh reasoned these arrangements gave everybody plenty of time

▲

Racing for Ireland in 1974:
L TO R: Killian Bushe, Mick "the Messer" Ahern, Hugh Coveney, me, and Harold Cudmore.

"During the ten-minute countdown to the start, the other crews were doing double-takes. Here they were with every man on deck furiously winding and grinding, while the Irish guest boat *Golden Apple* was apparently being sailed by a skeleton crew. Perhaps they thought the rest of the manpower was concealed below decks, ready to leap into action in a surprise tactic."

to get organized and develop a feel for the changeable conditions in the Solent and Channel before the actual racing began.

Then it all went wrong. The Beagle got held up by Her Majesty's Customs for a long time at Southampton Airport, and we had to dash for a taxi to get to Gosport for the opening race. Throwing ourselves out of the taxi, we rushed to the dock, pulling on our oilskins as we went.

But *Golden Apple* wasn't there. With the clock ticking down to the start of the first race, a 27-miler, the rest of the crew including Harry had decided they'd better slip the moorings and get out there. In the era before mobile phones we hadn't been able to alert them that we were running late, nor could we contact them out on the water. "Let's hire a motor boat," said Hugh. "We might make it." Meantime Harry was wondering how on earth he could race a One-Tonner with half a crew. Nobody was even sure if the rules allowed it.

During the ten-minute countdown to the start, the other crews were doing double-takes. Here they were with every man on deck furiously winding and grinding, while the Irish guest boat *Golden Apple* was apparently being sailed by a skeleton crew. Perhaps they thought the rest of the manpower was concealed below decks, ready to leap into action in a surprise tactic. In reality the entire crew was rushing around the deck, doing two jobs at once and trying to stay calm. Looking back, it was a tour de force of improvisation. Amazingly, *Golden Apple* cracked a perfect start and set off for the first mark in front of the entire fleet.

Now what? It's one thing for three people to manage a yacht upwind, which generally involves handling just two sails, but it's quite another to set spinnakers and other headsails for the downwind leg with their extra sheets and winches. Normally it takes three crew to go forward to hoist the kite and lower the jib, with all the others helping to trim the sails and tidy things up in the stern while somebody does the steering.

Ridiculously, as *Golden Apple* closed on the windward mark – an inflated rubber buoy with "RORC" stamped on it, she was still leading. And that was when the cavalry arrived, hurtling out from the dock in a high-powered launch. As the helmsman pulled up alongside we threw ourselves over the lifelines, then dived for the sheets and winches as the launch drove off in a cloud of spray.

Minutes later we arrived at the top mark, executed a perfect rounding, hoisted the staysail and spinnaker and charged off downwind, still at the head of the British fleet.

To general astonishment *Golden Apple* won the British One Ton trials: without exaggerating, she cleaned up. In the final race she was so far ahead that Harry was able to drop us off on the dock and set sail back to Ireland before the second yacht had completed the course. I don't think Hugh could believe it. His first serious attempt at a level-rating event had more than vindicated his decision to have me design his yacht and get Ireland on the international yachting map.

Full of confidence, we began to prepare for the world championship.

▶

In 1977 Harry Cudmore skippered a new *Silver Shamrock* to second place in the 1977 Half Ton Cup in Sydney, after losing his mast in the final race. He still managed to cross the finish line second in that race under an innovative jury rig, securing second place for the series. Representing Royal Cork Yacht Club, Cudmore and his crew went on to complete the 1977 Sydney Hobart Race.

I welcomed racing in bad weather
to show how well my yachts performed in any weather conditions.

Changing of the guard

AS WORD GOT AROUND about *Golden Apple* and my other designs, the pace began to heat up at my fledgling studio. Commissions were pouring into what was still a one-man operation, and I urgently needed help. Laurel and I had moved into an apartment in a rambling Georgian house called Coolmore, right beside the Owenboy River that feeds into Cork Harbour. With its vast rooms, high ceilings and tall staircases, the apartment was spacious enough for me to set up an office on one of the staircase landings, still using a door as an improvised desk.

Eager to get things moving, I applied to the Irish telephone company for a connection. "There's a nine month waiting list," I was told. "Come on, are you kidding?" I blurted. "Nine months," they repeated, "No sooner." Nine months! With more and more international clients contacting me, or trying to, this seemed like a lifetime. But the telephone company was adamant. They said I simply had to wait patiently and try to work my way around the problem. I got into the habit of saving as many pennies as I could in a bag, so I could make my calls from the nearest payphone, installed downstairs near the old staff entrance to Coolmore – that is, when nobody else was using it. If they were, which was more often than not, I just had to stand in the hall cooling my heels, with my bag of coins. A phone call to America, or even to Britain, consumed an entire bag's-worth. Obviously, this was a state of affairs that couldn't continue, so I contacted the state-owned phone company again, and with Hugh's help

▲

Kiwi yacht designers on the "catwalk" for a photo shoot to go with an article in the *Auckland Star*: I'm with Laurie Davidson, Bruce Farr and Paul Whiting.

Laurie, the oldest member of this group, has a lifetime of fast beautiful designs to his credit, including a winning America's Cup boat as his crowning achievement.

Bruce Farr followed me overseas. Bruce and Russell Bowler established Farr Yacht Design in the USA and have produced many winning designs, including multiple Round The World Race victories.

Paul was the youngest member of this design group, and like all of us he was also a race-winning yachtsman. He sadly disappeared in 1980 while sailing one of his race yachts across the Tasman Sea.

pulling a few strings, I finally got a phone within a few weeks.

I quickly realized I couldn't handle all this on my own. Fortunately, I met up with the person who would become my right-hand man and a pillar of the start of Ron Holland Design, as the business would be known. I'd first met Butch Dalrymple-Smith, son of a rear admiral of the Royal Navy, in Sydney when he was aboard Mexico's *Sayula*, winner of the inaugural Whitbread Round-The-World Race. Butch had dropped out of medical school to go sailing and had no intention of returning. Although only in his twenties, he was already a skilled ocean racer and knew a lot about yachts.

I ran into Butch again at Cowes at the finish of his victorious Whitbread. Because of my mounting workload, I was spending a lot of weekends on the Isle of Wight, talking to new clients and racing with them on the Solent. Over a few beers in one of the town's many High Street pubs, I suggested that he come and work for me. Among other things I urgently needed his university math skills. Also, I knew Butch would be good around the office: he's pretty much unflappable with a great sense of humor, qualities I knew we were going to need as we got busier and busier.

So without further ado he came across to Ireland where, having decided I needed a proper office, I was in the throes of converting an abandoned piggery and cowshed into a studio, directly opposite the Royal Cork Yacht Club on the other side of the Owenboy River. Butch had no long-term plan: he just wanted to be involved in yachting, and the relaxed atmosphere in the office seemed to suit him. We always worked to the sound of music, from Butch's and my extensive collection of vinyl LPs. I don't think we ever discussed money, which was even further down Butch's list of priorities than it was mine, but I must have paid him well enough because a few years later he decided to check his bank account to see how much was in it, and to his amazement he found that he had enough on deposit to buy, for cash, a house on the waterfront that was just down the road from the studio.

Butch could turn his hand to practically anything. With his civilized manners he was great with clients, particularly with the Americans who loved him; he was so knowledgeable that he could talk yachting with anybody. If I were away, which was much of the time, Butch effortlessly took control. Naturally inventive, he was always working on some extracurricular project or other, like the deafening hovercraft that he bought cheap from a local inventor so he could whiz across to the pubs on the other side of the river at Crosshaven. This was one of his crazier schemes. When the tide was in, Butch liked to cross the river in a rigid-wing sailboard that he had designed and built himself, but when the tide was out the hovercraft meant he could negotiate the muddy banks without getting his pants dirty.

▲

When I joined the Royal New Zealand Yacht Squadron in 1967, I could never have imagined New Zealand would win the America's Cup. I also could not have predicted at 70 years of age I would represent the Squadron in the 2017 6-Meter World Championship.

"We got a good start, and as we worked our way up the first beat to windward I was studying the hastily-assembled mast, and I didn't like the look of it one bit. 'Lars, do you think it's going to stay up?' I asked. He got up from the weather rail, slid over the deck to the mast and studied it for a while. 'No,' he announced, and sat down on the rail again."

Whenever he started it up the noise could be heard over half of Cork.

As you'd expect from a round-the-world sailor, Butch was good in an emergency. And we had plenty, mainly because we were so short-handed. As Irish yachting took off, everybody was working flat out and many things were being done at the last minute.

One early incident springs to mind. Butch had sailed into Cork from Cowes aboard *Golden Apple* (he couldn't afford a plane fare) on a tight schedule to deliver our latest design, *Silver Shamrock*, to La Rochelle for the Half Ton Cup. When he arrived he found boatbuilders George and Killian Bushe still screwing the deck down onto the hull. As for the mast, it was a bare aluminum tube with all the fittings and rod rigging still in boxes alongside.

Swinging into action, Butch helped George throw the mast together. Next they put *Silver Shamrock* in the water and measured her, a big job in itself. With the tide ebbing, they raced over to the Royal Cork to pick up stores for the trip to France, hurled them aboard and started the engine. Within minutes they'd run aground just outside the club.

Jammed in the mud, Butch and Killian threw themselves on the sail bags and fell asleep for a few hours until the tide turned and they could set off again. Butch took the first watch while Killian went below and started building the bunks so they could get some sleep between Ireland and France. They arrived there for official measurement at the last possible moment.

I flew over to La Rochelle to meet Butch and Killian for the first race to be joined by Lars Bergstrom, our mast and rigging expert, and my old *Ganbare* skipper (and now star yacht designer) Doug Peterson. He didn't have a "ride" so he decided to join "the Irish." We got a good start, and as we worked our way up the first beat to windward I was studying the hastily-assembled mast, and I didn't like the look of it one bit. "Lars, do you think it's going to stay up?" I asked. He got up from the weather rail, slid over the deck to the mast and studied it for a while. "No," he announced, and sat down on the rail again.

Sure enough, a few minutes later the mast collapsed over the side in three pieces as the rest of the fleet sailed straight past. After limping back to La Rochelle we managed to persuade a company called FranceSpar to loan us their factory, and it was decided that Lars and Butch would work through the night. I went back to the hotel in despair. I felt it just couldn't be done.

I turned up early next morning in a state of dejection. Another cock-up! But Butch, Lars and Killian were standing outside the factory, looking totally beat but proud, the rebuilt mast beside them. Elated, I helped them throw the mast back in the boat in time for the second race.

We never started the middle distance race because we had to make a few serious modifications to our still troublesome rig, which was never going to stay standing in the overnight race as it was. But we still ended up in the top ten despite a Did Not Finish and a Did Not Sail. And reporters loving a good story, *Silver Shamrock*'s trials and tribulations got us a lot more space in the newspapers and magazines than we deserved, and this attracted more commissions, mainly from France and elsewhere in Europe.

As the workload increased, Butch was soon joined by others who became the brain trust of the studio. Rob Jacob, a local artist, yachtie and sailmaker from Kinsale, was hired after he showed a portfolio of his artwork to Butch and me over a pint of Murphy's, County Cork's favorite stout, at the Royal Cork Yacht Club.

Next, an architectural draftsman named Pat Lynch took over the high-pressure job of completing the many detailed drawings that we dispatched to boatbuilders all over the world. As a bonus, he was a good rock bass guitarist.

Not long afterwards my brother Phil would join us as a project manager who could turn his hand to anything aboard a racing yacht. In the intervening few years since he had been entrusted to my care in the Sydney Hobart Race, Phil had put thousands of sailing miles under his sea boots, and he would take care of some of our racing yacht projects.

Finally two local teenagers, Helen Coveney and Joan McCarthy, took

▲

Doug Peterson and I are meeting here with German Frers during the 1970s. For a few years the three of us "owned" the IOR race yacht market. For the 1977 Admiral's Cup more than one hundred new racing yachts were launched from our combined three design studios.

I'm concentrating to stay ahead of the fleet, Killian and Butch supporting me. Following the success of *Golden Apple*, South Coast Boatyard commissioned me to design the Half Tonner *Silver Shamrock* to represent Ireland at the 1974 Half Ton Cup in La Rochelle, France. We did not win but everyone present saw that we were very fast, and racing design commissions started coming in.

"The regatta began brilliantly for *Golden Apple*. With Harry calling – well, yelling – instructions, we got off to a great start in the opening race and led the fleet up the first leg of the course. Sitting on the side deck with my legs dangling over the side, I vividly remember those few minutes."

over the hectic secretarial and bookkeeping work. Almost overnight they became indispensable.

The 1974 One Ton Cup in Torquay was the first serious international competition for *Golden Apple* – and for Ireland. It was another international affair with 34 yachts entered from Britain, France, America, New Zealand, Australia, Hong Kong and of course Ireland, among other countries. The One-Tonners being very much a development class where designers could express their ideas, I found a lot of interesting yachts tied up at the marina. Peter Nicholson of the British boatbuilding family had qualified his new aluminum *Brigante* which was said to be a specialist in the light weather that was expected in Torquay. George Stead, a regular crewmember on Prime Minister Ted Heath's *Morning Cloud*, had turned up with another lightweight flyer of his own design called *High Tension*. The most sought-after designer of the moment, Dick Carter, was represented by several boats including *Eleuthera* to be steered by John Oakeley, a former world champion in the Olympic Flying Dutchman class. And Olin Stephens was represented by a couple of his latest designs.

One of the most daring concepts was America's *Terrorist*, an aluminum yacht that boasted two unballasted keels that looked a bit like wings. During a tack, a crewmember winched one of the keels up and the other down. In the American trials for the One Ton Cup team she had apparently flown in a breeze.

Doug Peterson was represented by *Gumboots*, which I knew would be dangerous. Bill Green was in her crew. As well, Doug had several other new boats in Torquay. He was the man of the moment because of the success of *Ganbare* the year before.

A new wave of technology was also emerging: more boats were being built of composite materials that journalists variously described as fiberglass or polyester. Among developments in sailcloth there were see-through synthetic materials and Kevlar, then known as "Fiber B" sailcloth. And hydraulic technology was being used for the first time to control the rake of the mast – an innovation that would soon be outlawed – and the set of the sails. I look back on this championship as a period of intense and exciting development right across the spectrum of yacht racing.

The regatta began brilliantly for *Golden Apple*. With Harry calling – well, yelling – instructions, we got off to a great start in the opening race and led the fleet up the first leg of the course. Sitting on the side deck with my legs dangling over the side, I vividly remember those few minutes.

Anxious about how *Golden Apple* would shape up in such an elite international field, I was keeping a particularly close eye on one of Doug's boats. Crewed by Californian rock stars, including Olympic yachtsman and sailmaker Lowell North, she was one of the favorites to win the championship. As the wind dropped to between three and four knots, I saw that *Golden Apple* was matching her speed when Johnny Mac made a call for one of his latest headsails to be hoisted.

Not right now, I thought. This was a bit brave – the sail had never been out of its bag. But I kept my mouth shut. Let's wait and see, I thought.

Because we were right alongside the Californians, if we got the maneuver wrong we would be certain to slip into their dirty wind and be left in their wake. Our crew tiptoed to the foredeck to make the switch. Hugh had invested in the latest Twinstay system that allowed crews to hoist a new headsail before taking down the old one. Invented by American Tim Stearn, the system amounted to a minor revolution. Until then, all sail changes were "bald-headed" – that is, there was no headsail until the new one went up – but this new system meant the yacht shouldn't lose any speed during the maneuver. The hoist went to perfection and within minutes *Golden Apple* started to pull clear of the Americans. Lowell North was looking at us in surprise, and so was Tim Stearn who was also aboard Doug's design.

An unknown Irish yacht in the lead!

Trying to stay calm, we approached the first mark. "Hurry! Spinnaker up!" yelled Harry. What! Now? It seemed too early. Obediently, the crew

▲

Once a year Doug and I informally met to "talk boats." We joked about creating a yacht design cartel, but it never happened. We were just concentrating on where the next design commission was coming from and who would get it.

Following racing *Golden Apple* at the 1974 One Ton Cup in England, the next challenge was racing *Golden Delicious* at the Three-Quarter Ton Cup in Norway. Here Butch Dalrymple-Smith and Damian Byrne (on deck, me in the cockpit) consider the meaning of coming second in this major level rating Regatta.

rushed to hoist the kite. They did too good a job. The sail was up before we'd rounded the mark. Result? The wind got on the wrong side of the kite and blew it backwards. The cloth got hooked up on the turning mark and *Golden Apple* came to an abrupt stop. As we fought to clear the sail, swearing and cursing as we clawed it back off the mark, several boats sailed right around us.

But at least we'd proven we were fast.

The third race – a 150-miler to Lizard Point off Cornwall and back – turned out to be the most memorable, although not for the sailing. For the first time in the series, the breeze picked up and most of the competitors were reveling in the conditions, *Golden Apple* included. We were sailing fast, near the leading yachts, when a humanitarian emergency intervened.

As the fleet was heading back from the Lizard around 1 AM, the crews of several yachts, including *Gumboots*, spotted a boat ablaze. Owned by the Rogers brothers, boatbuilder Jeremy and medical doctor Jonathan, *Gumboots* was lying fourth at the time and leading the event overall. But the Rogers didn't hesitate, immediately ordering a change of course to provide assistance. With flames building and the entire complement now in the rubber dingy, *Gumboots* hove alongside and took the entire complement of four adults and three children on board while other yachts stood by. The rescue accomplished, *Gumboots* returned to Torquay under motor, put the survivors ashore, and promptly resumed the race, a long way behind. When the weary crew finally made port, the race jury would rule that *Gumboots* and the other yachts that abandoned the race for the rescue should be treated as though they'd finished the race, and be given points based on their positions at the Lizard. As France's *Bateaux* magazine would write, "Nobody complained about this decision."

Far from it: the Rogers brothers were widely admired for putting human life above a possible victory. After all, at the time of the rescue they had no idea what decision the jury would make.

As for *Golden Apple*, we never saw the burning boat, but after crossing the finish line we learned we were effectively out of the championship. In a protest meeting the jury ruled that we'd failed to give way to a rival in a classic port-and-starboard incident. The penalty? A loss of ten places, a bitter blow. But you've got to be philosophical in sailing – at least we hadn't lost our mast like *Terrorist*. Nor had we hooked a large plastic bag on the keel and dragged it around the entire 250-mile race, as one of Dick Carter's designs did.

The deserving winner was Doug Peterson's *Gumboots* ahead of *High Tension* and New Zealand's *Hati IV,* another one of Doug's designs. There

"As *Bateaux* wrote later: '*Golden Apple*, the One-Tonner from the drawing board of that other prodigy Ron Holland, was also very quick but drew too many penalties to worry *Gumboots*'... Its conclusion: there had been a changing of the guard in yacht design in which 'The eternal Carter-Stephens duel has become the Peterson-Holland duel.'"

was no doubt that my former shipmate of the 4 AM watch on *Spirit* had covered himself in glory: his designs finished first, third, fourth and sixth.

As for *Golden Apple*, we placed seventh, which wasn't too shabby in the circumstances. Without the ten-place penalty and hooking up the mark in the first race, *Golden Apple* would have been a genuine contender. Once again we got more publicity than we deserved – it's not every day a yacht gets its spinnaker stuck on a mark. The BBC even ran a complimentary documentary called *Gumboots and Golden Apple*.

As *Bateaux* wrote later: "*Golden Apple*, the One-Tonner from the drawing board of that other prodigy Ron Holland, was also very quick but drew too many penalties to worry *Gumboots*."

The magazine went on to point out that neither of Dick Carter's or Olin Stephens' designs had seriously featured in the championship. Its conclusion: there had been a changing of the guard in yacht design in which "The eternal Carter-Stephens duel has become the Peterson-Holland duel."

This was a heady verdict for both of us. Prodigies! Doug was 29 and I was 27.

But I got just as much satisfaction from Ireland's sudden leap into prominence in international yacht racing. Not only did I feel Laurel and I had done the right thing by moving to Cork, I knew I had justified Hugh's faith in me.

Imp from San Francisco ahead of
the Admiral's Cup fleet. Racing
for the "world championship" of
ocean racing.

Green-striped machine

DURING A PARTICULARLY BUSY DAY in the studio I got a call from Dave Allen in San Francisco. It was early 1976 and I hadn't heard from him in a while. He'd still been winning races with *Improbable* and I'd been forging a career as a designer, but we'd kept in touch. He treated me like a son and sometimes gave me helpful advice about business, including on one occasion warning me not to overwork, perhaps the most helpful advice of all.

"You sound tired," he said. "Get somebody to do the drafting for you." And I'd done exactly that.

But that call would become one of the most important of my life. "I'd like you to design a new yacht for me," he explained. "I want to win the SORC and make the US Admiral's Cup team."

The flaw with *Improbable*, as we all knew, was her weakness upwind compared to the latest IOR-designed yachts. To do well in these most competitive of all regattas, a yacht needed to be strong on all points of sailing.

"But I still want her to sail downwind like *Improbable*," he said.

OK, that's a challenge, I thought.

Dave knew that my designs were all-rounders that not only satisfied the often-contradictory imperatives of the IOR rules, but that also attracted the builders of series production yachts. Camper and Nicholson had already bought the production molds of another yacht, *Golden Delicious*, that was entered in the Three-Quarter Ton Cup for me to race in Norway, and started knocking out a slightly modified production version known as the Nichol-

151

son 33. When some of my bigger boats such as *Golden Dazy* and *Irish Mist* started winning important races, other boatbuilders came knocking on my door. Winning designs were good for sales.

I very much wanted to help Dave who had done so much for me, but the pressure in the studio was intense at that time. Just about every weekend one of my designs was hitting the water somewhere in the world. But there was also a problem with the measurement rules, which had just gotten more complex with the issue of an updated version of IOR Mark III. Dave's boat would have to be designed to this latest version if she were to succeed in the SORC and Admiral's Cup. Without a good rating she wouldn't have a chance, however quick she might be. *Improbable*'s rating, for example, was terrible simply because she was never designed to suit the rule book but to win one race, the downwind slide to Jamaica.

In addition to these issues we were already running late. If Dave wanted the boat to be launched in good time for the SORC the following year, we'd have to get the ball rolling within months, if not weeks. After getting my thoughts together, I wrote a long letter to him in which I drew attention to an exciting new trend towards wider-beamed designs. I was beginning to think that the narrow bows and sterns encouraged by the IOR had gone too far, and I could see a way to design a more moderately proportioned yacht without incurring an unfavorable rating. But, as I explained, I didn't want to rush things. It was important to first see how the new IOR edition influenced the latest designs.

Reluctantly, after looking at all the options, I followed up with another a letter in August. "The timing from my side doesn't allow for the design to be developed accurately," I wrote.

I knew Dave would be disappointed – and probably disappointed in me too – but we would not be able to produce the drawings until mid-October at the earliest. I'd also been in touch with my brother-in-law, Gary Carlin, who told me it would be impossible for his thriving Kiwi Boats company to build the yacht in time for the SORC. Gary had a hefty order book filled up mostly with my latest designs: all those late nights helping me build *Eygthene* were paying off. I could see an advantage in waiting if Dave could be persuaded to give up his dream of the SORC. This was because the One Ton and Two Ton Cup world championships were coming up and we could learn a lot from how my latest yachts performed in them. Based on these lessons, I was convinced I could then design him a faster boat.

But once Dave got his teeth into a project he didn't give up easily. In the meantime he'd also gotten in touch with Gary in Florida and suggested that he build two boats, a much more attractive proposition for Kiwi

▲

My intention when designing *Imp* was to improve my new IOR design racing yacht's performance when running with spinnaker set. I was not surprised *Imp* was a winner downwind, but I was surprised she could also win beating into the wind. A good all-round performing yacht and a great crew, a winning combination.

"I was beginning to think that the narrow bows and sterns encouraged by the IOR had gone too far, and I could see a way to design a more moderately proportioned yacht without incurring an unfavorable rating."

Boats. And, thinking like the good businessman he was, he then came back to me with the idea that, if the new boat proved a winner, we could co-own the production rights.

"OK," I said. "Let's go."

I could see why Dave was so successful in commerce. Despite the odds he was determined to make the project happen and would do so through creative solutions rather than coercion.

Then a wrench was thrown into the works. Ragnar "Ragga" Hakansson, my old crewmate from *Improbable*, turned up at Currabinny as Dave's project manager with a mission to get the new yacht off the ground as fast as possible. Ragga had been racing in Europe and jumped on a plane to Ireland as soon as he got the call from Dave.

But when Ragga arrived, eager to get started, I wasn't there. I was in hospital with a severe swelling on my forehead. The lump was feared to be a tumor of some sort, and although it turned out to be benign, it took an operation, heavy doses of antibiotics and four days in a hospital bed to bring the swelling under control before I could return to work, still pretty shaky. The medical opinion was that the lump was the legacy of rolling the car in Auckland during my apprenticeship days.

Once I'd recovered Ragga became invaluable. Within a few days my team produced preliminary drawings to send to Dave in San Francisco and to Gary in Florida, who had now agreed to take on the project after

"'All the numbers suggest we will have a very competitive and fun boat,' I wrote in what would turn out to be the biggest understatement since my teachers had said, 'Holland will never amount to anything.'"

some persuasion from my former mentor. We'd all agreed on a small Two-Tonner of just over 40 feet designed to the latest IOR rules. In the midst of the birth of my second daughter, Benna, for which Laurel flew to New Zealand (Laurel and I wanted to have a true-blue Kiwi in the family), we quickly advanced the project.

"All the numbers suggest we will have a very competitive and fun boat," I wrote in what would turn out to be the biggest understatement since my teachers had said, "Holland will never amount to anything."

Now we were able to get cracking on the other elements of the new yacht. After considering an experimental fractional rig with a big mainsail, we settled on a more conventional masthead configuration because we were too pressed for time to thoroughly test the first concept. Dave flew to Florida to sign a contract with Gary in late October. Based on a quick turnaround, the deal rewarded Kiwi Boats handsomely if they got the job done by the deadline: to make the first race of the SORC, she had to be in the water by January. Gary estimated it would take 4,000 man hours to build Dave's dream yacht.

By now the project had been designated as Holland Design No. 26. As soon as construction started, Ragga returned to Florida and threw himself into the fray with the Kiwi Boats team. He worked late most nights, sometimes to the point of exhaustion. He was greatly helped by his fellow Swede Lars Bergstrom, who was also based in Florida. Then in his early forties, Lars was one of the most creative people I have ever met. With my encouragement Hugh Coveney and Johnny Mac had used Lars' rig concept with success on *Golden Apple*, and he was always coming up with new ideas. While building then flying his own power glider, *The Windex*, he was a consultant on rigging and mast structures. He was an authority on aerodynamics in aircraft, and he and his business partner Sven Ridder often applied their knowledge to the design of keels and rudders. At that time he was already working on the first of the carbon fiber rudders that would become highly controversial a few years later. Lars was also a capable ocean racer in his own right who would later beat the old clipper ship time from New York to San Francisco, a voyage of 14,000 miles around Cape Horn, in a 60-footer that he designed for boatbuilder Warren Luhrs.

While I was engaged on other earlier design projects, the two Swedes gave Gary and his boatbuilders a lot of help in ensuring that the hull of the yacht was exceptionally strong, fair and light – all prerequisites for a fast boat no matter how well she was designed – and extremely light in the bow and stern. Two people could easily lift the hull by the stern when it was under construction. And it was all done without detailed drawings, just the preliminary ones. Lars and Sven were also developing a concept for Gary Carlin that would become an intense point of discussion in global yachting circles. It would become known as a "space frame." Based on what some called load-path engineering, and incorporating what others described as a geodesic frame, Gary had already tried out the idea on a successful Quarter-Tonner that I designed called *Business Machine*, which was a spin-off from *Eygthene*. Since then and with Ragga's help, Lars had developed the technology further.

Essentially, the space frame was an interlocking structure of struts and tubes and rigging that was built into the interior of the hull to absorb the loads at the points of greatest stress, such as the forestay and backstay, shrouds and mast step. So instead of the boat having to be built like a tank to contain the loads –"belt and braces," as the saying goes – she could be constructed lighter with the confidence that the stresses would be channeled through the space frame.

While Lars and Sven were designing the space frame, Dave had a lot of people, all specialists in their own field that I had recommended, working flat out. Mast maker Tim Stearn had been entrusted with the spars and rigging. Steve Taft, a regular crewmember on *Improbable* and boss of the North Sails loft in San Francisco, was developing her sail wardrobe. Together they were trialing the latest idea in headstays – that is, the rigging running from the masthead forward to the bow.

Ron's boats are ruling the waves

Today one in every three boats built for the competitive ocean racing circuit is first conceived in the tranquil studio beside the water's edge at Currabinny, Co. Cork, where Ron Holland and his team of young designers work to the background beat of pop music in a converted old stone cow shed and piggery.

A decade ago Holland, a self-described ex-boat bum, was trying to break into the elite business of yacht designing. Hugh Coveney invited him to Cork to design a boat. The rest is sailing history — "Golden Apple" won the Fastnet Race and launched Holland's international career.

In every year since then his boats have won at least one world championship in the half-dozen or so classes which compete in offshore racing.

At the moment a million dollar cruiser being built near Venice for Prince Rainier of Monaco comes from the Holland drawing board.

● Our picture shows Ron and his team standing from left, Rob Jacob, Ron Holland, Pat Lynch, Butch Dalrymple-Smith, sitting, Helen Coveney, Joan Sammon and Mary Keohane.

▲

Ron Holland Design team "ruling the waves."

STANDING L TO R: **Rob Jacob, Ron Holland, Pat Lynch, Butch Dalrymple-Smith.**

SEATED L TO R: **Helen Coveney, Joan McCarthy, Mary Keohane.** In front of the converted pig shed during the early "crazy years," before the yachts became bigger and more complex and we needed to expand the team.

"I'd had numerous calls from yachting journalists, and there was a lot of buzz among the yachtsmen hanging around the club. Now it was a matter of seeing whether *Imp* could live up to the hype that surrounded her. It didn't take long. Next day, although the crew had no time to tune her up, *Imp* won the opening race comfortably to the general consternation of the other hotshot entries."

With the project shaping up, Dave was in his element. A member of the Christian Science faith, he derived a deep spiritual satisfaction from his yachting endeavors. For him sailing was almost an expression of his religion, an activity that allowed him to demonstrate his belief in social responsibility and good works. That was why he didn't throw his money around. Unlike a lot of successful boat owners, he didn't pay the crew to race but made sure they were accommodated together, including wives and girlfriends, in a house rather than in an impersonal hotel. He liked a family atmosphere. Although Dave paid for non-racing tasks such as delivering the boat from one port to another, he disliked the way money was becoming such a big element of top-level yachting, a sport he loved for its own sake. One of his regular crew, Bill Barton, who would write a book about *Imp*, remembers, "Every crewmember became as close as family to David Allen. He had a knack for fostering respect and cooperation and instilling confidence in each of his crew and even in the support group of wives, girlfriends and his own kindred." That's certainly how I felt about him.

By December 1976 I had run the numbers through the latest IOR rule book with the aid of a new computer, and I came up with her rating. "With all the variables going our way, we will achieve a rating of 31.3," I wrote Dave. These were great numbers because they meant I'd been able to achieve the refined hull design I wanted, but without falling foul of any serious IOR rating penalties.

After a furious few weeks when Gary put all available manpower on the job, the yacht was finally finished. It helped that the boys didn't have to bother much about building an interior. Apart from the tubes and struts running in all directions, the yacht was stripped to the bone; just a few sheets of canvas for bunks, and other bare necessities including a very public (to save weight) toilet.

Already named *Imp* after a classic 55-footer that had smashed up on rocks in Tiburon, California (Dave, who wasn't superstitious, just liked the name, and it reminded him of *Improbable*), she was launched on January 28 at Snead Island Boat Works. The crew motored down to St. Petersburg Yacht Club screwing on bits and pieces as they went, trying out sails and generally putting everything in working order as fast as they could. To say things had been cut a bit fine would be an understatement: the opening race of the SORC, the Boca Grande Race, was coming up the very next day.

I was already at St. Petersburg, ready to sail aboard another of my latest Two-Tonner designs, *Jack Knife*, as I'd promised her owner, but I was more than interested to see how *Imp* had turned out. As soon as she was tied up, I hurried to the yacht club to have a look at her and her stunning green-striped hull. Modest though he was, Dave wasn't averse to making an impression. I was struck by the appearance and the quality of the finish, especially in view of how rushed the whole project had been.

In the previous weeks the word had gotten out about the yacht with the space frame. I'd had numerous calls from yachting journalists, and there was a lot of buzz among the yachtsmen hanging around the club. Now it was a matter of seeing whether *Imp* could live up to the hype that surrounded her. It didn't take long.

Next day, although the crew had no time to tune her up, *Imp* won the opening race comfortably to the general consternation of the other hotshot entries. And thereafter she carried on as she'd started. *Imp* was beaten only by far bigger yachts in the second race, the long-distance race to Ft. Lauderdale. In the third race, the Ocean Triangle across the Gulf Stream to the Bahamas and back with its powerful currents, the crew came down to earth a bit with a second place finish to a tough German crew aboard *Champagne*, one of Doug Peterson's latest Two-Tonners, but already *Imp* was becoming the number one topic of conversation. The next race, the Lipton Cup, was a 30-miler that produced light and shifty winds, quite different conditions from the opening races. Yet once again *Imp* triumphed. She was now leading her class by a wide margin and seemed to be unstoppable.

▲

The Lars Bergstrom-inspired "space frame" for *Imp*. The goal was to build a light hull and deck that would remain rigid and not flex when loaded by sailing forces. The aluminum-tubed space frame ensured this, and *Imp* was fast. Interior amenities? None – we wanted to save weight.

"OK," I said to Dr. Greenberg, owner of *Jack Knife,* which had been trailing *Imp,* "let's give them a run for their money in the 193-miler from Miami to Nassau." And we did, at least until around midnight when they cleared out as the wind fell light. *Imp* won her class, beating a Sparkman & Stephens-designed 46-footer, *Pirana.* I was now feeling very confident about just how good this yacht was. Dave, myself, Ragga, Lars, Gary, Tad and everybody else involved had come up with something special.

When *Imp* cleaned up in her class in the final race, the Nassau Cup, which took the fleet just 31 miles out to Booby Rocks and back, we had undisputed confirmation. Although there were other fast boats in the SORC such as *Sweet Okole*, a One Ton flyer from the drawing board of fellow New Zealander Bruce Farr, *Imp* had become the talk of the bar. And although tradition has it that the SORC is designed as a regatta of different classes and isn't meant to have an overall winner, the press paid no heed. As far as the journalists were concerned, *Imp* was the runaway victor.

"*Imp* Wins Southern Yachting Title" headlined the *New York Times*.

Her success even rated a mention in *Sports Illustrated*. On the other side of the Atlantic, British Olympic gold medalist Iain MacDonald-Smith described her as "the sensation of the whole fleet," and yachting journalist Jack Knights judged *Imp* to be "head and shoulders above the rest as the unassailable champ."

Very gratifying indeed but, proud as I was, I knew much of her success was down to her crew as well as to her design. They knew each other well, understood their job, and had logged many racing miles together. In Ragga they had not only an able racer but somebody who probably knew more about her construction and handling characteristics than anybody. They had a talented and experienced ocean racer as skipper, the unflappable Skip Allan. And of course they had Dave who pulled everything together.

But how would *Imp* perform in the very different conditions of the Admiral's Cup with its tricky tides? Good as she was, surely the green-striped machine couldn't maintain her winning streak.

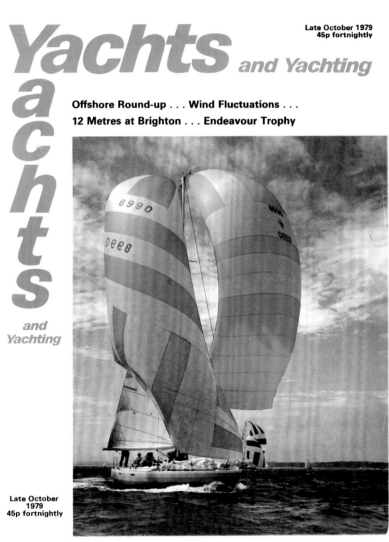

Yachts *and Yachting*

Late October 1979
45p fortnightly

**Offshore Round-up . . . Wind Fluctuations . . .
12 Metres at Brighton . . . Endeavour Trophy**

Yachts and Yachting

Late October
1979
45p fortnightly

During 1977 and 1979 the green yacht was winning most of the IOR races she entered. *Imp* was featured on the cover of many sailing magazines.

In 1977 we had more than 30
special new racing yachts building
around the world. They were all
hoping to represent their country
in the Admiral's Cup.

IOR frenzy

I ALWAYS LOOKED FORWARD to going to Cowes, and particularly for the Admiral's Cup.

It was July 1977 and I had arrived a few days before the first race. The pace back in the studio had been so hectic that it was a relief to escape. I was wandering around the narrow streets of the historic town absorbing the atmosphere, when I turned a corner and was startled to see a large photograph of myself hanging in the window of a grocery store of all places. I can't remember exactly what the caption said, but it was something about a famous yacht designer who had a lot of boats entered in the Admiral's Cup. Getting over the surprise, I turned another corner and was confronted by a large poster of *Imp*. That really stopped me in my tracks. Dave Allen's latest project had apparently been installed as one of the favorites to win the Admiral's Cup. I remember I could have bought the poster for a tenner.

Ever since arriving aboard *Improbable* for my first visit to Cowes six years earlier, the place had become almost a pilgrimage for me because of its sailing history. It was everywhere. Known locally as "The Castle", the Royal Yacht Squadron building occupies the prime position overlooking the harbor, sitting alongside a hillside with an immaculately tended lawn. If you didn't know it was a yacht club, as it has been from its foundation in 1815 by a group of gentleman sailing enthusiasts from London, you might think it had originally been a fortress. Lined up in front is an intimidating row of polished bronze cannons.

161

▲

Encouraged by the success of *Golden Apple* in England, a friend of the Carlin family (my new parents-in-law) Dr. Gerald Murphy asked me to design him a 41-foot racing yacht. He intended to represent Bayview Yacht Club in a challenge for the Canada's Cup, a race series between Canada and USA in yachts of the same IOR rating. Only two yachts racing in five races, and first across the finish line three times wins.

In 1974 a 41-foot yacht was a big boat. In Ireland a sister yacht *Irish Mist* was under construction to represent Ireland in the Admiral's Cup. Two important 41-foot racing yachts! Things were looking good for the new Ron Holland Design.

Golden Dazy was built in wood and epoxy resin by the Gougeon Brothers in Bay City, Michigan, the biggest yacht they had ever built.

After struggling in preliminary races, Dr. Murphy asked successful Australian skipper John Bertrand to take charge. *Golden Dazy* started winning races, including the 1975 Canada's Cup.

In the summer Cowes practically exists for sailing. The streets boast more yacht chandleries per square mile than any other place I know, and during the Admiral's Cup there are probably more yachties per square mile than anywhere else. I also owed a lot of my design projects to Cowes. In the short time since Ireland had made its brilliant but checkered debut at the top level of yacht racing, I had received a number of commissions from local residents, including one from Sir Max Aitken, son of Canadian-born press baron Lord Beaverbrook, and an ex-Spitfire pilot. He was known to everyone simply as "Max."

In the course of designing a Two-Tonner named *Knockout* for Max I spent many an evening at his Cowes home, The Prospect, overlooking the Solent and Cowes Harbour. A dashing and genial host, his dinner parties were legendary for their beautiful women and famous men, many of whom held titles in society. Sometimes I almost had to pinch myself as a reminder that I wasn't imagining it all. On one of these occasions I found myself with my sailing girlfriend Pippa Longley talking yachts with Prince Philip, and was seriously impressed by his knowledge of sailing.

Having had a lot of success with *Knockout*, Max followed up with a commission for a 65-foot racing schooner to be built by Souter's boatyard in Cowes. Unfortunately, I had just started on the design when he suffered a massive stroke and the project was cancelled.

The house next door to The Prospect belonged to Uffa Fox, a true son of Cowes who was the father of many original dinghy designs. A long way ahead of his time, he practically invented planing hulls – boats that sit up on the water and skate along the surface instead of plowing through it like displacement hulls. In this way he prefigured the foils on which the recent America's Cup catamarans fly at speeds that even he could not have imagined. From his drawing board came a number of small boat designs – the first planing International 14, the Flying Fifteen, National Twelve, National Eighteen, Firefly and Albacore among them – some of which became highly successful classes. Perhaps the most thrilling of them all was his International Canoe, a flying pencil of a boat that was steered by a very wet man sitting on the end of a wooden sliding seat, rather like a diving board sticking out over the side. The International Canoe isn't for the faint-hearted, but Uffa Fox liked to sail them single-handed across the Channel and back just for fun. He also put his flair and knowledge to many good causes including, during the war, a 24-foot lifeboat that could be dropped from an aircraft to ditched airmen floating in the sea. And, although it has been long forgotten, it was Uffa Fox who conceived the first British rowboat, *Britannia*, that crossed the Atlantic under nothing but guts and brawn.

"I was on the receiving end of commissions from current and new clients in the USA, Bermuda, Europe, Australia, New Zealand, South America and South Africa. In a single day Spanish hotelier Guillermo Cryns put in an order for three yachts – an 85-foot cruising yacht, a One-Tonner, and a Quarter-Tonner that would be series-built in Spain."

He followed that up with another oarpowered design, *Britannia II*, in which an intrepid crew crossed the Pacific. It's my regret that I came too late to Cowes to meet the great man – he died in 1972 – but I had read all his books and often passed by his house and thought of him.

The 1977 Admiral's Cup was the biggest and busiest ever, with no fewer than 19 teams, each composed of three yachts. That was 57 new yachts. Never before or since has the event mustered such a fleet. Hundreds of yachts were tied up in the marina in Cowes Harbour, and many cruising yachts had dropped anchor wherever there was space. The founding fathers of the Royal Yacht Squadron would have been amazed to see what they'd started.

In the lead-up to the event, the phone had been ringing off the hook. (Having finally got lines hooked up, we no longer needed to save coins for the public payphone at the bottom of the Coolmore stairs.) I was on the receiving end of commissions from current and new clients in the USA, Bermuda, Europe, Australia, New Zealand, South America and South Africa. In a single day Spanish hotelier Guillermo Cryns put in an order for three yachts – an 85-foot cruising yacht, a One-Tonner, and a Quarter-Tonner that would be series-built in Spain.

But surely one of the most unexpected commissions came from a certain Mr. Takeda in Japan. He called to say he wanted a Quarter-Tonner and a Half-Tonner as a first step in promoting yacht racing in his home country. Over the next few years I would come to see a lot of Mr. Takeda.

▲

We often had notable visitors come
to the Strand Farmhouse studio,
including this group during the
Round Britain and Ireland Race.
L TO R: Peter Bateman, Tony Fair-
child, Selwyn Parker, Daniel Forster,
Laurel Holland, Chay Blyth, Keith
Taylor, Jeff Holgrave, Naomi James,
Rob James, Ron Holland, Barbara
Binder, Butch Dalrymple-Smith.

Naturally I said yes to all these commissions. Hectic as life was, it was also exciting. Everybody in our rapidly expanding studio was on a high as the work and the clients poured in. Our list of visitors was turning into a mini Who's Who of European, British and American industry, and we liked to make the most of these distinguished arrivals.

When Pehr Gyllenhammar, chief executive of Sweden's Volvo Automotive Group, notified us of his impending arrival in a Falcon jet, we contacted the startled local Volvo agent in Cork and gave him the news. Rising to the occasion as the Irish always do, he immediately put Volvo's top model at his disposal and provided a driver for the duration, greatly impressing the boss.

The local community soon grew accustomed to welcoming these captains of industry as well as celebrities from most sectors of the commercial and creative worlds. The taxi drivers did a thriving business shuttling them to and fro between Cork Airport, Cork City, hotels and pubs in the nearest village of Carrigaline, and then to our design office in the Strand Farmhouse, the converted piggery overlooking Cork Harbour.

A particular beneficiary of this high-level influx was our local publican Finbar Coogan whose establishment, known simply as Coogan's, did a booming business many a night. The visitors loved it: an authentic Irish pub in which everybody mixed on the same level. As time went on Finbar became a celebrity in his own right. Although he wasn't a yachtsman, he began to find himself being quoted in the newspapers as something of a waterfront sage by journalists looking for a line or two. The highpoint of his fame would come when our studio received a telex from a consortium in Japan urgently requesting his contact details.

"Why?" we asked. "We would like Mr. Coogan's help in organizing a challenge for the America's Cup", was the reply. "We read Bob Fisher's story about Mr. Coogan and we need to talk to him."

There was never a dull day. Out of the blue our secretaries fielded a call from an American advertising man named Stuart Woods, who said he wanted to race the Observer Single-Handed Transatlantic-Race – the OSTAR – and could we please give him some advice? Although I was inundated with work, we agreed to meet in the Grand Hotel in Crosshaven and discuss this bold venture.

Over lunch in the dining room, with its picture windows overlooking the marina and my new Currabinny studio, our caller put his cards on the table. Stuart, who was a couple of years older than me, explained he'd approached me because he was thinking of buying a production version of my *Golden Shamrock* design, and racing her in the OSTAR.

"I liked the fact that he didn't pretend to know more than he did, which was pretty much nothing. As he would write later, Stuart didn't have much time for pretense. 'It's all too easy to casually throw out a few technical terms in conversation and give someone the impression that you know more than you do,' he declared."

"Interesting," I said. "Go on."

His grandfather had died and left him a modest legacy, which he hoped was enough to get started. He explained rather apologetically that he'd hardly done any sailing: his experience was limited to playing around in a ten-foot plywood Mirror Dinghy, a boat for beginners. He lived in a cottage in Galway and had bought the dinghy to race on Sunday afternoons against kids. He'd never gone offshore in a yacht of any kind. When you came down to it, all he'd really done was read a few books on single-handed sailing and studied celestial navigation. And now he wanted to do the OSTAR, which among other things required him to complete a 500-mile single-handed, nonstop voyage before he was even allowed to enter the race.

"Do you think it's possible?" he asked. I could tell my opinion was important to him.

I liked the fact that he didn't pretend to know more than he did, which was pretty much nothing. As he would write later, Stuart didn't have much time for pretense. "It's all too easy to casually throw out a few technical terms in conversation and give someone the impression that you know more than you do," he declared. "This is done every day in yacht club bars."

I couldn't have agreed more.

Yet I couldn't help admiring his enthusiasm and sense of adventure – after all, this was exactly what had inspired me when I was younger. I suspected Stuart was expecting I would try to talk him out of it. Certainly the odds were stacked against him. In less than a year he had to buy and fit out the yacht, get used to handling her, and somehow do the qualifying 500-miler.

If he had any chance of making the OSTAR, time was already running out.

"Let's go and talk to Barry Burke," I suggested. We drove around to the South Coast Boatyard where Barry was constructing production versions of *Golden Shamrock* as fast as he could. I'd re-jigged them to be more comfortable and roomy than the original racing boat, designing in a higher and longer coach roof that provided more shelter and a more roomy and comfortable interior. I was thinking this would be a good yacht for Stuart.

Barry had a busy assembly line going. He'd already sold nine boats, and more orders were coming in. He was under a lot of pressure, and reluctant to slow down the assembly line to build a non-standard yacht. An OSTAR boat would need modifications to allow her to be sailed single-handed. Also, as Stuart explained, he didn't want an all-out racer but a fast cruiser, with among other things a more comfortable cockpit that boasted seats and lockers.

"Why don't you modify one off the assembly line?" I suggested to Barry. "You could put two guys onto it." Although Barry clearly didn't want to take on any more work, he gave Stuart some helpful information about prices and specifications, so Stuart left the boatyard with some information to get him started. If Barry could eventually be persuaded to build a customized yacht, he had a rough idea of the likely timetable. We returned to the hotel, where we tossed around a few more ideas, and after thinking it all through, Stuart said finally, "I think I can do it."

"I think you can too," I said. "It's an exciting project and I'd like to be involved."

Over the next few months Stuart threw all his energies into the preparations. A good advertising man, he managed to talk Barry into a deal that would deliver the Half-Tonner in just enough time to attempt the 500-mile shakedown voyage. Next up, Johnny Mac readily agreed to make the sails. So, with the main issues sorted, Stuart raced off to the London Boat Show with a limited budget and snapped up a lot of essential equipment at heavy discounts.

As he would write later: "There were only two and a half days left of the show, and I had to buy or at least research virtually every piece of equipment that would be needed for my yacht. I bought a sextant, instruments, a hand-bearing compass, a VHF radio-telephone, clothing, a wetsuit, books, and much else from a long list. I carefully researched life rafts and inflatable dinghies, emergency radio transmitters, self-steering, and electronics."

▲

The centre of our universe: the Strand Farmhouse, Currabinny, County Cork. The Ron Holland Design studio occupied the old renovated pigsty, and the Holland family lived next door in the farmhouse by the river's edge. Here Kelly is sailing our Mirror Dinghy across the river to the Royal Cork Yacht Club.

And with a novice's enthusiasm he was also working like crazy on the interior of his yacht. Keeping up the tradition established by *Golden Apple*, he had already christened his yacht *Golden Harp*. By now Stuart had moved to Cork to be closer to the project, to a gamekeeper's cottage on the Coolmore estate at Drake's Pool. One day he turned up at the studio with some sketches he'd put together. Essentially, he wanted to cram a lot into what was a small space – *Golden Harp* was only 30 feet long – and he had come up with a plan that provided for just one bunk, with most of the space forward given over to the storage of sails.

I took one look at the sketches and saw he'd made the common and understandable error of forgetting that the interior of a yacht is determined by the shape of the hull.

"It won't fit," I had to explain. "The sides of a boat are round, not straight."

With the dimensions being wrong he had to start all over again, which he did. Still, I had to admire Stuart's tenacity.

Eighteen months after he'd broached the project to Barry Burke, *Golden Harp* was launched and Stuart went sailing every hour he could spare. (During all this, I would learn later, he was sporadically writing a novel based in his native Georgia.)

With help and advice from my team at the studio who were all experienced yachties, he quickly improved his competence to the point that, in the nick of time, Stuart completed his 500-mile qualifier to the Azores and back and was allowed to enter the OSTAR.

But he was unlucky. That particular OSTAR turned out to be a wild race, with one storm after another sweeping through the fleet and knocking out yachts by the score. Of the 125 boats that crossed the start line, only 73 made the finish in Newport. Tragically, two skippers were lost at sea and several boats broke up and sank.

To our relief Stuart made it, against the odds. With so little experience he must have been scared out of his wits more than a few times. Later on he would describe the adventure in his first book called *Blue Water, Green Skipper* – and it's still a great read. Perhaps because of the self-confidence he'd achieved from the OSTAR, Stuart would soon turn to writing full time. His first novel, *Chiefs*, became a blockbuster television series starring Charlton Heston.

Today Stuart is an award-winning author of more than 50 novels that regularly feature on the *New York Times* best-seller list. As well as flying his own Citation M-2 jet (we've shared an interest in aviation, influenced by Johnny Mac) he has owned and sailed a variety of different yachts.

Throughout the frenzied build-up to the 1977 Admiral's Cup, Hugh

Stuart Woods practicing single-handed sailing with *Golden Harp* at the entrance to Cork Harbour, before racing to the Azores in order to qualify for the single-handed transatlantic race.

Coveney remained my most valued client. I still shared his and Johnny Mac's mission to put Irish sailing on the international map. Encouraged by *Golden Apple*'s performance in the One Ton championship, he had decided to do one better and commissioned a 44-foot racing yacht for taking a serious shot at the Admiral's Cup.

I put my latest thinking into the design, and brother Phil supervised most of her construction and fit out. Instead of the yacht being built in Ireland the job was handed over to UK boatbuilder Joyce Marine in Southampton, who did a fine job in hand-crafted aluminum alloy. Christened *Big Apple*, the yacht proved she was quick in her first races, and we had high hopes for her in the Admiral's Cup where she would have two sister boats, *Mandrake* and *Marionette*, representing Italy and Britain respectively.

Then Irish bad luck struck again. Just six weeks out from the event, on a wild afternoon Phil and a skeleton crew including Clayton Love, co-owner and accomplished ocean racer, were delivering *Big Apple* to Cowes via Guernsey's Beaucette Marina. This is a unique harbor, blasted into existence by the Royal Engineers in 1968, when they used explosives to blow a hole in the cliff that let the sea into an old quarry. From the sea the entrance looks narrow because of the towering cliffs on either side, painted white to make the harbor more visible from the sea. Yachtsmen are advised to call the marina before entering the harbor because of a shallow reef lying just outside.

Known locally as "the sill," the reef is flat, invisible and dangerous. When the tide's out you can't be sure there's enough water under the boat, so yachts are supposed to tie up to a buoy identified by the symbol of an anchor, and wait until it's safe. As a rule of thumb, you want around ten feet of water over the sill to be sure you can take a yacht across in any waves. But the seas were building and the crew wasn't confident about tying up to the buoy and waiting it out. Then Phil noticed depth markings indicating the water level, which seemed to show there wasn't enough water to cross; but the markings were too indistinct to make out. After a fair amount of discussion the general consensus was that it looked deep enough, although nobody liked the swirling currents that were visible.

"I think we should give it a go," suggested Clayton. "OK. But let's do it under motor – and fast," said Phil, and there was general agreement for this action. Phil wanted to be sure there was enough way on to steer *Big Apple* accurately through the narrow channel. If she slowed too much, she would be knocked off course by the current and waves.

With the sails down, they started up the engine and headed for the entrance, eyes peeled for telltale broken water. Suddenly *Big Apple* hit the sill. With a bang that nearly threw half the crew overboard, Ireland's big hope for the Admiral's Cup shuddered to a dead stop and immediately began to list steeply. Water poured inside in torrents. When Phil looked over the side, he was horrified to see that half the hull had been ripped out.

Big Apple had not come anywhere near clearing the sill and had struck about halfway up the keel.

There was nothing the crew could do: *Big Apple* was jammed on the reef and sinking fast. They had to abandon ship and entrust themselves to the currents and rocks below.

When they jumped off the yacht, they were hugely relieved to find the sill was so close below the surface that they could just stand there and wait for rescue from shore, while they watched *Big Apple* settling fast into the water. Within a few minutes she had slipped off the sill and only the top half of the mast was visible.

Big Apple looked to be wrecked, along with Ireland's Admiral's Cup hopes. It seemed impossible that she could be retrieved from the rocks and rebuilt in time. As soon as he got ashore, Phil found a phone and told Hugh the bad news. He still considers it to have been one of the hardest things he has ever had to do.

Once he got over his shock, Hugh flew into action and organized *Big Apple*'s resurrection from her watery grave. The very next day shore-based rescue services refloated the yacht with balloons, and towed her alongside

▲

My "race winning look" for 1979. Who says yacht racing is not fashion conscious? Note the depth sounder on deck and close at hand, a must for successful Admiral's Cup racing during the inshore day races, where shallow water offers reduced adverse current.

◀

Big Apple leading the Admiral's Cup fleet out of the Solent following the start of the 1977 Channel Race, Harry calling strategy and me on the helm. We went on to win, the first Irish yacht to win an Admiral's Cup race: another Irish challenge to the British yachting establishment. A special moment.

the harbor wall where she was hoisted out by a crane. The extent of the damage was considerable. Apart from the gaping holes in her side, the rigging was crumpled and the keel badly bent. Only the sails were intact, still in their bags. At considerable expense Hugh arranged for *Big Apple* to be lifted aboard a freighter and shipped all the way back from Guernsey to Southampton, where an alerted Joyce Marine undertook a breakneck rebuild. Incredibly, the boatbuilders put *Big Apple* back in one piece in time for her to make Cowes for the Admiral's Cup.

But where was *Imp*? I couldn't find her anywhere. After asking around I discovered that my hot design, one of the favorites, was still somewhere mid-Atlantic. Although the crew was arriving in ones and twos at the house that Dave Allen had rented for the duration, they didn't have a boat to race. Now that he was a bona fide representative of America's Admiral's Cup team, Dave had planned the campaign down to the last detail, but not even he could have predicted the problems that befell his wonder yacht.

As Bill Barton would tell the story in his book, *Imp* had sailed out of Jacksonville, Florida, in good time to make Cowes. Ragga was skipper for the delivery trip across the Atlantic and everything looked good for an uneventful voyage. Then, a few days out, *Imp*'s experimental carbon fiber rudder snapped off in big seas somewhere off Bermuda. She started plunging and rolling, completely out of control. The ever-resourceful Ragga attempted to make a jury rudder by lashing floorboards to the spinnaker pole, but the improvisation didn't work and the crew had no option but to radio the US Coast Guard for help. The next day, as the boat continued to wallow around helplessly, making most of the crew seasick, a US Navy plane turned up, closely followed by a US Coast Guard cutter steaming along at 14 knots. Towards evening the cutter took the stricken *Imp* in tow.

Suddenly Dave's careful planning had been thrown into disarray. It was a long way back to Bermuda, especially as the yacht continued to veer all over the ocean behind the cutter, surely testing the patience of her captain as well as that of *Imp*'s crew.

It took about 18 long hours to make port. Immediately after they had they tied up, Ragga jumped ashore and phoned Dave in his office in San Francisco. Minutes later my brother-in-law Gary got a call at Kiwi Boats.

"Make another rudder and get it to Bermuda as fast as you can," Dave ordered.

In the all-hands-to-the-pump style that's typical of boatbuilding yards just about everywhere, Gary's business partner Tad Belknap toiled through the night to build the rudder, a job requiring considerable skill.

"Then the Fates intervened once more, when *Imp* ran into a dead flat calm. It lasted for day after interminable day. As the sails flapped uselessly to and fro, the engine was doing all the work. If the absence of wind wasn't enough, with a considerable distance still to go the fuel began to run low, until eventually stocks were down to just four hours."

Then he jumped on the first flight to Bermuda he could find and presented his handiwork in person to Ragga.

Equipped with the brand-new rudder, the crew set out once again with what they considered to be an even chance of making Cowes in time.

Immediately they ran into another problem – the rudder blade wasn't accurate. That is, it had been asymmetrically shaped. Or to put it more bluntly, bent.

Kiwi Boats just hadn't had enough time to do the job properly. The result was that in any kind of breeze *Imp* tried to dive off to weather or to leeward, and the only way the helmsman could hold her reasonably true to course was by rigging up a three-to-one tackle system to give more purchase on the tiller. As Bill put it, "The system helped us wrestle the tiller."

To speed up the crossing, they also turned on the engine, the extra speed through the water improving the flow of the wind through the sails, and *Imp* was able to maintain a higher average speed.

Then the Fates intervened once more, when *Imp* ran into a dead flat calm. It lasted for day after interminable day. As the sails flapped uselessly to and fro, the engine was doing all the work. If the absence of wind wasn't enough, with a considerable distance still to go the fuel began to run low, until eventually stocks were down to just four hours.

"[The crew] felt hopeless, dejected," Bill would write. "*Imp* seemed doomed not to make England in time."

"'If you don't believe me, please come with me,' I pleaded. 'And I'll give you a tour of his boat if you like.' The clock was ticking and I was getting desperate. The policemen looked at me skeptically. 'Follow us!'"

Then the law of the sea – namely, that you help those in distress – saved the day. A Polish trawler hove into view over the horizon, and spotting *Imp*'s crew waving in desperation, diverted from her course and pulled up alongside. Yes, the captain agreed, after the crew explained their predicament, he would be glad to help. The seamen promptly passed down four cans of diesel – 20 gallons in all - plus a bonus of some freshly caught mackerel for dinner. The price of this barter? A couple of issues of *Playboy* magazine.

With the cans safely lashed down, the crew fired up the engine again and wound it up to full throttle. Not long afterwards the wind finally reappeared, and *Imp* made her escape. Thereafter they made good time, and in mid-July the crew entered the English Channel and eventually sighted the Needles off the west end of the Isle of Wight. Menacing though they are, the Needles must have seemed a sight for sore eyes. *Imp* tied up in the Cowes marina just in time for the waiting crew to make final preparations for racing.

Excited as I was to see how *Imp* performed in the challenging waters of the Solent, I didn't have much time to spend with Dave and the crew. My main preoccupation remained *Big Apple*, on which I would share the helming duties, and with my other designs in various Admiral's Cup teams. I had eight yachts involved in the Admiral's Cup, not counting others entered for the yachting jamboree known as Cowes Week, and they kept me very busy in the days leading up to the event.

In addition Ted Heath, former Prime Minister of Britain, had become a client. After campaigning three earlier yachts, all called *Morning Cloud* and designed by Sparkman & Stephens, he had entrusted me with *Morning Cloud IV* in the hope of making his country's team for the Admiral's Cup. A bigger version of *Imp*, but without the space frame, she was constructed in aluminum. In the last few months I had spent many hours with the sailing-obsessed Sir Edward – or "Mr. Heath" as I always called him – during her development. He fully understood the technicalities of sailing, including the rigging and sails, and regularly plied me with questions. I could see why he'd once run a country. As he told me, he'd come to yachting quite late in life and enjoyed it for the complete break it gave him from the pressures of politics. Mr. Heath had also gathered around him an able and loyal crew headed by Peter Nicholson of the boatbuilding family, Owen Parker, sailing master on all the *Morning Clouds*, and Anthony Churchill, who had been with Mr. Heath when they had won the Sydney Hobart Race.

Because he was usually surrounded by people in suits, I think Mr. Heath came to enjoy the more informal relationship we shared. He even tolerated my occasional lateness.

On one occasion my flight from Cork was delayed and I was driving at high speed in my MG sports car, which I kept in London, to a small boatyard, Maitland Marine, in Woking, where *Morning Cloud* was under construction. Knowing Mr. Heath's punctilious habits, I was worried he might be waiting for me. On the verge of panic, I was pushing the car as fast as I dared when a police siren howled behind me, and I was pulled over. Wrong as I knew I was, I was fuming at the delay. Two policemen got out and strolled up to the window. "Do you realize, sir, you are travelling at 20 miles an hour above the speed limit for this stretch of road?" "Yes," I confessed. "But I'm in a hurry to get to a boatyard in Woking. I've got an appointment with Ted Heath. I'm his yacht designer."

"Pull the other one", one policeman said, starting to write out a ticket.

"If you don't believe me, please come with me," I pleaded. "And I'll give you a tour of his boat if you like." The clock was ticking and I was getting desperate. The policemen looked at me skeptically. "Follow us!" They'd decided I was genuine. They jumped back into their car and, lights flashing, escorted me all the way to the boatyard where I arrived just five minutes late, to find Mr. Heath's personal security detail waiting impatiently in the parking lot. This was a time when tensions over the IRA were at their height, and a former Prime Minister's schedule was timed to the minute. But when they saw I had an "official" escort they couldn't help grinning. They exchanged words with the police, who promptly ripped up the ticket.

▲

Portrait by photographer Guy Gurney, of Edward Heath at the helm of his latest Ron Holland-designed *Morning Cloud*. Looking happy after winning another race.

And I kept my promise: I showed the policemen around the boat.

The new *Morning Cloud* turned out to be as fast as Mr. Heath and I had hoped, but she narrowly missed selection for a hot British team, to the surprise of many of the pundits who attended the trials and thought she should have been included. Shaking off his disappointment, the highly competitive ex-prime minister had come to Cowes to prove a point. He would take on the fleet in Cowes Week that concluded with the Fastnet Race.

Despite her late arrival, *Imp*'s crew had managed to prepare her thoroughly for the series. The day before the opening race she was hauled out to have her bottom polished, and they'd gotten the surface as slick as Teflon before she was put back in the water at dusk. In the run-up to the Admiral's Cup most waterfront sages saw *Imp* as the boat to beat because of her runaway victory in the SORC. But these waters are so treacherous with their vicious tides and currents, rocky shores, dangerous headlands and often unpredictable winds, that anything can happen. As I knew from bitter experience, it's quite possible for yachts to be parked up in a flat calm while others are battling force seven gales just a few miles away. And that's without taking into account the commercial shipping traffic. The Solent and the English Channel are busy waterways plied by supertankers and other vessels that regularly carve their way straight through the racing fleet. Commercial vessels have priority. All in all, the Solent is a place that has humbled even the best crews and yachts, and only Dave Allen and Skip Allan of *Imp*'s Admiral's Cup crew had raced there before.

▲

Celebrating with Herbert Dahm and Hans Beilken aboard the 72-foot Jongert sloop *Inspiration*. *Inspiration* is Dahm's own private cruising yacht that's also enjoyed racing success, including winning the Jongert Regatta in 2007, and Les Voiles d'Antibes three times.

▲

Mr. Heath's latest *Morning Cloud* narrowly missed gaining selection for the 1979 British Admiral's Cup team. Her experimental carbon fiber rudder failed in the Channel Race so she did not start in the ill-fated 1979 Fastnet Race. Here she's racing flat out with Mr. Heath alongside helmsman Larry Marks and crew boss Owen Parker; no doubt discussing race tactics.

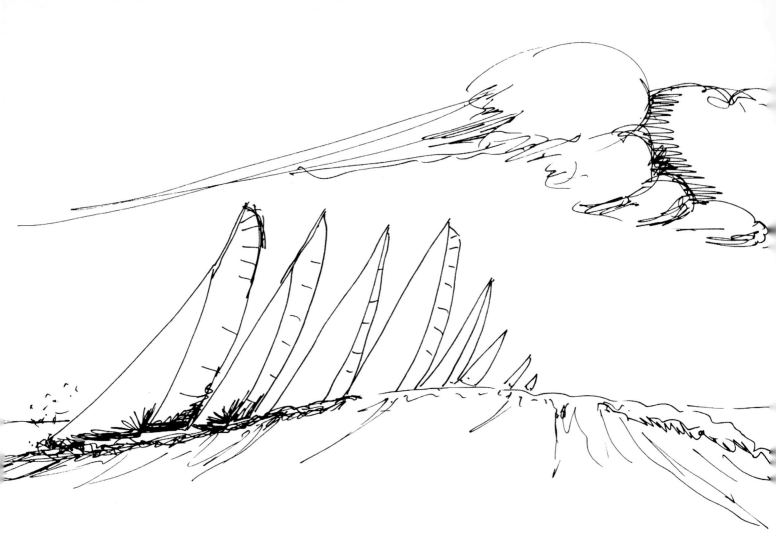

Against the best racing yachts in the world, *Imp*, one of the smallest yachts, a fast design with a crew who sailed her very well, was winning races in all wind conditions.

Dave's day

IMP MADE AN IMPRESSIVE but not outstanding start to the Admiral's Cup, placing fourth on corrected time in the first race, a short prelude to the main event. Considering the vagaries of the Solent, I was pleased for Dave and the crew.

Next up? The important 225-mile Channel Race that has broken the heart of many a good crew. Sure enough, in light winds veering wildly around the compass, *Imp* got on the wrong side of a shift and found herself in a seemingly hopeless position after just ten miles of racing. She was lying nearly last. Hundreds of yachts were ahead of her, practically stern to bow in a long line with gaily-colored spinnakers up. There and then, Dave's entire Admiral's Cup campaign could have been over. Because the race counts for extra points, no yacht can recover from a dismal result in the 225-miler.

But instead of resigning themselves to the situation, with Skip doing wonders on the tiller the crew got down to work in a virtuoso display of downwind sailing. As Bill Barton recalls: "We worked each zephyr, often rolling clumps of five or six boats at a time… we kept *Imp* marching and passing boat after boat after boat until, finally, we moved right up with the leaders. By the turn at St. Catherine's Point (southernmost edge of the Isle of Wight) we had passed hundreds of boats." It was a feat that few crews have achieved, before or since.

During the night the fleet crossed the Channel to France, and *Imp*, now lying in a respectable position, began the long 50-mile beat back across the Channel in fast-rising winds and rough seas. These were conditions in which she reveled, and making up place after place, she crossed the finish line at Gilkicker Point off Gosport in the early hours of the morning. When the race committee did the numbers, *Imp* was placed third on corrected time. So far so good. In a regatta that rewards consistency, a fourth and a third were good results to have in the bank.

Through all of this racing, Dave spent little time on deck. He stayed down below in his role as navigator, working long hours to calculate and plot the fastest course. He regularly stayed awake throughout the night while others went below and slept, ignoring the system of watches that he'd set up for those doing the physical work up top. I suspect that, as an old fighter pilot, he loved to labor over the charts because it brought him back to days of action when navigational skills were a matter of life and death.

Yet, however competitive the racing, Dave never neglected his spiritual life. At two o'clock one morning Bill Barton slipped down below and found him, barefoot and wearing only a T-shirt and underwear, bent over the chart table as the boat banged and crashed through the waves. This time though, instead of poring over charts of tides and currents as Bill assumed he would be, he saw Dave was reading his Christian Science lesson for the day. While Dave wanted to win as much as anybody, he also kept things in perspective.

In the third race, another inshore battle with the Solent's uncooperative tides and currents playing havoc with tactics, *Imp* was unlucky. Had the clock not intervened, she would have cemented a place near the top of the standings with another banker result. Much to the crew's frustration, with *Imp* doing well again the race ran over the time limit and was declared void, meaning no yacht was awarded any points.

For the fourth race of the series, the Solent excelled itself. As much bigger yachts were knocked flat in wild conditions and driven off course by roaring tides, *Imp* performed another Houdini act. Stuck again near the back of the huge fleet, the crew somehow managed to fire *Imp* through hundreds of yachts once again to finish in a respectable eleventh place. As for the hastily rebuilt *Big Apple*, she more than justified my hopes. She won the race on corrected time, the first time Ireland had taken the honors in the Admiral's Cup.

By now *Imp*'s boat speed and crew work were becoming hot topics in Cowes's crowded pubs. The conditions could hardly have been more different from the SORC series, but here they were, time after time maneuvering the yacht through an armada of yachts.

"Instead of taking the standard tactic of a long, safe – and slow – turn around all the becalmed yachts so *Imp* didn't get stuck like them, Skip took a deep breath. With the spinnaker still up, he aimed the boat straight between the pack and the rounding mark, approaching at a rate of knots while the other crews including us on *Big Apple* looked on in disbelief."

In the next race, a rerun of the voided inshore one, the boys did it all over again. As *Imp* bore down on a crucial turning mark known as West Ryde Middle Buoy in light weather, Skip saw that dozens of yachts including *Big Apple* were stuck there, unable to clear the mark. Their sails blanketed by other boats, they'd lost the wind and stopped dead. It was an expensive parking lot.

Instead of taking the standard tactic of a long, safe – and slow – turn around all the becalmed yachts so *Imp* didn't get stuck like them, Skip took a deep breath. With the spinnaker still up, he aimed the boat straight between the pack and the rounding mark, approaching at a rate of knots while the other crews including us on *Big Apple* looked on in disbelief.

Skip was putting his faith in three things apart from God. First, split-second crew work to drop the kite. Second, a space somehow opening up. And – well, divine intervention. He got all three. Identifying a hole in the pack at the last minute, he dove straight into it. As they hit the space the crew dumped the big sail in a flash. Skip threw over the tiller, narrowly avoiding a number of yachts, and brushed by just clear of the mark. Within a few seconds, *Imp* was sailing away completely unscathed. She'd overtaken about twenty boats in fifty yards.

Imp crossed the line in fourth position. Not fourth on corrected time, which would have been another banker, but fourth overall. The papers now dubbed her the "Pocket Rocket." When I met the crew in the bar later,

"My designs had dominated the rankings of the top ten yachts. The all-conquering *Imp* meant that we had won consecutive Fastnet Races, as Three-Quarter-Tonner *Golden Delicious* had taken the honors in 1975. *Iorana III*, a 41-footer racing for Austria, placed third. And, a hectic few weeks after being rescued off the Beacette reef, Ireland's *Big Apple* ended up seventh, a result I still consider not much short of miraculous."

they were still high from pulling off another Houdini act.

Next up was the Fastnet, the granddaddy of them all. Counting triple points, it usually decides the winner of the entire series. So far *Imp*'s crew had demonstrated their ability to handle just about any conditions from flat calms to strong winds, but such was the Fastnet's reputation for destroying reputations, that the boys were treating the race with respect. The stakes were high. If they didn't make any mistakes, *Imp* could well end up as the top-scoring boat in the Admiral's Cup.

In the meantime, gales were forecast.

It quickly turned out the forecasts couldn't have been more wrong. In the slowest Fastnet on record, the crew of *Imp* and other yachts ran low on food as they drifted down the Channel and into the Irish Sea, in often glassily calm waters. With little wind or no wind in the sails they were helpless to influence events. They whiled away their time by playing backgammon on the deck, making jokes about each other and watching the stars. Dave probably read his Christian Science book from cover to cover.

But the conditions were the same for everyone, and when *Imp* finally rounded the Fastnet Rock the crew looked at the yachts nearby and the penny dropped. She was right up there with the big boys. Designed to be nimble and quick off the wind especially with her spinnaker set, *Imp* had obviously made exceptionally good time in the light weather, accelerating rapidly through the puffs and ghosting through the lulls. According to race radio, *Imp* lay fourth – that's fourth overall. As Dave set a course for the finish line at Plymouth, the boys put away the backgammon and worked every single gust of wind. One of the most prestigious prizes in yachting awaited them. When the cupboard was down to peanut butter and crackers, *Imp* crossed the finish line in the late morning of the sixth day, the crew hungry and exhausted.

As the rest of the fleet crawled home during the day, the race committee did their tallies, calculating the finishers' handicaps. When it finally became clear that no competitor still out on the course could possibly overtake *Imp* on corrected time, she was given the ultimate accolade: top yacht of the 1977 Admiral's Cup.

I had enjoyed a good Admiral's Cup too. My designs had dominated the rankings of the top ten yachts. The all-conquering *Imp* meant that we had won consecutive Fastnet Races, as Three-Quarter-Tonner *Golden Delicious* had taken the honors in 1975. *Iorana III*, a 41-footer racing for Austria, placed third. And, a hectic few weeks after being rescued off the Beacette reef, Ireland's *Big Apple* ended up seventh, a result I still consider not much short of miraculous.

I attended the trophy presentation the following day and watched as Dave stepped jauntily onto the stage, wearing the *Imp* uniform of white pants and green-striped shirt, to receive the coveted prize for the Admiral's Cup Fastnet victory and the Myles Wyatt Memorial trophy for top-scoring boat in the Admiral's Cup series overall. Holding them high above his head, he was grinning from ear to ear.

For Dave, it was a personal triumph. He'd taken charge of the project and pushed it through against all the odds, when it could have gone sideways several times along the way. The construction schedule was so tight that *Imp* could have been launched too late to make the SORC and lost any chance of selection in the American team. And if he hadn't got Kiwi Boats to throw everything into making the replacement rudder, asymmetrical though it was, and flying it out to Bermuda, the project might have slipped hopelessly behind schedule. In so many of his actions you could see the quick-thinking fighter pilot at work. But not even Dave could have organized the fortuitous arrival over the horizon of the Polish freighter. If it hadn't been for the willing assistance of the Poles, *Imp* might never have made it in time to Cowes.

Johnny Mac flies his fabric-
skinned single-engine Beagle
Airedale between the mountains
of Corsica on our way to Rome.

Mr. Takeda

I SOMETIMES WISH DAVE HAD MET MR. TAKEDA. Although wartime ene-mies, I think they would have had a lot in common and gotten along well together. And like Dave, Mr. Takeda would exercise a profound effect on my life.

Just about every week prospective clients were calling the studio, and sometimes knocking unannounced on the door of the piggery after trave-ling long distances. But no caller was more of a surprise than Mr. Takeda. He was that rare thing in those days, a sailing-obsessed Japanese. As he explained over the phone in halting English, he had set himself a mission: almost single-handedly he wanted to promote the sport in his country.

Not long after the 1977 Admiral's Cup he offered a proposition. He wanted some of our smaller designs, the Quarter and Half-Tonners, to be constructed in Japan. He would organize the builders. It turned out that he had already established useful commercial contacts with the marine in-dustry in New Zealand, where presumably he'd heard about our success. So now he wanted to add our designs to his growing portfolio. Would I please come to Japan and see him?

"Certainly," I said. "When would you like to see me?"

My expenses were hefty, but I always believed the expenditure was more than justified by the results. You can't beat personal meetings. Not only did Mr. Takeda's proposition sound like a promising long-term project, I had also never been to Japan. So, in due course I traveled there

185

Mr Takeda wanted Japan to go sailing. He invited me to help him and I had several exciting visits to Japan in the early years of Ron Holland Design. This was before there were any English train station signs, so it was easy to get lost. Only the little kids spoke any English.

with my new wife Joanna Keltner, another Florida girl whom I had met when she was holidaying in Ireland. Sadly my relationship with Laurel had broken down, partly because I was away so much and no doubt partly because of the relentless pressure of work. She had moved back to our house in London with our daughters Kelly and Benna.

Just as Laurel had, Joanna supported me in my work and was full of practical ideas for the business. I adopted many of these but, to my regret a few years later, not all of them.

I retain a clear recollection of that first meeting with Mr. Takeda. After landing at Narita airport, we caught a train into Tokyo where he was waiting for us on a crowded platform.

"Why he so sad?" he asked Joanna almost immediately after greeting us. Why am I so sad?! I didn't understand what he meant. Did I appear jet-lagged? Or did he see some inherent sadness in me of which I was unaware?

Later, as I got to know him, I would come to understand how perceptive Mr. Takeda was. (I always addressed him as "Mr. Takeda" although he always called me Ron.) He certainly got under my skin with that observation because from then on I began to reflect on what he'd said. Perhaps I should do something about this sadness, I thought. Was I working too hard? Yes, definitely. Was I traveling too much, away from home for some of every week? Absolutely. Should I take some time out and seek an answer? Certainly. Partly because of this one remark, I would begin to develop a spiritual life that I had unknowingly neglected. Thus Mr. Takeda became one of my most fascinating clients, and in time a mentor. Elderly and aristocratic in manner, he had fought in the Second World War as a fighter pilot and survived the appallingly high fatality rate of Japanese fliers, albeit with burned and damaged hands and forearms.

Perhaps it was his wartime experiences that made him so determined. As he told me in many long conversations, he was fighting an uphill battle against vested interests. The fishing industry wielded all the power on the Japanese coast and was firmly opposed to marinas being constructed in ports along the coast for mere pleasure boats. But Mr. Takeda wasn't a man to give up.

As good as his word, Mr. Takeda organized boatbuilders for my designs, and over a ten-year period many of our yachts hit the water in Japan. This was a time when Japan was beginning to look outwards and was developing products, everything from electronics to vehicles, whose technology would amaze the world. I visited him several times and it was exciting to travel around Japan, dropping in to visit boatyards, sometimes in his company, and seeing how rapidly the nation was changing.

"As the Quarter-Tonners broached left, right and center, and sometimes capsized, the masts the Japanese builders had specified for my designs just couldn't take the strain. One by one they began to break. It was carnage. By the time the regatta was over, not a single Ron Holland-designed yacht was sailing."

In the 1970s few Japanese spoke English, and the authorities saw no need to put up road or other signs in English. One result was that when Joanna and I got off at the wrong train station, which we did more than a few times, we always had trouble finding our way back to the right one.

Largely because of Mr. Takeda's efforts the Quarter Ton Cup world event was awarded to Japan in 1978 against all the odds, and predictably a lot of our Japan-built designs were entered. For Mr. Takeda this was exciting and satisfying, the showcase for which he'd long dreamed. One up on the fishing industry!

Unfortunately the weather did not cooperate.

The regatta, which took place at a small port town called Sajima on the Miura Peninsula, started well enough when a champion skipper from New Zealand, Mark Patterson, steered Mr. Takeda's personal Quarter-Tonner *Vargo* to victory in the first race. Normally fairly stoic, he was delighted. Unfortunately his joy didn't last past the second race, when *Vargo* lost her mast in wild conditions.

Thereafter things went from bad to worse. As the Quarter-Tonners broached left, right and center, and sometimes capsized, the masts the Japanese builders had specified for my designs just couldn't take the strain. One by one they began to break. It was carnage. By the time the regatta was over, not a single Ron Holland-designed yacht was sailing. Every single mast had given up the ghost.

OVERLEAF: *Mandrake* and *Aries* racing in the 1978 SORC. During 1976 I designed three racing yachts at 44 feet in length, at that time our biggest designs. All three won Admiral's Cup selection for their country, *Big Apple* for Ireland, *Marionette* for Britain and *Mandrake* for Italy. International yachting commentators took notice!

The way it was – always fixing something. Johnny Mac and Butch were good at fixing!

Although I was bitterly disappointed, probably even more so than Mr. Takeda, these failures weren't my fault. As every yacht designer knows, sometimes to their detriment, you can only advise on the strength of the rig that should be installed in a yacht and just hope that the boatbuilder is listening. The masts that had been supplied were simply not up to the conditions for this particular world championship. It was a painful lesson in how little control I had on the construction in far-off locations like Japan.

But Mr. Takeda did not give up, and largely because of his enthusiasm and prodding Japan would enter a team in the Admiral's Cup, and later in the America's Cup.

In the years leading up to the 1979 Admiral's Cup we were once again frantically busy and our staff nearly doubled in size, up to 15 at the peak. Nearly 30 of our designs competed in selection trials for various national teams and I felt I needed to be everywhere, giving advice and support to clients, boatbuilders and crews all over Europe, Britain and America. It was rather ironic, I often thought. Here I was, a yachtie who had started out just wanting to go sailing, now spending half my time in the air.

Most of my flights were by scheduled carriers, and particularly by Aer Lingus with whom I would take a weekly flight from Cork to London to visit boatyards and check on the integrity of the construction of my designs. After finishing my business in England, I would fly on to Europe or the USA to visit clients and visit more boatyards, and race in various regattas. The pressure of work was such that I once had to fly Aer Lingus between Cork and London on Christmas Day. When I boarded I was surprised to find I was the only passenger, and the cabin crew, many of whom I knew from earlier flights, joined me for Christmas dinner and drinks. In some ways it made up for not being able to spend the day with my family.

Often I flew on my clients' private jets, definitely the ideal way to travel. No boarding calls, no delays, no fuss. You just show up and step aboard when you need to go.

Every so often Johnny Mac, who lived and worked on the other side of the Owenboy River, would invite me along on delivery trips around Europe and Britain with a wardrobe of sails he'd made for his many clients. He didn't own a jet – Johnny Mac's personal transport was the Beagle Airedale, a little four-seater that could carry fuel for three hours max. For a pure flying experience the Beagle, which was then about 15 years old, was hard to beat. Also, being aloft with Johnny Mac was a pleasure. A former RAF ace who used to fly Phantom jets among other elite aircraft, he was a pilot's pilot. One day he suggested I join him on a flight to Italy where he planned to drop off several suits of sails for his growing number of customers there. I didn't hesitate. Single-engined, the British-made Beagle's official cruising speed was around 130 miles per hour. With only fabric separating the occupants from the elements, it was real seat-of-the-pants flying. I knew this would be fun – when the regulations permitted, Johnny Mac loved nothing better than to fly low.

We took off from Cork airport, heading for Rome by a roundabout route, in clear skies and favorable winds. We flew over the Irish Sea and St. George's Channel, then across Wales and England before stopping at La Rochelle to meet some sailors and the owner of a boatyard.

Early next morning, after topping up the tank Johnny Mac decided to do some low-level aviation. We headed south towards the Mediterranean coast at about 1,000 feet or sometimes lower, buzzing above one farm after another and scattering animals in all directions. As we flew along the south coast of France from west of St. Tropez, over Cannes, Antibes and Nice, heading for Monaco and the Italian border, he took the Beagle down to below 200 feet. A former member of the RAF's ace Red Arrows aerobatic team, Johnny Mac had fingertip control of the aircraft. I could tell from the happy expression on his face that this was the kind of flying he loved.

When we reached the Italian border we turned right and set a course out to sea towards the Corsican mountains, a jagged line of around fifty rocky peaks rising to nearly 9,000 feet. Instead of attempting to take the Beagle over the top, Johnny Mac simply flew straight between them, angling through one canyon after another, the snow-peaked mountains soaring above us on both sides and the valleys spread out below. Buckled into the right-hand seat, I was riveted by the magnificent spectacle. You don't see this at 45,000 feet! Landing at Bastia in Corsica late at night, we had to wake up the fuel guy at his house so we could pump another three hours' worth of juice into the Beagle.

Leaving Corsica behind next day, we flew over the sea again on our approach to Rome. Dusk was falling. Johnny Mac started talking with the air traffic controllers at our destination airport of Rome Fiumicino. He was working off an RAF manual.

Although English is supposed to be the international language of the air, Johnny was finding it hard to understand exactly what the Italians were saying, and I certainly couldn't help. As he struggled to interpret their instructions, I could hear them becoming more and more animated.

At one point, wondering why this aircraft was so slow, the controller asked: "Do you 'ave diplomatic clearance come 'ere?" "Yes," replied Johnny Mac instantly. We didn't of course, but what else can you say when you're

▲

Ready to fly across Europe. John McWilliam often invited me to join him in his small twin engine Piper plane, taking sails from Cork in Ireland to his clients in various European locations. Flying low level across France to the Mediterranean. If I wasn't sailing, this is the way I wanted to travel!

OVERLEAF: When you have a twin-engine plane you don't need a fancy car, that's what I was thinking. The first and only new car I ever owned was the little Renault. Another thought – when you own a big twin-engine plane you can't afford a fancy car!

RON HOLLAND

PORTRAIT
OF THE ARTIST AS
A YOUNG MAN
BY MICHAEL LEVITT

"At gunpoint we were ordered out of the Beagle and marched off to a nearby office where the head of security was waiting for us. As we entered, he was peering out the window at the apron, trying to find the aircraft that was causing all the trouble."

running low on fuel? Despite the babble Johnny made a perfect touchdown and switched onto ground control. It was then we knew something was up. If anything, ground control was more excited than the control tower had been, yelling into Johnny Mac's earphones. What was going on?

Following what he thought was the correct procedure, he taxied our tiny aircraft onto the concourse and parked under the wing of an Alitalia Boeing 747. Suddenly, to our shock a convoy of army trucks, bristling with soldiers holding machine guns, hurtled out from behind the main building and had us surrounded in a few seconds.

"We must have done something wrong here," muttered Johnny Mac laconically.

At gunpoint we were ordered out of the Beagle and marched off to a nearby office where the head of security was waiting for us. As we entered, he was peering out the window at the apron, trying to find the aircraft that was causing all the trouble. As we waited he kept looking until he finally lowered his gaze and spotted the little Beagle, practically hidden by the 747. Shocked, he started talking to us rapidly, gesticulating wildly.

But what was wrong? What rule, or rules, had we broken? Eventually, after much confusion we got the message. We had landed at the wrong airport! This was Rome Leonardo da Vinci, which was strictly reserved for commercial passenger jets, not fabric-covered, single-engined light aircraft. Yet what could we do? We'd landed and that was that.

Johnny Mac did his best to placate the authorities but they clearly weren't in a mood to overlook the fact that we'd broken every rule in the book. We could be in big trouble here, I thought.

Eventually, after some discussion common sense prevailed. We obviously couldn't take off in the dark, so the head of security and the other officials agreed the Beagle could stay where it was. To our relief they decided not to fine or imprison us, although they seriously considered both options, and they gave us permission to go off and find a hotel for the night on the condition that the offending aircraft was gone first thing in the morning.

So we went to bed, taking care to set our alarms, and just after daybreak we took off from Leonardo da Vinci and duly landed at the right airport, the one reserved for general aviation. Warned in advance by their colleagues at the big airport, security gave Johnny Mac another going over. But when he finally delivered the sails to his Italian customers and told them the story, they thought it was the funniest thing they'd heard in a long time. The trip turned out to be a huge success. Our Italian hosts were so impressed we'd come so far in our own private plane that they pulled out all the stops to make us welcome. Even better, they gave Johnny Mac orders for new sails that were far in excess of his wildest dreams.

But I obviously couldn't rely on Johnny Mac and the Beagle to get me around Europe every week, much as I enjoyed it. So, with the studio in a more or less permanent IOR-fueled overload, I gave in to my fascination with aircraft and decided to buy my own. Anyway, I argued, I had spent so much time in airports chafing at delays that I decided enough was enough.

So, after briefly owning a smaller aircraft, I splurged on a Cessna 402B fitted with long range tanks. Seating eight, she was a twin-engine and equipped for all-weather flying capability. Some of the seats could be easily removed if we needed to take equipment or sails with us, which we often did. Because I did not yet have my pilot's license (that would come later), I hired Englishman Hugh Woodsend, a highly experienced pilot, to take over the controls. Hugh was also a computer programmer and his skills would come in useful when the studio entered a new age with computer-aided design.

The aircraft soon proved its worth as a timesaver because we could fly on our own schedules and land at smaller airports closer to boatbuilding yards. The Cessna took us as far afield as Sweden, northern Finland and Italy. Also, I was able to defray some of the costs by flying Irish business friends from Cork to their own appointments in Europe. Expensive though it was to run my own plane, I was fulfilling a dream and for me that was more important than accumulating money.

▲

Wrong airport! Looking out of place, our Beagle near a Boeing 747 at Rome's international airport. The Italian authorities were not happy we landed here.

As the 1979 Admiral's Cup neared, we ended up with 29 designs striving for selection, not as many as Doug Peterson's 35 designs but quite enough for us to handle. (The third most sought-after designer was the Argentinian, German Frers, with about 17 new yachts to his name.) As well as designing them and supervising their construction to ensure they complied with the specifications, we would also crew on them. Because Butch, Phil, Rob Jacob and I were all seasoned racers, we could make an important contribution to our yachts' success.

Butch had agreed to crew on *Aries*, a 46-footer that had won selection for America. It was owned by Mike Swerdlow, one of our youngest clients, an ex-math teacher who had made a fortune in property in South Florida and enjoyed nothing more than spending it. He would eventually commission three yachts from us, and Butch became our point man with Mike. He was usually picked up from JFK Airport in a limo and driven into Manhattan by chauffeur George, and after talking boats at Mike's penthouse apartment above the uptown Westbury hotel, was taken to highly informal meetings in freewheeling nightclubs. At one meeting the owner and his friends met Butch at the door wearing nothing but bathrobes. Hey, this was the 1970s in New York!

As for me, I was going to stick with Hugh Coveney and do my bit on *Golden Apple of the Sun*, the new Irish Admiral's Cupper for which we had high hopes.

▶

Our first design for Mike Swerdlow was the Palmer Johnson-built Two-Tonner. This *Aries* won lots of races and encouraged Mike to build two more of our racing yachts.

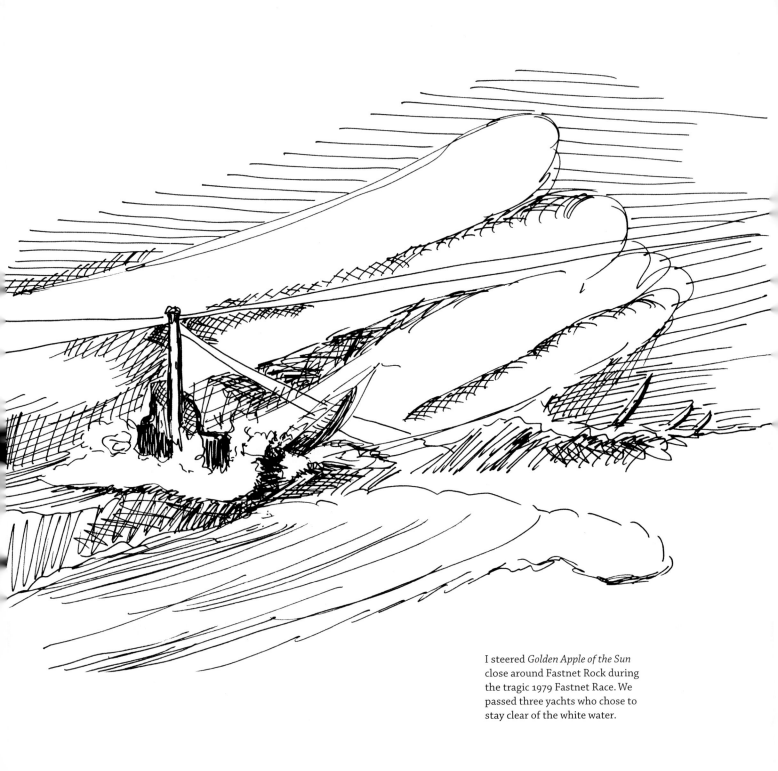

I steered *Golden Apple of the Sun* close around Fastnet Rock during the tragic 1979 Fastnet Race. We passed three yachts who chose to stay clear of the white water.

White water

IN ALL MY YEARS OF RACING I had never witnessed seas like those besieging the Fastnet Rock. There was white water everywhere. *Golden Apple Of The Sun* was sailing on an Atlantic of heaving foam.

As tall as cliffs, nearly vertical waves bore down on the lighthouse, crashing against the rocks and rebounding back into the sea. The waves smashed against each other and turned the waters around "The Rock", as sailors know it, into a treacherous place for a yacht, indeed for any vessel. No boat could survive such turmoil if she got trapped in it and was swept against that grim-looking wall, and certainly not a light-weight racing yacht like ours.

And the wind!

Storm-force gusts shrieked through the rigging, forcing us to ease the sheets on the mainsail when they threatened to overpower us. It was taking every ounce of my concentration to steer through the deep troughs and towering crests of ever-steepening seas. Every one of the ten-man crew was on deck – it felt safer to be up on the rail, wet as it was, than to be clinging to a bunk down below as the yacht crashed and banged off one wave after another. The only way to make ourselves heard above the din was to yell directly into each other's ears.

Golden Apple (we always used the short version of her name) was heading into her second night in the Fastnet Race and the sky was darkening by the minute. Menacing clouds hurtled past overhead. I had to peer into the gathering gloom to pick out the shape of the waves. Still, I was enjoying being on the helm. We were about to sail around The Rock and head for the finish line at the entrance to Plymouth Harbour. Despite the ferocious conditions, our spirits were lifted by our high position in the race. *Golden Apple* was excelling herself in the race, the climax of the 1979 Admiral's Cup. The yachts nearby were all much bigger and giving us hours on handicap. I snatched a glance around us and could not see any yachts of our size anywhere in sight. We might be winning the Fastnet, I thought.

The race had started in light airs off Cowes, and our brains trust, led by Harry Cudmore and Olympic gold medalist Rodney Pattisson, had elected to split from most of the fleet and take a bold westerly course pretty much straight up the middle of the English Channel. Their thinking was that we'd leave our competitors to fight it out among themselves along England's South Coast.

As we predicted most of them had elected to short-tack inside the Portland Race near Weymouth and battle a hostile tide around each headland. Although *Golden Apple* would be pushing against the current in the Channel, we would at least have clear air and – a bonus – be free to sail on the favored tack.

As dawn broke on the second day, we knew we had made the right decision. Based on handicap, the boats around us should have been much further ahead.

Golden Apple was flying.

It was during the afternoon that the winds had begun to increase and for the last few hours we had been reaching fast under spinnaker in gusts of 25 knots. Big green seas sluiced straight across the deck, drenching the crew. It took all our sail-trimming and helming skills to hold the small spinnaker: the pole was jammed right up against the headstay. We knew there was no latitude for error in these conditions, but we weren't worried either. We were comfortable pushing a yacht hard in wild conditions.

Hugh, the man who had been instrumental in bringing me to Ireland, could hardly keep the grin off his face. Not a single yacht had overtaken us all day, not even the higher-rating ones. We were racing the socks off his Admiral's Cupper.

But we weren't stupid. A little while earlier the gusts had increased in force and, after the yacht had wiped out several times in what's known as a broach, we elected to drop the spinnaker. A potentially dangerous event: each broach had thrown *Golden Apple* onto her side and everybody had to make a grab for the lifelines to save themselves from falling into the sails and rigging, or worse, into the sea.

"Keeping the lighthouse to port, I steered for the white water. I caught a few concerned glances from the crew as the yacht hit violent cross-currents from the waves smashing back from the rocks, and began to buck and heave like a bronco. I gripped the wheel as hard as I could, and others clung to any handhold they could find."

Not long afterwards we had to change down yet again, this time to a small reaching genoa and reefed mainsail. For a short time that made life a little safer, but as the wind increased in speed again even these sails became too much, and the foredeck crew had to fight their way up to the bow once more to replace the reaching genoa with the tiny No. 4 jib.

Yet still the gusts grew in strength: we'd had blasts of more than 40 knots across the deck. This was nearing full storm force. The seas turned even steeper and bigger.

The image of The Rock that evening is burned into my memory. As we bore down on it the lighthouse keepers switched on the beam, sending a ghostly wagon wheel of yellow spokes across the white water. I steered directly for the lighthouse, estimating the yacht's leeway would push us clear of the turmoil before we prepared for the rounding. Since I was on the helm, it was my call and I had made a decision.

Big as the seas were, I was determined to take *Golden Apple* as close as I dared and slip inside the few other yachts that were lying just ahead, their stern lights coming and going in the breaking waves. I had noticed that although they were much bigger than us, they were standing further out to sea and giving The Rock a wider berth. I knew what I was doing, or at least I hoped I did. Familiar as I was with these waters, I had never before rounded The Rock in a full gale.

Keeping the lighthouse to port, I steered for the white water. I caught a

▲

This Daniel Forster photograph reminds me of the 1979 Fastnet Race aboard *Golden Apple of the Sun*: as dawn broke all we could see was white water.

few concerned glances from the crew as the yacht hit violent cross-currents from the waves smashing back from the rocks, and began to buck and heave like a bronco. I gripped the wheel as hard as I could, and others clung to any handhold they could find.

Judging the moment, I yelled "Ready about," and threw the wheel over, flipping *Golden Apple* onto starboard tack for the rounding. The crew scrambled up onto the starboard side and prepared to ease the sheets as soon as we cleared The Rock and the lighthouse. I glanced under the boom and saw for the first time the space between us and The Rock. All of a sudden it seemed a little too close for comfort.

On her new tack the yacht took a few seconds – too many seconds – to get back up to speed. The helm felt soft as the rudder struggled to bite in the froth and foam. Glancing back, I could see a black trail that our passage had carved in the whiteness. I was struck by a fleeting thought that the other yachts outside us were probably watching and wondering if we'd taken leave of our senses.

Eventually *Golden Apple* picked herself up, and although thrown about like a toy, began to plough her way through the turmoil. That was a bit scary, I thought.

As soon as we were clear of The Rock we set a course for the Scilly Isles from where we would head for the finish line off Plymouth. Looking back in the gathering darkness, I could make out other yachts far behind us.

"We just killed those guys," I yelled. And I was right. Later we would learn that the lighthouse keeper had recorded us as leading the race on corrected time.

Tired from my stint on the helm, I handed the wheel over to Harry Cudmore for his one-hour trick: it was impossible to concentrate longer than that. He was dripping wet in his oilskins – there was no place to hide from the green water and flying spray – and he hooked himself to a lifeline, planted himself squarely in the cockpit on his sea boots and seized the wheel. *Golden Apple* tore into the night like a scalded cat.

Right through the darkness there was no letup from the conditions, and at dawn the wind was still screaming with gusts shrieking through the rigging at 60 knots or more. The breaking waves continued to roar down on us, each one towering above a yacht that suddenly seemed fragile against these elements.

I had lost my confidence that *Golden Apple* could handle these conditions. I had never seen seas like these and I hoped never to see them again. They marched out of the horizon, white water tumbling over the top as though they were breaking on a beach. When they reached us, they loomed momentarily high above the beam before sweeping over and under the boat, throwing her around like a rag doll. Line after relentless line, they stretched as far as the eye could see, both ahead and astern. There was no reprieve.

I knew that if this was happening to us, it meant the entire fleet in the Fastnet Race was fighting a violent storm. For the first time, I began to fear for the fate of some of the smaller yachts that simply didn't have the waterline length to get up and over these waves. After a shouted conference on deck, we decided to reduce sail to a triple-reefed main and a pocket handkerchief of a storm jib, the smallest sails we could set. Experienced though we were, I sensed the mood among us had changed. Yes, we were still racing for victory in one of offshore yachting's greatest classics, but we had moved past a sense of exhilaration that we were winning. To a man we had come to realize the situation had turned dangerous.

Steering *Golden Apple* had become a gamble with disaster. The key to steering her in such extreme conditions was to treat the boat as though she were a 15-ton surfboard. You had to angle her down the wave so she didn't bury her nose in the bottom of the trough, or she might somersault stern over bow. Known as pitchpoling, it's probably the most feared event in all of big-boat sailing. When a yacht pitchpoles, anything can happen. Even if attached to lifelines, the crew can be tossed so hard and fast that the hooks snap and they are hurled into the sea. If anybody's down below, they can easily be knocked unconscious and trapped by water pouring into the cabin. Worse, no rig can be designed to withstand the terrific impact of a big boat doing a somersault. The mast usually crumples, sometimes on top of anybody still left on deck.

But if you've managed to steer the boat to the bottom of the wave without mishap, there's another technique. You should steer a little fuller in the trough – that is, a few degrees more off the wind – so the boat doesn't lose momentum as she comes back up the wave out of the sheltered wind in the trough. And finally, at the top of the wave you should feather her into the stronger wind while easing the main so you slow down a little and keep the hull in contact with the breaking water. If you don't, the yacht may end up traveling too fast, flying over the crest and jumping into thin air before crashing down into the next trough. Many a yacht has broken her back after falling off a big wave into a void. I knew *Golden Apple* had been built with integrity – one of the best boatbuilders, the highly skilled Killian Bushe, was on the crew – but these conditions will break any yacht if she's not handled correctly.

When I'd finished my latest turn on the helm I went below, not to sleep because that was out of the question, but just to lie down, even if my head was resting on a soaking wet pillow. My back and arms were aching from two days and nights of turns on the wheel. And I was sore and bruised from a fall. It had happened while I was relieving myself over the side while clinging to the backstay – the standard procedure – when somebody yelled "Breaking wave!" Jeez, it must be a big one, I thought. Aren't they all breaking? And then it hit, knocking me clean off my feet. If it hadn't been for my crewmate Neil Kenefick, it would have been worse. Reacting fast, he grabbed me and unceremoniously threw me to safety into the bottom of a water-filled cockpit.

As I lay in the windward bunk, hanging on like grim death in case a wave hurled me straight across the cabin, I began to grow concerned, seriously concerned. In my thousands of miles of deep-sea racing, I had never seen waves so steep, so confused and so perilous, not even in the much-feared Bass Strait during the Sydney Hobart, or even in the Gulf Stream during the hurricane-hit Bermuda Race.

The noise down below was so deafening it did nothing to settle my fears. Our triple-reefed mainsail had been pretty much permanently eased to spill wind, yet it was flogging so hard, making a sound like gunshots, that it was shaking the boat from stem to stern. If we hit anything, we'll sink like a rock, I thought. But even if we don't hit anything, these vibrations are going to rip the yacht apart. I came to a decision.

"Taking another turn on the helm, I kept a wary eye astern for a rogue wave, the one that can so easily catch you by surprise. Although we might be over the worst of the storm, the seas remained monstrous. I'd not been long on the wheel when somebody shouted above the screaming of the wind, 'Big wave coming!'"

Trying to ignore the fact that my crewmates might think I was a wimp, I clambered out of the bunk and struggled to the hatch, gripping whatever handholds I could in a cabin tilted at a crazy 40-degree angle. I shoved open the hatch to see a drenched Harry on the helm.

"Harry, this is madness," I yelled into the storm. "We've got to slow her down." Normally fearless, Harry didn't hesitate. He took one look at me and yelled, "Right lads, mainsail down."

There was no hesitation among the crew either. It's no mean feat to lower a mainsail in a full storm but they had it done in double-quick time, and reduced to the lone storm headsail, *Golden Apple* finally stopped shaking herself to pieces.

I returned below, slightly relieved. But two hours later the conditions began to stabilize a little, and after another yelled debate about the conditions we decided it was time to return to racing mode. We broke out the triple-reefed mainsail again and *Golden Apple* began to fly once more. A glorious victory awaited, just a few short hours away.

Taking another turn on the helm, I kept a wary eye astern for a rogue wave, the one that can so easily catch you by surprise. Although we might be over the worst of the storm, the seas remained monstrous. I'd not been long on the wheel when somebody shouted above the screaming of the wind, "Big wave coming!" It had become a familiar warning but I remember thinking once again, Jesus, this must be a beauty.

Crash! A wall of white, gray and turquoise water – I still remember the colors – burst over us and knocked *Golden Apple* straight on her beam ends. I wrenched the wheel hard to stop her from broaching and lying side-on to these huge seas, a dangerous position for boat and crew. In my anxiety, I must have overdone it. Above the din of the wind and waves, I heard a loud bang. With a sinking feeling, I immediately knew what had happened. The carbon fiber rudder shaft had snapped. Confirming my fears, the wheel went limp in my hands.

With the rudder useless, *Golden Apple* ran out of control, careering straight down a vertical wall of water. We were staring down an abyss, the stern lifting high above the bow. To save myself from being hurled into space, I let go my grip of the wheel and grabbed the steering pedestal with both arms, clinging to it with all my strength. Hang on tight, I told my-self. This could be a pitchpole.

With another crash *Golden Apple* buried her bow in the bottom of the wave and her stern lifted ominously higher. The entire crew was holding on for dear life to anything that would stop them being thrown into the void. White water engulfed us.

After seconds that felt like minutes, she popped back out of the wave like a cork.

"We've lost the rudder," I yelled. "No steering." The others looked at me aghast.

Killian shot below to check our steering and reappeared in a few mo-ments. "Yes, the carbon shaft is broken," he yelled. "It could damage the hull. Split the hull open." We hardly needed to be told. Flapping around out of control, the jagged edges of the shaft could cut through the wood-en hull like a can opener. Meantime *Golden Apple* was plunging along, veering this way and that, completely at the mercy of the waves.

Everybody knew what this meant: our race was over. And *Golden Apple* and her crew were adrift, heading towards the jagged rocks of the Scilly Isles, one of the most dangerous shores in the English Channel.

the
BEKEN
file

Keith Beken

A development of my *Imp* design, *Impetuous* survived the Fastnet Race gale to help the Australian team win the 1979 Admiral's Cup.

As close as I dare in the storm:
Golden Apple Of The Sun at Fastnet
Rock lighthouse in 1979.

Aftermath

EVERY DETAIL OF THE ENSUING HOURS, day, weeks and months remains burned into my memory.

Still shocked at the loss of our steering system, I looked at the crew, all of us haggard with fatigue from two days of all-out racing in conditions none of us would ever forget. Hugh was stunned and disappointed, as well he might be. We were all thinking that one of the greatest prizes in yacht racing had been snatched from our grasp on the brink of victory. To rub salt into our wounds, the wind was quickly moderating and our wind gauge was registering below 30 knots for the first time since we'd rounded The Rock. And we were drifting helplessly into the deadly embrace of the Scilly Isles.

Known and feared among all those who sail in these waters, the rocks around the Scilly Isles have claimed hundreds of sailing vessels over the centuries, most of them before the invention of Harrison's clock that made the calculation of longitude more accurate for ships returning from the North Atlantic through the Channel.

And now we were as vulnerable as any of those ships.

It was late afternoon and dusk was approaching fast. Night would fall in a few short hours. Rather than issue a mayday call, standard procedure for a yacht in trouble, we tried to jury-rig a steering sweep with the spinnaker pole for *Golden Apple* in the hope of extricating ourselves from the predicament. But despite our best efforts the boat was still drifting fast out of control, entirely at the mercy of seas that, despite the moderating wind,

▲

The Fastnet lighthouse in more pleasant weather than when *Golden Apple* raced around The Rock in the Fastnet Race of August 1979.

▶

Following *Golden Apple*, *Silver Apple* and *Big Apple* Hugh Coveney felt he needed to honor his countryman William Butler Yeats. For the *Golden Apple of the Sun* Admiral's Cup campaign, Hugh wondered if the transom was big enough for the poem? Yes, we all agreed!

were still steep and dumping white water all over us. What now? I thought.

Then, to our disbelief a cargo ship came charging out of the mist of flying spray, steaming straight towards us. When she was twenty yards away, she stopped and hove to. What was going on? We didn't have long to wait. A few minutes later a snub-nosed Royal Navy helicopter hovered into view, rotors beating louder and louder as it approached barely a hundred feet above the waves. Next, another Royal Navy presence loomed low over the horizon in the form of an Orion search and rescue aircraft, practically skimming the waves. It's getting busy out here, I thought.

Pleased as we were to see all this rescue firepower, we didn't understand why *Golden Apple*, stricken as she was, and her shipwrecked crew were receiving so much attention. Hugh scooted down below, grabbed the VHF radio transmitter and began to talk directly to the helicopter crew as they hovered above us, a technique requiring serious skills in strong winds and big seas like these without a proper reference point for the pilot.

"Do you need help?" they asked.

"Not really," Hugh said in a master class of understatement. "We've lost our rudder and we can't steer. We've tried to jury-rig the boat but it's not working in these seas. We're drifting out of control. But we're still OK."

"Copy that," said the pilot. "But the weather's going to deteriorate again and this is your last chance. I recommend we hoist you up to safety. It's now or never."

A crestfallen Hugh emerged from the cabin and shouted the news above the chopper noise, the whistling of the wind through the rigging and the crashing and banging of the yacht as she wallowed up and down. Leave the yacht? For any yachtsman it's a stark and terrible choice. After all, there's an unwritten rule that you never abandon a boat that's still afloat. It took a few minutes for the enormity of it all to sink in.

Leave *Golden Apple of the Sun* out here!

But with the helicopter's rotors thrashing overhead the decision made itself. If we didn't abandon ship now, we'd probably end up in a watery grave on the rocks of the Scilly Isles. And there's another unwritten rule that Hugh had to take into account: a skipper's primary concern is the safety of his crew. Also, I had to admit, a safe flight to a warm dry bed in a naval base sounded extremely attractive now that our race was over.

So without exception we agreed to take this golden offer, and Hugh dashed back down below to hook up with the pilot again. "Yes, we'll abandon the yacht," he said.

On deck we were already preparing for the evacuation, a new experience for all of us. Harry raised a laugh by suggesting we leave a note to say: *Gone*

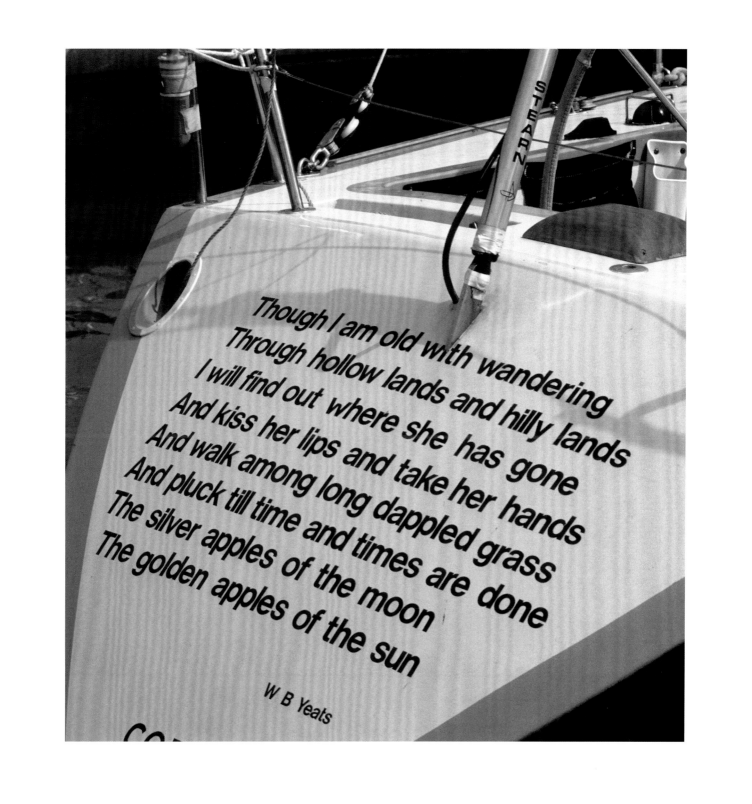

Though I am old with wandering
Through hollow lands and hilly lands
I will find out where she has gone
And kiss her lips and take her hands
And walk among long dappled grass
And pluck till time and times are done
The silver apples of the moon
The golden apples of the sun

W B Yeats

"Both yacht and raft were locked in a potentially fatal embrace, drifting sideways at around three knots. We were much safer on the yacht, I realized. The noise was deafening. With the chopper roaring directly overhead and the wind screaming through the mast and rigging, it was impossible to think straight."

for dinner, will be back soon. That was when the trouble started.

Because we had to be winched to safety in a harness, the helicopter crew could not risk the rescue wire getting entangled in the mast and rigging, which were flailing around wildly. At best a snared wire would force the crew to release the harness into the sea, leaving us stranded on the yacht with no further hope of rescue, while at worst it could drag the helicopter itself down into the sea with all its crew.

The pilot ordered us to deploy the life raft first and paddle clear of the yacht, giving the wireman a clean drop into the sea from where he would hook us up and hoist us to safety, one by one. None of us had ever used a life raft in these conditions. In my experience hardly any racing yachtsmen did so even in practice, simply because the possibility of being rescued just never entered their mind. And even in the unlikely event that we might have practiced the maneuver, it wouldn't have been from a yacht that was leaping up and down in huge seas.

But with the chopper eating up precious fuel, time was marching on and we didn't have time to read any instructions. Hoping for the best, we released the life raft from its container behind the helmsman's location. The wind caught it immediately, making it flap around like a sail. It took all our combined strength to prevent our only means of survival being blown clean over the side. Next, we had to inflate it. How do we do that in these conditions? I wondered.

Keenly aware that the helicopter crew was watching us impatiently from above, we made a start and, grunting with the effort, finally got some air into our puny-looking craft. We just hoped it was enough. Hanging on desperately to any handhold we could find in case it flew away, we launched the raft over the lifelines into the sea on the lee side. One by one, we tumbled into it. This is crazy, I thought.

Suddenly, we found ourselves in a worse predicament.

Nowhere near fully inflated, the life raft immediately sagged alarmingly under the weight of the ten of us. Breaking seas poured straight over the sides, swirling around us. Jammed tightly together, we were sitting in water up to our armpits. I became all too aware that our special waterproof clothing, which I had helped design, wasn't all that waterproof. I was freezing. Now half under water, the raft could capsize at any moment and tip all of us into the sea.

Then *Golden Apple* joined the party.

Because we'd been forced to launch the raft on the lee side, away from the wind, the yacht was drifting down on top of us. In a highly unequal contest we were being pounded by fifteen tons of wood and fiberglass and were at imminent risk of being submerged under the hull. In our waterlogged oilskins I didn't have much faith in our chances. Powerless to paddle our unwieldy, half-swamped life raft out of harm's way, we just sat there helplessly. Both yacht and raft were locked in a potentially fatal embrace, drifting sideways at around three knots. We were much safer on the yacht, I realized.

The noise was deafening. With the chopper roaring directly overhead and the wind screaming through the mast and rigging, it was impossible to think straight. None of us could hear what the other was saying. There had been moments during the racing of the last two days when I'd been alarmed. Now I was genuinely scared.

It was the pilot who came to our rescue. Seeing our predicament, he somehow maneuvered the chopper around to the leeward side of *Golden Apple*, and held it at an angle so the downdraft of the blades hit the side of the hull. Bit by bit, in this way he was able to push the yacht away from the raft. As a demonstration of piloting skill, it was deeply impressive and I've never been so grateful for another person's proficiency.

As *Golden Apple* wallowed away on her own, the wireman dropped out of the skies with the harness, hooked up the first of us and rode him back up to the helicopter. Within seconds he returned and deftly secured the next. One by one, the crew disappeared into the chopper until only Hugh and I were left, watching our beautiful racing yacht drifting further and

Author Jerry Grayson flew the Royal Navy helicopter that hauled me and my *Golden Apple* crewmates to safety during the 1979 Fastnet Race storm.

further away. The embodiment of all our hopes, she had weathered everything the storm and her crew could throw at her, except for the failure of an experimental rudder.

As the wireman came down to hook me up, Hugh yelled into my ear above the screaming of the wind, the roaring engine and thrashing rotors, "Holland, who would have thought it would end like this?" I had no answer.

Within a few seconds I was scrambling into the utilitarian safety of the chopper cabin to join the rest of the crew. Soon afterwards Hugh joined us and the pilot set a course for land. It was only now, on our flight to safety over a storm-swept Irish Sea, that we learned from the helicopter crew what had been happening in those last few hours. It was a tale of carnage.

"30 yachts missing," we were told, "Several capsized and many crew feared drowned. Boats are in trouble all over the Irish Sea as far north as Dublin and Liverpool." We were shocked to the core and utterly depressed. As I looked out of the window at the still mountainous seas, the truth hit me for the first time, so preoccupied had we been with our own survival.

Of course! If we had trouble in our 43-footer, what it would be like out there in a 30-foot Half-Tonner?

That's when I began to fear the worst. I knew that many Half-Tonners had started the race, including several of my designs like the Nicholson 33 *Grimalkin* sailed by the Sheahans, father and son, and four crew. In breaking waves of this size, it would be almost impossible for such a small yacht, barely twice the size of a dinghy, to survive in these seas, however skillful the crew might be.

Shaken at what we'd heard, we were dropped off at Coldrose Royal Navy Air Base in the far west of Cornwall. As soon as I could, I called Laurel and my design team back in Currabinny to reassure them that *Golden Apple*'s crew were all in one piece, and asked about the safety of the other Irish yachts. I can't say I was reassured. Nobody really knew who was safe and who wasn't.

Then at the staff's insistence we were ordered to take a hot shower and were put to bed, almost as though we were children. Given what we'd been through, I was simultaneously amused and annoyed.

Next morning we woke to a day of relatively calm weather and dramatically smaller seas. The morning news was full of the tragedy, and we learned that many of the surviving yachts had run for cover and found safe harbors all along the Welsh and southern Irish coasts. But the reprieve in the weather had come too late for 15 yachtsmen, drowned at the height of the storm despite the heroic efforts of the crews of the Royal National Lifeboat Institution and the Royal Navy, who had mounted one

◄

My new design for Mike Swerdlow, the 47-foot *Aries*, secured a place on the 1979 USA Admiral's Cup team, and survived the 1979 Fastnet Race despite the *NY Times* reporting the *Aries* crew missing. Here *Aries* is "peeling" spinnakers in the Nassau Race. Racing yacht crews had developed the routine to change sails without sailing "bare headed". Previously it had required sailing slowly for a few minutes with no headsail or spinnaker set. That was no way to win a race!

life-saving mission after another at considerable risk to their own lives. The Irish lifeboats had been out all night saving yachts and their crews, including my brother Phil and the rest of the crew aboard an Irish 40-footer called *Regardless*, another of my designs. Owned by property developer Ken Rohan, a personal friend, she'd gotten into trouble when, among the leaders, her carbon rudder had also failed. So close yet so far.

We would also learn that the finish line off Plymouth had turned from what was usually a happy occasion into one of anxiety and fear. Many of the relatives of those still at sea had waited by the telephone for hours on end, or spent all day and all night by the harbor, hoping against hope their loved ones would return safely. As yachting writer John Rousmaniere remembered when he crossed the finish line aboard *Toscana*, a Swan 47-footer, "The wharf was crowded with silent, solemn women and men staring blankly out toward the Channel." It was one of his fellow crewmembers, ex-Royal Navy captain John Coote, who had radioed officials the day before with the memorable words: "People are dying out here." It would become almost an epitaph for the lost.

We knew some of those lost, people with whom we had sailed or shared a beer after a race. As I feared, one was the owner of the Nicholson 33 *Grimalkin*. I learned much later that she had somersaulted not once but twice, rolled right over and been dismasted. The father, David Sheahan, had slipped off the deck, drifted away and drowned. One of his crew also died.

Fortunately some of the bad news turned out to be wrong. The normally accurate *New York Times* reported that Butch had been lost with the rest of the crew of *Aries*, including her fun-loving owner Mike Swerdlow. As it happened, to our huge relief Butch was very much alive and *Aries* had come through the storm unscathed.

In this tragedy the results of the race hardly seemed to matter, but American cable television mogul Ted Turner's 61-foot *Tenacious* won on corrected time, a position *Golden Apple* might have taken if the rudder had stayed where it was.

As for our runaway *Golden Apple*, we heard she was safely back in port after being retrieved by a Cornish fishing boat before she'd run aground on the Scilly Isles.

And then came the inquest, the most sobering such exercise that the yachting fraternity has undertaken, before or since. As well as the death toll, the tally was 24 boats abandoned and five sunk. As the inquiry conducted by the Royal Ocean Racing Club and the Royal Yachting Association determined, the main element of the Fastnet tragedy of 1979 was of course the storm, a freak occurrence that had not been predicted and that

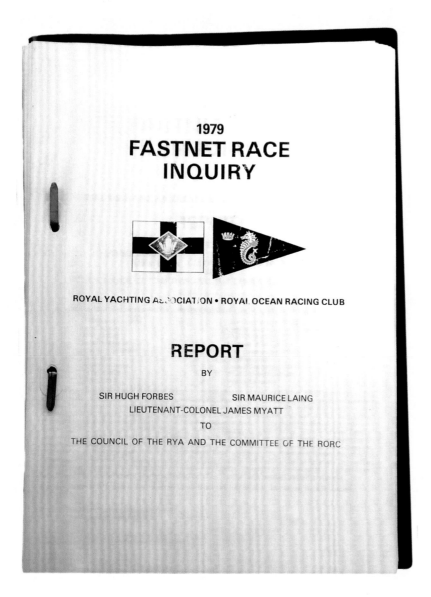

Butch went to London to face the 1979 Fastnet Race inquiry, representing Ron Holland Design and our clients.

"The ferocity of the westerly winds – 60-knot-plus gusts – and the freak breaking seas had taken the entire fleet by surprise. It was also established that the relative shallowness of the Irish Sea contributed to the calamity because it 'tripped' the waves, making them extremely steep."

had engulfed the fleet so quickly that boats had no time to run for safety. Many smaller yachts would have prudently elected to do so rather than confront those conditions if the weather forecast had warned what was on its way across the North Atlantic.

The ferocity of the westerly winds – 60-knot-plus gusts – and the freak breaking seas had taken the entire fleet by surprise. It was also established that the relative shallowness of the Irish Sea contributed to the calamity because it "tripped" the waves, making them extremely steep.

But also, as yachting writer Rousmaniere pointed out in his book *Fastnet Force 10*, some of the crews just weren't ready for the conditions. The prevailing emphasis in yacht racing at the time was on speed, not safety. This was especially true in the case of a classic event like the Fastnet where a victory might happen once in a yachting lifetime, even for the very best. Owners and crews wanted to win, an ambition in which survival skills ranked a poor second. Partly because so many of our designs were represented in the Admiral's Cup we were invited to attend the inquiry, and it was Butch who did the honors.

As a veteran ocean racer who had survived the storm, Butch had a lot to say and it fell to him to explain how the carbon fiber rudder shafts had failed in the Fastnet as well as in earlier races, including the one that had given way on Mr. Heath's new *Morning Cloud* in the Channel Race, a particularly galling event for me because of the publicity it inevitably attracted.

For Ron Holland Design you might say the rudders became Exhibit A. It was Gary Carlin, with the help of Lars Bergstrom among others, who had developed the technology. Always trying to do things better for his clients, Gary had created a way of reinforcing the high-stress areas of the hull and deck with laminates of carbon fiber tape. So impressive were the results that Gary and I agreed; he should do the same with the rudders.

So he replaced the heavier steel and aluminum rudder shafts with these laminates. In theory, huge weight savings would result. Even better, these savings would be made at the bow and stern where excessive weight contributes to a yacht's propensity to pitch and "nod" in choppy waters, a motion that slows a boat down.

As a fan of car racing I was attracted to the idea of using these latest materials. I had met and talked with Formula One teams during the Monaco Grand Prix at a period when they were starting to use carbon fiber, and it seemed the way to go. Unfortunately, the integrity of the production process wasn't high enough, and the bond between the carbon fiber and the resin had failed. The main problem lay in a lack of production experience, rigorous analysis of methods of construction, and use of full-scale testing that is taken for granted in, for example, the aircraft industry where the consequences of structural failure are catastrophic. The yacht industry simply lacked the budget to follow suit. Because these rudders were experimental, they should have undergone the same kind of brutal testing to destruction that was common in aviation as well as in car racing, a sport which had learned through its own failures to be much more professional about durability and safety issues. I was thankful that none of our designs had suffered structural failures in the hull, which can quickly send a yacht to the bottom.

Our own shortcomings were reflected right across the yachting industry. In terms of analytical tools, design and construction had for too long been a seat-of-the-pants exercise. The experience of individual firms rather than hard-headed analytical rigor, preferably from independent consultants, had been standard practice. All too obviously that now had to change. And it did.

After I had returned to Currabinny I received a phone call from senior figures in Formula One, and from the RAF at Farnborough where carbon fiber had been invented. "You guys are giving us a bad name," they said bluntly. "Why don't you come over and talk to us?"

They were referring to the yachting industry's generally inexperienced use of carbon fiber and wanted to show us how it should be done. Although I was a yacht designer and not a boatbuilder, I encouraged Gary to meet

▲

It's not always possible to win when experimenting with lighter masts. Sometimes we didn't get to the finish line under sail!

▲

In 1979, although experimental carbon fiber rudders were breaking, my designs were still winning many races.

with the Farnborough people, and because I knew I could play a useful role in the boatbuilding yards I wanted to know all I could about this new material. At the end of the day, a designer is no better than the quality of the construction of his yachts, and I firmly believed the yachting industry should invest more heavily in construction processes, materials, stress-testing and engineering for the purpose of making boats stronger and safer. My approach to yacht design was mostly intuitive, and always would be, but I still saw the need for more rigor and discipline.

And so, in one positive outcome from that terrible race, the 1979 Fastnet started the ball rolling. Although not deliberately, the IOR rules had tended to encourage lighter and less stable designs. Clearly, less stable yachts are more prone to capsize, which is what had happened to the smaller boats in the Fastnet. On this issue I was convinced that the IOR had to move in the opposite direction and promote stability rather than penalize it as it had done.

Everybody learned a lot from the experience. One of the most insightful analyses came from Jim Kilroy, the hyper-competitive Los Angeles property developer whose 79-footer *Kialoa III* was looking good for outright victory until a running backstay blew out, forcing him to sail conservatively so they could keep the mast in the boat. With Jim confined to his bunk with busted ribs, *Kialoa* got home safely before the worst of the weather struck. A tough sailor frightened of nothing, he wasn't foolhardy though. A veteran of hurricanes in the Caribbean, and some of the wildest seas anybody could encounter in the Sydney-Hobart, he took strong issue with race organizers over their failure to make two-way radios mandatory. Among several other pertinent points, he wrote, "Failure to have a disciplined and mandatory plan for the use of radios limited not only the security aboard... but also made problems of rescue much more complicated."

The '79 Fastnet eventually slipped off the news pages, but the repercussions continued for years. For me it turned out to be a watershed. I never competed in another major long-distance ocean race. I gradually left behind the slippery pole of IOR racing in favor of bigger – and more profitable – private cruising yachts.

It didn't happen overnight. We continued to book commissions for racing yachts that would become highly successful, including New Zealand's *Swuzzlebubble*, winner of the overall prize in the next Admiral's Cup in 1981. And perhaps surprisingly, nobody seemed to hold the rudder failures against us. The competitive mentality of our racing clients was such that they understood what we'd done and why – I always explained the risks – and I'm sure they saw lightweight composite rudders as the future,

"At the end of the day, a designer is no better than the quality of the construction of his yachts, and I firmly believed the yachting industry should invest more heavily in construction processes, materials, stress-testing and engineering for the purpose of making boats stronger and safer."

which is exactly what happened. Once the manufacturing problems were sorted out, they became standard for performance sailing yachts.

No, my main reason for the change of direction was creative. I could see yachts were going to get bigger, and I had some ideas that I believed would rewrite the rules of global cruising under sail. After all, I had spent a lot of time on the world's oceans, and I had learned a lot that I could apply to sailboats designed for a more leisurely form of sailing.

I suppose I was entering a different phase of my life. Although I was still young, in my early thirties, the years since I had left school at the age of 16 had been full, much fuller than I could possibly have imagined. Everything had happened so fast. Without ever really having had time to take stock, I had gone from the young penniless wannabe designer of *Eygthene*, with little going for me except ambition and hope, all the way to a sought-after designer of some of the world's most successful racing yachts. It was as though my life had been in a state of constant acceleration.

In my rare moments of leisure I sometimes wondered what had happened to the kid who loved square riggers, and could name all the spars and ropes of these wonderful old sailing ships. Then out of the blue it all came flooding back.

A childhood dream come true.
Crossing the Bay of Biscay in
a square-rigger.

Tall ship *Eagle*

THE U.S. COAST GUARD'S TALL SHIP *Eagle* sailed majestically into Cork Harbour on a long voyage from America. A three-masted barque built in Hamburg in 1935, and impeccably maintained, as you'd expect from such a prestigious service as the U.S. Coast Guard, she was a magnificent sight that instantly reminded me of everything I had learned from the histories and Royal Navy texts that Marie Clay had handed me for remedial reading.

Her white hull gleamed and a gold-painted eagle adorned the bow. In no time a crowd gathered on the dock to admire her, and I was one of the first to arrive. It was 1981, two years after the fatal Fastnet. I had met one of the *Eagle*'s permanent crew during the SORC series off Florida, and he obviously hadn't forgotten where I lived because I soon got a phone call from him.

"Would you like to come aboard for dinner?" he asked. Would I ever!

The last time I had gotten myself aboard a tall ship was when I was a kid. The Chilean square-rigger, the four-masted barquentine *Esmeralda,* made one of her then regular visits to Auckland, and totally enthralled, I went down to the dock several times just to stare at her. I must have kept pestering my mother until she took me aboard during an open day for the public, and dragged her around the ship, listening intently as the guide described the names of the spars and rigging. I committed them all to memory.

So, jumping at the chance to get aboard my second-ever tall ship, I spent a congenial evening at the captain's table talking the technicalities

223

▲

My first time aloft aboard a square-rigger. In 1981, I joined the USCGC *Barque Eagle* at the invitation of Captain Martin Moynihan, and we crossed the Bay of Biscay on passage from Cork to Lisbon.

▶

Eagle under full sail, wind power pushing her along at 10 knots.

of square-riggers and yacht design. I found that in all those years I'd hardly forgotten anything, and it turned out to be a great conversation.

As the night drew on the captain suggested, "Why don't you join us? We're sailing for Lisbon tomorrow and we've got a spare berth." Although I was swamped with work I accepted immediately, and turned up next day with some clothing thrown into a sea bag. I was assigned to one of his cadets, a bright-eyed and bushy-tailed 21-year-old named Sandy Stosz.

"Sandy will watch over you," the skipper said. "We don't want you to do anything silly like falling overboard." He was only half joking.

On the third morning out of Cork the *Eagle* was crossing the notorious Bay of Biscay, and anxious to miss nothing of this special voyage I was up on deck early. Allowed on to the control bridge deck, I watched as the cadets, high aloft, trimmed the big banging sails, their feet precariously balanced on nothing but ropes.

"What do you think?" the skipper asked me, pointing up at all those acres of canvas.

I couldn't help myself. "They're over-trimmed," I said. "They're sheeted in too tight, especially the jibs and staysails. All too flat."

"OK," he said. "Go and tell the watch leaders to slacken 'em off a bit."

Really? Obediently, I found the watch leaders and gave a few instructions. The cadets scrambled to the lines and eased the sheets, and I returned to the bridge. "What's the result?" I asked. "We've picked up an extra knot," the skipper said with a grin.

I felt like I'd earned my berth. An extra knot is a lot for a massive displacement hull like a tall ship. *Eagle* wasn't in a hurry, but I've always thought that no sail-powered boat should go slower than she has to.

For the rest of the voyage I spent much of the time climbing up and down the rigging, listening to the wind as it screamed aloft when the barque rolled to windward, then fell eerily silent when she rolled back to leeward. I spent a lot of time with Sandy, who literally showed me the ropes. She impressed me as a natural leader and she had an obvious love for the sea. When I disembarked at Lisbon, thanking her for keeping an eye on me, I was sorry to say goodbye to Sandy and to USCGC *Eagle*. I never imagined I would see either of them again.

I wasn't in the slow lane for long. For years, well before the 1979 Fastnet, Jim Kilroy had been tearing up the world's ocean races in *Kialoa III*, a Sparkman & Stephens-designed 79-footer made of aluminum. To date the New York studio had created all his yachts, but I'd heard rumors that Jim was considering a new *Kialoa* – a Hawaiian word that means "long white canoe" (or, I later learned, "beautiful young woman"), and I wondered

Dec. 10ᵀᴴ, 2016

Dear Ron,
  This book will always
remind you of our adventures
sailing in the Barque Eagle.
  Fair winds,
  Sandy Stosz

A gift from the admiral – a book about the tall ship. I count myself lucky to have sailed aboard the U.S. Coast Guard barque *Eagle* on three occasions.

whether I might play a role in the new sailboat.

So during the 1979 Southern Ocean Racing Conference series, which took place a few months before the Fastnet Race, I had approached him and his New Zealand skipper, the tough and capable Bruce Kendal, and asked if I could jump aboard *Kialoa III* for a transatlantic race that was due to start from yachting-dominated Marblehead on the New England coast and end in my home county of Cork in Ireland. I could have gotten home much faster by plane, but it was a perfect opportunity to learn about this emerging breed of bigger yachts. And, you never know, I hoped I might get an inside track on the design commission.

Having come to sailing relatively late, Jim was a man who liked to do it his way. Not only did he own, skipper and steer his yachts, he prided himself on racing with a crew of amateurs, albeit unusually capable ones. In a rapidly professionalizing sport this was highly unusual, and I also wanted to see how this worked.

A heavy fog descended on the fleet almost immediately after the start from Marblehead, and we didn't see any sign of our main rival, the 75-foot *Ondine*, for a whole five days. When the fog finally lifted we glimpsed her emerging from the gloom in mid-ocean. *Kialoa* crossed narrowly in front before the fog descended again and *Ondine* disappeared once more from view.

A natural leader, Jim was very much in command and loved nothing better than taking the helm. You would never imagine he was approaching his sixties. A high achiever by instinct, he had been a collegiate track star and an accomplished surfer before entering the work force. Jim was still tall, fit, white-haired and handsome with a charming manner. Yet he'd earned his success the hard way.

Born in Alaska, he was the youngest of three children raised in the backwoods of that state pretty much single-handedly by their mother. Seeking a better life in the city, the family left the frozen wastes on the back of a dog-hauled sled containing their entire life's possessions. When they finally made it to Los Angeles, his mother worked nights as a telephone operator at the *Los Angeles Daily News* to help make ends meet. While she answered the phones, the kids did everything they could to pull their weight. Between them they repaired bicycles, delivered newspapers and served tables to bring in a few dollars. I never met his mother, but Jim revered her and paid her fulsome tribute in his book *Dare to Win*. He certainly inherited her capacity for hard work. Spotting the potential of a booming Los Angeles, Jim made a fortune in property development around the airport and Southern California. I had many conversations

▲

For my 2012 and 2017 passages aboard *Eagle* I am thankful for the invitations to Rear Admiral Sandra Stosz, now a Vice Admiral, my cadet shipmate on my 1981 *Eagle* passage.

"Not long after we docked at Crosshaven, Jim visited my design studio to say he would entrust us with the job of designing his new yacht. And he made it clear she had to be the fastest yacht afloat, a 'maxi-yacht' (the term was new at that time) that would demolish the opposition."

with Jim during the Marblehead-Cork race and I soon learned that he hated to lose.

Not long after we docked at Crosshaven, Jim visited my design studio to say he would entrust us with the job of designing his new yacht. And he made it clear she had to be the fastest yacht afloat, a "maxi yacht" (the term was new at that time) that would demolish the opposition. It was the runaway success of *Imp* that had convinced Jim and Bruce, on whose advice he relied heavily, that he could hand us the commission for *Kialoa IV*.

Imp had become a showcase for us. As Jim and Bruce explained, they had been impressed by her success in the SORC and the Admiral's Cup in that year, and they saw the new *Kialoa* as another *Imp*, only bigger. Like *Imp*, she would incorporate the internal aluminum space frame that the creative Lars Bergstrom had dreamed up to buttress the hull and structure at the points of greatest stress.

After *Kialoa* had returned to her home port in California, Bruce flew out to Cork to hammer out the many details. I suggested the IOR rules would allow 81 feet, a couple of feet longer than *Kialoa III* and certainly the biggest ocean racer ever built at that time. Everybody agreed and we got down to work.

As we expected, Jim made it clear he intended to leave little – well, nothing – to chance. This was in his nature and background. An aviation engineer by training as well as a pilot, he'd learned his trade with the

Douglas Aircraft Corporation after the Second World War, before turning to property development. He had a disciplined mind and he took a close interest in every stage of the project; for instance, on the crucial issue of what materials would be used in the yacht's construction. At first he favored the lightweight aluminum that had served him so well, but *Imp* was constructed of the new composite materials and this interested Jim. For our part we preferred composites, because being lighter they were inherently faster, assuming there was no compromise in strength.

The composite we most favored was Kevlar, the fiber first synthesized at Dupont in 1964. Put on the market from the early 1970s, it was proving to be stronger and stiffer than any known material relative to its weight. Even so, in the conservative yachting industry there was considerable skepticism about its properties. Gary Carlin wasn't one of the skeptics and had been working with Dupont for quite a while; the relationship was one of the reasons for Kiwi Boats' success. As for Jim, he wasn't convinced but at least he had an open mind.

In order to persuade him of the merits of Kevlar, we set up an experiment. It took place in the Kilroy Industries parking lot across from LAX airport. There were just four of us present – myself, Bruce, *Kialoa* crewman Terry and a deeply interested Jim, his engineer's instincts fully aroused. The object of his curiosity was a panel of Kevlar laminate. We placed the laminate over the curb at the edge of the parking lot. Terry handed the broad-shouldered Bruce a sledgehammer and we all stood well back.

Raising the hammer as high as he could, Bruce brought it down on the panel with a tremendous blow. But instead of smashing into a thousand pieces, as I think Jim expected, the panel remained intact and ricocheted right across the parking lot. When we went to examine it, there was hardly a mark to be seen. Jim was seriously impressed.

Mainly on the strength of the demo, it was decided the new boat would be made of these so-called "exotic" materials, and we all got down to work. Butch and I fully appreciated that the commission would test the expertise of Ron Holland Design and Kiwi Boats to the limit. At over 80 feet the new *Kialoa* posed an entirely new set of challenges for all the parties involved.

For lay people this is a difficult thing to grasp. "How hard can it be," I'm sometimes asked, "to design a sailboat that's just a few feet longer than another one?"

The answer lies in the volume. As sailboats, and especially racing ones, are made longer, it's not just a question of adding a few feet to the overall length and telling the boatyard to get on with it. A sailboat isn't like a

▲

At the conclusion of my third passage aboard the US Coast Guard tall ship *Eagle*, Captain Matt Meilstrup handed me this *Eagle* medallion. I'm proud to be able to include it in my story.

▲

I commissioned Vancouver marine artist John Horton to create a painting for my private collection: the clipper ships *Taeping*, launched in 1863, and *Ariel*, launched in 1865, racing up the English Channel to London with a cargo of tea from China.

piece of elastic that can be stretched here and there. With every extra foot in length, there's a corresponding increase in height and width.

In short, the volume increases as a cubed calculation. Thus, a 40-footer will have roughly four times the volume of a 30-footer, not just a quarter more as you might expect.

Also, our brief was to create a yacht that was as light as possible for her length while being immensely strong. There could be no sacrifices made to structural integrity or overall rigidity. The rigidity or stiffness of a yacht is an essential element in her success because it means that the horse-power, if you like, provided by the wind in the sails, is transmitted directly into the hull in a way that propels the boat forward with the least amount of wastage. *Imp* had proven this.

The stiffer the hull, the faster the propulsion. Hulls that flex from the pressure of the sails' horsepower won't win. And they are liable to breakage. Think of a bicycle whose frame could bend whenever pressure was applied to the pedals.

Another vital consideration in a sailboat's strength is her speed: the faster she sails, the greater are the stresses she must withstand. That's why, although we weren't entirely convinced that the new *Kialoa* would need an aluminum space frame now that Jim had opted to build her out of composites, we decided it was better to be safe than sorry.

In terms of design we had no doubt Jim's maxi would take us into the red zone, but at least some things had changed in our favor. At that time most of the bigger yachts doubled up as cruisers and boasted comfortable interiors, on the basis that it wasn't considered quite fair to turn up to the start in a stripped-out racing machine.

But Jim made it clear that *Kialoa IV* wasn't to be a cruising/racing hybrid but a no-compromise racer. In other words, a stripped-out racing machine.

For Gary this was the biggest construction project his relatively young Kiwi Boats had taken on. In the wake of *Eygthene* he had established his business in a shed located in a farmyard near Plant City, inland from Tampa Bay. As well as *Imp*, his most famous construction project, he had turned out Quarter- and One-Tonners, all of them to my designs, and now which boasted owners all over the United States as well as in Mexico and Greece.

For the *Kialoa* project Gary decided to move the business to a bigger shed at Largo, closer to Tampa Bay. Gradually Jim's yacht took shape there, with Bruce closely involved and acting as project manager. I regularly stopped in to visit Kiwi Boats to check on progress and got more and more excited as the new *Kialoa* approached completion. From Heathrow Airport it was a long flight with multiple connections, but tired as I usually was, I always hurried straight to the boatyard as soon as I arrived.

I'll never forget one particular trip. There it was, the hull sitting on a cradle without its keel and rudder, but the lines still looked beautiful, exactly as I had envisioned. I couldn't wait to get up on deck for a closer look, and before talking with anybody I raced up the wooden steps leaning against the hull. I was stepping onto the deck, ten feet off the concrete floor, with one foot in the air and the other on the ladder when the ladder started to move. For a horrifying moment, I was suspended in midair. Hoping to save myself, I somehow found a purchase on the ladder and kicked off backwards in what felt like a slow-motion backwards swan dive.

Unfortunately I didn't do a complete somersault and land on my feet, like you see in the movies. I fell the entire ten feet like a sack of spuds and crashed onto the concrete on my back. According to the shocked bystanders, I did what they call a dead-cat bounce and lay motionless. Well, I've had a good life, I clearly remember thinking. It's a wheelchair from now on.

When the paramedics turned up, they lifted me carefully onto a stretcher and transported me to a local clinic where, to my amazement and relief, they declared me to be still in one piece.

"You can leave," I was told.

They were the best words I'd ever heard. Shaken and bruised, I was driven back to the site, this time for a more cautious examination of *Kialoa*. The explanation for the moving ladder was all too banal. It just happened that the construction crew, unaware that I was on the steps, was simply shifting it to a different place on the hull at the exact moment I was about to step aboard.

The new *Kialoa* was launched off the St. Petersburg Yacht Club with Laurel doing the christening honors at Jim's kind invitation. The SORC was looming and Jim, Bruce and his crew of ace amateurs got right down to testing the *Kialoa IV* against her predecessor in the waters of Tampa Bay.

Typically, Jim had drawn up a detailed work-up program that was managed by Bruce and ex-Sparkman & Stephens designer Dave Pedrick. He also brought in extra serious talent, including aviation engineer Alan Pucket of Hughes Aircraft, who had become one of America's leading brains in defense technology during the Cold War. I'm sure he enjoyed putting his knowledge to work on a beautiful sailboat rather than on weapons of war.

This team put *Kialoa* through her paces in every imaginable condition, compiling a whole range of performance data on computer printouts that

▲

I was invited to join *Eagle* for the third time in 2017. Here I'm at the wheel with her commanding officer, Captain Matt Meilstrup, and executive officer, Commander Brook Millard.

The first composite maxi racer, *Kialoa IV,* racing around the Hawaiian Islands.

"The yacht was crashing into the waves and spray was hurtling over our heads. It was rough and uncomfortable but *Kialoa* was flying along at over ten knots in bursts, a new experience for me, Jim and the crew. Even better, our deadly rival, the 73-footer *Windward Passage*, then the champion maxi, lay astern of us, exactly where Jim wanted her."

covered speed, tacking angles and anything else you could think of. No yacht had ever been subjected to such a robust and detailed analysis, but this was Jim's way and it worked. One thing became immediately clear in the testing: in all but the lightest conditions she was significantly faster than *Kialoa III*. But testing is one thing and racing is another.

Kialoa IV's first serious trial came in the 1981 classic SORC race from St. Petersburg to Fort Lauderdale for which I was invited aboard. Now, although there were now many of my designs on the water around the world – production boatbuilders, including Nautor Swan in Finland, were buying up my plans wholesale – a sense of apprehension always accompanies me (I suspect other designers feel the same) when I first step aboard one of my yachts before an important race. Particularly one as high-profile as this. The conversion of a racing yacht from a set of drawings, detailed though they may be, to the real thing is a lengthy and sometimes nerve-wracking process that doesn't always end with a boat that exactly reflects the designer's intentions.

I will never forget that debut race. There I was, sitting on the windward rail with the rest of the crew, my legs dangling over the side as *Kialoa* bashed up the east coast of Florida against a strong northerly wind. Over 20 people were on board and they were getting more than they bargained for. Like me, most of them were lined up on the rail where we served as ballast.

Kialoa was being sailed flat out, close-hauled in big seas aggravated by the Gulf Stream current that was flowing at three or four knots against the strong wind. The yacht was crashing into the waves and spray was hurtling over our heads. It was rough and uncomfortable but *Kialoa* was flying along at over ten knots in bursts, a new experience for me, Jim and the crew. Even better, our deadly rival, the 73-footer *Windward Passage*, then the champion maxi, lay astern of us, exactly where Jim wanted her.

As I clung to the lifelines, spray stinging my face, I couldn't help but reflect on the loads being imposed on what had been described in the yachting press as *Kialoa*'s "experimental Kevlar hull" and aluminum space frame as she pounded up and down. Despite all our thinking and planning, I couldn't repress the question, Have we designed in enough safety factors? Well, I concluded, this race is going to tell us – or not.

Then Jim invited me to take over the wheel, a massive thing more than six feet in diameter, and I braced myself against the steep, 30-degree angle of heel. Occasionally *Kialoa* would leap straight off the back of a particularly big wave, fly through the air, all 30 tons of her, and crash back into the Gulf Stream with a bone-shaking crack that practically rattled your teeth.

With *Windward Passage* hanging on grimly astern, Jim wasn't about to slow down. Then, without warning, *Kialoa* did her bucking bronco act, jumping off one of the biggest waves so far. The wheel kicked back and threw me onto the cockpit floor on my backside, right at the feet of a startled movie maker, Dick Enersen, who was aboard filming a documentary. I scrambled back up and grabbed hold of the wheel again before *Kialoa* veered off course. She didn't miss a beat. "Can we go faster?" asked Jim. "I'll do my best," I replied.

Kialoa IV beat all the other maxis into Fort Lauderdale and, predictably, Jim was delighted. More importantly from my viewpoint, she was clearly bulletproof and the "experimental" hull had more than proven itself. Over the rest of the SORC regatta *Kialoa* fulfilled that opening race's promise, crossing the line first in all six events against nearly 90 other sailboats, and setting two course records. And I knew that yes, she could go faster. As other deep-pocketed owners saw how the 81-foot *Kialoa IV* was tearing up the oceans, they began to knock on our door. Almost overnight the studio acquired a reputation as the preferred choice for maxi yachts, especially for the Whitbread Race that was making the headlines. In seemingly no time we fielded commissions for three more maxi racers for this wild circumnavigation.

And then I was drawn straight back into the fast lane again, the fastest I had ever found myself in.

yes!

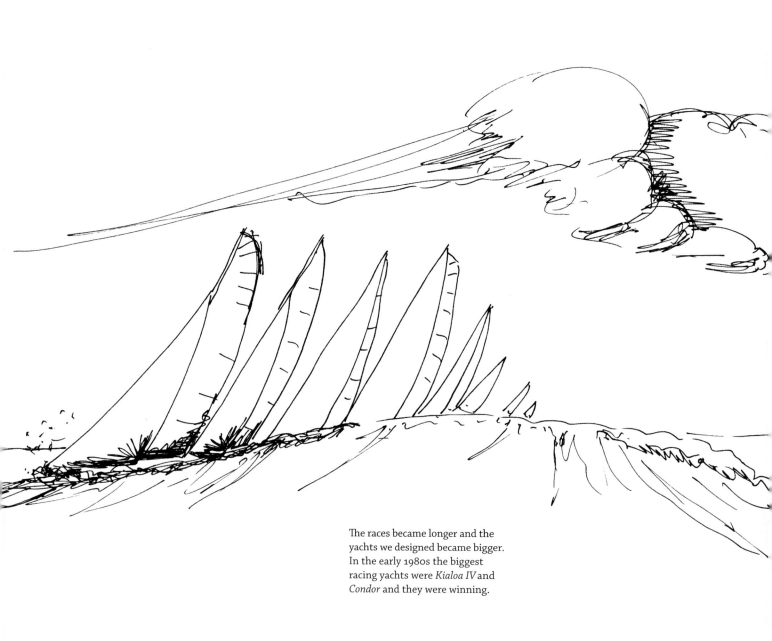

The races became longer and the
yachts we designed became bigger.
In the early 1980s the biggest
racing yachts were *Kialoa IV* and
Condor and they were winning.

Heavy weather

ROUND-THE-WORLD YACHTIE Rob James walked into the studio and announced he wanted us to design a 65-foot trimaran. He had sponsorship from Colt Cars, at that time the British arm of Mitsubishi, and intended to race the trimaran in the next Round Britain and Ireland Race which would take place in 1982. His crew would be his wife, Naomi.

A 65-foot trimaran! I had never designed a multi-hulled yacht. I had only sailed on two of them, a small Hobie Cat and a 40-foot cruising trimaran, and nothing had changed my views about multihulls. I considered the new wave of big racing trimarans, especially the ones designed in France, as exciting but also unsafe: they often capsized despite their wide beam.

And I had a low opinion of their all-round sailing capabilities. Although they could fly off the wind, they were pathetic at tacking upwind compared to a maxi like *Kialoa IV.* I suppose my views hadn't changed much since we used to have intense debates at the Atkinson yard all those years ago about the relative merits of conventional single-hulled yachts – that is, with keels – versus unballasted multi-hulled craft. One of the boatbuilders, Ken, was a fanatical multihull man who used to describe yachts with keels as "lead mines" while I always thought of multihulls as not real ocean-going yachts.

Yet despite my views, the challenge of designing a big racing trimaran was irresistible, a commission Butch and I couldn't turn down. The prospect of helping create a multihull of this caliber was exciting enough, but

239

I had noticed that the French multihull fraternity was attracting deep-pocketed corporate sponsorship, and I saw this as a highly viable commercial model for other big racing boats.

I knew Rob very well. He and Naomi – actually Dame Naomi – lived near my studio in Currabinny. They regularly dropped by to see us and talk yachts. Having also raced the single-handed transatlantic event, Rob was recognized as one of Britain's most accomplished deep water sailors, while Naomi had achieved worldwide fame as the first woman to accomplish a single-handed, non-stop circumnavigation of the globe. I thought of Naomi's 272-day, 30,000-mile round trip as one of the greatest but unlikeliest voyages ever. Encouraged by Rob, a man she'd only just met but who saw the steel in her, she set off with no prior offshore experience. She didn't even know how to navigate, and for her first few months at sea she kept confusing latitude with longitude.

Despite being capsized, among other close calls, she managed to get her 53-footer around Cape Horn and all the way back to Dartmouth, England, to the boom of welcoming cannons and an audience with the Queen. So between them Rob and Naomi certainly had the credentials.

Compared with what they'd done, the Round Britain and Ireland Race was a mere jaunt of 2,000 miles, with four stops of 48 hours along the way. It was a double-handed event: all the yachts have a crew of just two, even the biggest ones. The race is held every four years, and I knew there would be some serious competition for Rob and Naomi in the 1982 version. We'd heard that a lot of multihulls – trimarans and catamarans – were being built for the race. And there'd be some rivalry in this race: Rob had won the last Round Britain with ex-British paratrooper Chay Blyth, who was mounting a separate challenge this time.

So we took on the challenge for the new 65-foot trimaran, motivated by our conviction that we could do better even though we had made our name in the completely different world of IOR racing. In my opinion the French multihulls raced by professional sailors had inefficient rigs: the masts were too short because of the fear of capsizing. For *Colt Cars GB*, as the trimaran would be named, I gave her what I considered a proper racing rig with a much taller mast, technically known as a seven-eighths rig, while increasing the volume of the outrigger hulls to reduce the risk of capsizing.

More radically, Butch, Rob and I agreed to give *Colt Cars GB* a deep retractable centerboard that we believed would make her much faster on what was multihulls' weakest point of sailing. "I want her to fly upwind," I told Rob. "We'll give Chay Blyth a fright." But how to design this radical

"For *Colt Cars* GB, as the trimaran would be named, I gave her what I considered a proper racing rig with a much taller mast, technically known as a seven-eighths rig, while increasing the volume of the outrigger hulls to reduce the risk of capsizing."

lightweight keel? Fortunately, living not too far from us in West Cork was Francis Costin, a structural engineer specializing in aircraft. So Butch and I went to see him and sought his expertise. A convivial person, Francis uncorked a large bottle of rum and we talked well into the night about lightweight but strong centerboards. By the time we'd emptied the bottle, Butch and I had learned a tremendous amount about structures and car racing that we took back to the Strand Farmhouse next day, nursing severe hangovers.

The construction design details for *Colt Cars GB* were entrusted to Cowes-based SP Systems, structural engineers and experts in the application of the new breed of composite materials such as Kevlar. We also suggested to Colt Cars managing director Michael Orr, who was bankrolling the project, that he should hire New Zealand boatbuilder Tim Gurr. A no-nonsense guy with experience in America's Cup yachts, Tim knew a lot about the intricacies of how composites should be used in hard-raced yachts. Michael agreed and Tim was flown into Cowes to set up the construction facility and get started.

Michael Orr was a dream sponsor. Determined to do the job properly he handed over a fat budget for Rob to manage, and even gave him a powerful Mitsubishi to drive around in Ireland. Too powerful, because Rob managed to do a 360-degree spin in it while driving my children, Kelly and Benna, to school on a wet morning. He returned to the studio in a shaken

▲

Colt Cars GB. The fastest trimaran, winning the 1983 Plymouth
to Vilamoura Race. With her deep
centerboard and high-aspect rig,
she was faster than a maxi racer
to windward. This was a new experience for multihull racing yachts.

state: "That car's just too uncontrollable," he announced. Michael didn't stint on the luxuries of life either. At Colt Cars headquarters, an elegant manor at Cirencester, west of London, lunch was always silver service. He also had at his command two aircraft; a Jet Ranger helicopter and a twin-engined King Air whose controls the pilot once handed to me on a flight back to Cirencester.

Rob was anxious to get sailing as soon as possible. At the age of 36, he liked nothing more than to get his teeth into a project, and would sometimes drop by on Sundays to discuss details of design and construction. Rob was much more than a client: he and Naomi often joined us for a beer in the pubs at Crosshaven, and as I got to know him we became close friends. As a veteran ocean racer he left nothing to chance. Like us, he was determined that *Colt Cars GB* would not only win the Round Britain but make the multihull fraternity sit up and take notice. During the entire design and construction phase we kept the boat's secrets to ourselves, especially the keel and rig.

Colt Cars GB was launched in late 1981 and more than justified our expectations. I first stepped aboard her after racing on *Kialoa IV*, and was amazed at her performance compared with the big maxi yacht which was over 20 feet longer. The tri accelerated like a rocket, and went upwind like a scalded cat thanks to our deep retractable centerboard. Despite giving away so much in length to *Kialoa*, she was even faster than the maxi close to the wind. Although I'd hoped for this, I was surprised.

In a hard and wild Round Britain Race *Colt Cars GB* shocked the rest of the field. With Rob and Naomi racing her to the limit, she beat Chay Blyth into second place and left the other multihulls well behind. When seasickness-prone Naomi stepped ashore at the finish in Plymouth, she vowed never to go ocean racing again. And who could blame her? Fast trimarans can be extremely uncomfortable.

But Michael had already set his sights higher. Now that his yacht had won the Round Britain, he wanted Rob to take on a bigger challenge, the Whitbread Round-The-World Race, in a single-hulled maxi yacht that would also be called *Colt Cars GB*. Hardly had Rob and Naomi tied up when Michael set things in motion, commissioning us to design the maxi for the next Whitbread in 1985 and establishing a boatbuilding facility near Plymouth in the west of England. I'd never seen Rob so excited by a project. Here was a chance to win the most prestigious ocean race in the world in a boat that he would skipper. But then fate intervened.

With a delivery crew of four, Rob was sailing the trimaran from Cowes to Salcombe, east of Plymouth, late in the season for an overhaul. As they approached the harbor around 5 AM, Rob went forward to drop the mainsail. The netting gave way and he fell straight through into the very cold water.

Despite the best efforts of the crew to haul him back aboard, it proved impossible. A racing trimaran is a notoriously difficult vessel to stop or even slow down, and *Colt Cars GB* kept on accelerating away every time they tried to secure Rob and haul him aboard. As the cold weakened him, Rob became unable to help in his own rescue and eventually, unconscious, he drifted away.

I got a call later that day – March 22, 1983 – with the terrible news. I shall never forget that call. It was the first time a close friend had died at sea. Our studio grieved not only for Rob, who was almost like one of our team, but for pregnant Naomi. They were one of the happiest couples I had ever met.

Rob's death knocked the enthusiasm out of Michael Orr, a warm-hearted man. If Rob couldn't run the Whitbread project, he wasn't interested. He canceled the entire program even though the boat was almost finished.

For months afterwards, there was a sadness at Currabinny. The office wasn't quite the same without Rob's irrepressible enthusiasm. A grieving Naomi, who gave birth two weeks after the drowning, was far too upset to visit us, and we understood why. Rob had spent so much time at our studio that the place would only have reminded her of how much she'd lost. The memories were too raw.

I never lost my skepticism about these big trimarans which were still capsizing and breaking up during big offshore races, and I didn't want to do any more. They were just too scary. I wasn't happy about risking our design studio's reputation which had been built on single-hulled yachts. So we retired from multihulls while, you might say, we were still winning.

Personally this was a hard time because my father died a few months later. Mum still lived on Auckland's North Shore where Philip and I had both grown up, and I often thought back to all the work Dad and Mum had put in at the Torbay Boating Club, purely to provide a healthy interest for their sons. But life had to go on.

▲

Rob and Naomi testing their new
65-foot trimaran *Colt Cars GB*.
A very fast 65-foot yacht that was
not easy to sail with two people,
but they won races with her.

Our clients wanted larger yachts.
At over 100 feet in length, I thought
Whirlwind XII was the ultimate
design challenge, but in the 1990s
sailing yachts kept getting bigger!

A whirlwind experience

I KNEW OF NOEL LISTER BY REPUTATION before he turned up at the studio. Just about everybody in sailing, particularly British sailing, knew of him.

By the early 1980s he and his wife Sylvia had owned no fewer than eleven yachts of ever-increasing size, all of them named *Whirlwind*. The Listers were renowned for their love of cruising and playing golf in exotic locations. With their children and friends they had crossed all the world's oceans, their current boat being a Swan 76-footer from the drawing board of Sparkman & Stephens and built by Nautor of Finland. The Listers had certainly gotten their money's worth from that particular *Whirlwind*, cruising her all the way from Britain into the Pacific as far as Tahiti.

Noel was much more than an ocean voyaging yachtsman. For him sailing was a part-time activity that he sandwiched in between an exceptionally hectic business life. He was an entrepreneur who had jointly founded and developed one of Britain's biggest companies, the MFI furniture chain, which had revolutionized interior décor across the U.K. with its flat-pack, home-assembled products. I once read that so popular was MFI furniture that six out of ten British children were conceived in its bedroom suites. In the early 1980s his company was just 15 years old but profits were heading upwards of £40 million, and Noel had decided he had sufficient spare cash to put a large chunk of it into yet another *Whirlwind*.

In sailing, as in life, this was a man in a hurry, which suited me perfectly. Even if some of my clients didn't care much about fast cruising, I did.

247

"All things being equal, fast boats are safer boats because their speed means they can stay out of trouble, keeping away from bad weather systems. It's a point I've often hammered home. A yacht able to sail at ten knots or faster can generally avoid bad weather, and is certainly more likely to do so than a slow cruiser."

All things being equal, fast boats are safer boats because their speed means they can stay out of trouble, keeping away from bad weather systems. It's a point I've often hammered home. A yacht able to sail at ten knots or faster can generally avoid bad weather, and is certainly more likely to do so than a slow cruiser.

As well as owning the 76-foot *Whirlwind*, Noel had acquired *Imp*, probably the most famous racing yacht I had ever designed. He used her for adrenalin-boosting entertainment when he was in England in between his long distance voyaging, and was apparently sufficiently impressed with *Imp*'s performance to approach us for his new boat. He was also influenced by the success of *Kialoa IV*, which you might describe as a bigger *Imp*.

Ron Holland Design now consisted of twelve staff. After nearly 20 years at Currabinny we'd moved the office to Kinsale, partly because a house I had long coveted came up for sale on the nearby Bandon River and I grabbed it.

One of Ireland's most picturesque villages, Kinsale also had the added attraction of being a local sailing hub. Geographically it wasn't a big move – Kinsale is just 20 minutes by car from Currabinny – but it marked a change in my life.

Joanna and I felt the shift would give us a good start. Although Joanna was only 21 years old when we married, she was commercially astute far beyond her years, much more of a natural business thinker than I was.

I was basically besotted with boats and sailing and never really thought of myself as a businessman. As time went on, I was taking more and more of her advice.

Noel and Sylvia flew over to Kinsale, where we discussed the broad concept of the new *Whirlwind*. In principle at least Noel's brief was simple: he wanted a fast cruising yacht that would circumnavigate the globe. A former army officer raised in India, Noel held a world view when it came to sailing, and Sylvia, who was always up for an adventure, clearly felt the same. A circumnavigation! An exciting change from our racing yachts, I thought. "What length are you thinking?" I asked. "At least a hundred feet," he said.

Wow! My brain went into overdrive. In the early 1980s nobody was building, let alone designing, 100-footers. To the best of my knowledge, only one sailing yacht of around that length had been launched in the past 20 years: a 120-foot steel ketch built in Germany to a Dutch design, she was a very different boat from the one Noel was proposing, with nothing special about her. If we could pull off this project, the new *Whirlwind* would become one of the biggest sailboats since the America's Cup J-Class yachts of the 1930s.

When I broke the news to Butch, his typically low-key reaction was: "Things just keep getting more exciting around here. We won the Quarter Ton Cup, won the Half Ton Cup, produced winning Admiral's Cup designs, got the commission for Ted Heath's new *Morning Cloud*, then we did *Kialoa* and *Condor* (another maxi), and now we've bagged a 100-footer? OK."

Exciting as the commission was, I could foresee plenty of problems. There were practically no books or research available to the yachting industry that would help us create a high-performance, sail-powered craft of this magnitude. Winches, masts and spars, running rigging, sails, hydraulics to power them all: none of these had even been invented for a 100-footer. No amount of human muscle could handle a boat of these dimensions without hydraulic power. So pretty much everything would have to be custom designed and manufactured. Butch and I made some back-of-the-envelope calculations and immediately saw that the stresses and strains on such a yacht could not be contained unless the industry raised its game several notches and developed equipment capable of doing the job.

But Noel wasn't finished. During discussions that sometimes took place over a game of golf at Bandon Golf Club, Noel being proficient and me hacking away as you'd expect from somebody who only played once every second year or so, he stipulated that this particular *Whirlwind* must be sailed by a small professional crew.

▲

After moving the design studio to Kinsale, I purchased Rock Castle on the Bandon River. Here with Aisli and Nikki, enjoying rowing lessons off the boathouse. Getting ready for bigger things.

▲

The J-Class yacht *Endeavour* visits Kinsale: Aisli and Nikki on the wheel. This was special. When I was a kid sailing off Torbay I could never have imagined one day to be sailing aboard *Endeavour*.

"How small?" I asked, expecting him to say anything from six to ten. By general agreement even a 60-footer needed a crew of at least six brawny individuals, and preferably eight, for serious offshore voyaging.

"Four," he said.

I nearly dropped my club. "Four?"

"Yes, including the cook."

I was starting to feel sorry for the cook. She (or he) would have to be extremely versatile, probably spending as much time on deck hauling sails and grinding winches as preparing food in the galley. A crew of four!

The implications for sailing one of the world's biggest sailboats with such limited manpower were many. In practically every activity – anchoring, mooring, hoisting, reefing and trimming the sails, among scores of other essential tasks such as keeping the yacht tidy and maintaining all her systems – a four-man professional crew would have to function pretty much flawlessly to get the job done. That was assuming the industry could come up with the technology. I tried to reason with Noel, but he wouldn't budge. His 100-footer would be crewed by four and no more.

Next came the issue of what yard would be prepared to take on the construction of a 100-foot aluminum sailing yacht. Because cost is a major consideration this is always the owner's decision, but I still felt entitled to make a suggestion.

"We should at least consider Wolter Huisman's yard in Vollenhove, or Jongert, both in Holland," I said. "They would be the best for aluminum. And Wolter Huisman has been building yachts in aluminum for a long time." Jongert had just built their first aluminum yacht to my design, a 73-footer, but Huisman's longer experience with the material was in their favor.

Boatbuilding was in the Huisman family's blood. Wolter was the nephew of the founder, Jan Huisman, who had established the yard in 1884, exactly 100 years ago at that time. Originally located in the lowlands beside the Zuider Zee, the yard specialized from the very beginning in small wooden yachts, fishing boats and general working craft. Like many Dutch companies the family was deeply involved, with Wolter's wife Ali and his three daughters all holding important roles.

Wolter wasn't a man to stand still, and convinced that aluminum would become the material of choice over wood and steel at least in Holland, he had gone to night school to study how it should be done. He must have been a fast learner because by the mid-1970s, just as my design studio was getting established in Ireland, the yard was building the 65-foot *Flyer* in which Connie von Rietschoten would win the 1977-78 Whitbread Round-

"'How small?' I asked, expecting him to say anything from six to ten. By general agreement even a 60-footer needed a crew of at least six brawny individuals, and preferably eight, for serious offshore voyaging. 'Four,' he said. I nearly dropped my club. 'Four?' 'Yes, including the cook.' I was starting to feel sorry for the cook."

The-World Race. A few years later the Huisman yard followed that up with the 76-foot *Flyer II* in which Connie repeated the feat in 1981.

Just as Noel was searching for a boatyard that could build his 100-footer, Huisman was changing direction again. Wolter had discerned the dawn of a new era. Having created his reputation with racing yachts, he'd started taking on commissions for bigger, luxurious boats that would be used for leisure. Although more intricate because of their beautiful interiors, these projects were also more lucrative.

The chain-smoking Wolter was Dutch through and through. He was thorough, highly organized and direct. If he didn't like a client's suggestion, he didn't hesitate to say so. I'd worked with him for years on various IOR racing projects, including the construction of one of my 50-footers. Called *Midnight Sun*, she was a big yacht for her day and the yard had done a great job. Right then *Volador*, a luxury 76-footer from the drawing board of Argentinian designer German Frers, was taking shape at Huisman, and Noel decided to visit Vollenhove to see for himself. He came away sufficiently impressed that Huisman could stretch things a bit – well, a lot – for his dream boat and signed the yard up, much to our relief. Although Noel and I had also visited Jongert, the other Dutch builder I had recommended, we both believed Huisman was the place for this very big fast cruising sailboat.

At that stage we'd finished the basic design work and had enough data for Huisman to start cutting metal, a four-month job that was the first

▲

At 50 feet in length *Midnight Sun* was a big commission for our studio, and our first design built by Wolter Huisman for Swedish yachtsman Jan Pehrsson.

step in the building program. Around the same time Noel contracted another Dutchman, Peter Sijm, to take care of the interior and overall styling. Peter normally did most of his work with the family-owned Jongert group, but Noel happened to like his sense of aesthetics. So Peter temporarily jumped ships.

As project manager and point man Noel engaged a German yachtsman, Jens Cornelsen, because he was too busy running MFI to supervise all of it himself. He already had the skipper lined up, a highly respected Aussie named Mike Koppstein who'd been involved in building and racing an 82-foot maxi called *Nirvana*. As Mike told me later, he also was relieved that Huisman had gotten the construction contract, partly because of the complex control systems that would need to be developed. He knew how tough it would be to sail a yacht that was 21 feet longer than *Nirvana*, but with 24 fewer crew! Now that everybody was on board, *Whirlwind XII* could get started. Incidentally, she had now grown to 103 feet.

When the news got out about the yacht, the reaction varied between disbelief, skepticism and even hostility. A 103-foot family cruising sailing yacht! Because the loads on a yacht increase exponentially with size rather than linearly, many waterfront sages were convinced that she just wouldn't work. As America's Cup enthusiasts know, the old J-Class yachts needed over 30 crew, and that was just for inshore racing.

The mast – over 100 feet in length for a small-crewed 103-footer – would fall down, people said. She would break in half under the enormous loads required to keep the rig in the boat. It would be impossible to control the sails – and so on. And only four professional crew! Ridiculous!

Ignoring the critics, we got on with the job. I could see their point but we'd pushed the envelope for years and we believed we could do it again. We did have the maxis as a starting point. Essentially we gave *Whirlwind* a hull similar in shape to that we'd used for the maxis, while making it bigger to accommodate all the weight that a circumnavigating 100-plus-footer would need in the form of fuel, water, stores and spares, not to mention an intricately detailed interior that Peter Sijm was already working on.

One of the biggest headaches was the shrunken size of the crew. Although there were existing hydraulically-driven sail furling systems, there was nothing on the market powerful enough to do the job with a yacht this big, with just four crew on deck including the chef. Whenever we raised concerns, which we did over many dinner discussions, about how so few people were expected to handle so much sail, Noel just batted them away. "It's going to be four and that's it," he said.

Early on it was agreed the only way to furl the mainsail was to roll it

▲

Sailing trials aboard my first Huisman-built design, the 50-foot racing yacht *Midnight Sun*. Standing by, ready to take over from Wolter Huisman. Yachting fashion was different in "the old days."

"And then we came to the sails. *Whirlwind*'s wardrobe would be gigantic, the biggest in the world. The loads would be through the roof. A maxi racing yacht applied loads on the jib sheets of over a ton, but this yacht would have to handle loads approaching three tons."

straight into the mast. Known as an in-mast furling system, this wasn't entirely new, but nothing had been attempted on this scale. There were a lot of genuine worries: for instance would the sail be twisted out of shape and jam as it rolled into the stick? Similarly, the giant headsails would have to roll up. To do all this, the crew would need push-button power winches in every available place. That meant hydraulic power packs of a magnitude and efficiency that was then off the scale. How much oil would they need, how much water cooling, and how much electricity? Where would all this technology come from? Somewhere during these discussions Noel threw another curveball. His 103-footer would have to complete a tack in forty seconds. Forty seconds! Even nowadays that's no easy task.

As Mike recalls, "That simple maneuver would require the runners, lazy and loaded jib sheets, the headsail furlers and the mainsheet to all run at the same time. And I might add Noel wanted all this to happen with a 24-volt DC battery bank." I was beginning to see why Noel was such a successful businessman: in his eyes practically nothing was impossible. To put it another way, the only answer he liked was yes. You couldn't help but admire his convictions.

And then we came to the sails. *Whirlwind*'s wardrobe would be gigantic, the biggest in the world. The loads would be through the roof. A maxi racing yacht applied loads on the jib sheets of over a ton, but this yacht would have to handle loads approaching three tons. Fortunately, English sailmaker John Channon from Hood Sails came to the rescue. At a factory in West Cork, not too far from us, he was working with new ultra-strong materials that we thought just might do the job. So Hood got the commission to build this enormous wardrobe.

As for the in-mast furling and associated equipment, eventually Wolter took it all on himself through an equipment company called Rondal that he'd recently established. Soon he would come up with the biggest hydraulic furling systems ever seen to that date.

Early on in the planning Noel and I discussed the vital component of the keel. For our 80-foot racing yachts we'd learned that a keel depth of 13 feet was about right to keep the yacht sailing at the most efficient angle and reduce its leeway, the sideways movement of a sailboat. A deeper keel would be better for bigger sailing yachts so we made our calculations and suggested a draft of at least 20 feet.

"No," said Noel. "I want to be able to anchor in harbors that might have shallow bottoms. And I will definitely want to drop the hook close to the beach."

"You mean close to the first tee," I joked.

"I don't want the draft to be any deeper than your maxis," Noel decreed.

Reluctantly I agreed, and over my initial misgivings I designed a 13-foot-deep keel. Wolter suggested we try a keel design by his friend Henry Scheel. This concentrated the lead weight close to the bottom of the keel, but also located the sailing balance differently than my keel design. Later, after sailing observations, *Whirlwind*'s keel would be improved with more lead ballast and fitted with aircraft-like winglets that improved the shallow keel's windward sailing performance. These wing appendages not only reduced her leeway but also made her more balanced on the helm. As the speed increased, she could be controlled with less rudder angle.

Fortunately, a new era was at hand in the form of computer-aided design, known as CAD. If the hulls of great yachts were transparent, people would be stunned by the detail, complexity and intricacy of the aluminum structure and what a hull conceals: wires, pipes and ducting running around the inside, all of it essential to the yacht's performance. The detail was so great that it was just about impossible to do it all by pen and paper. So at the suggestion of one of my most high profile clients, Volvo boss Pehr Gyllenhammer, we turned to the American Intergraph Corporation.

Founded 12 years earlier by a group of IBM engineers who had developed guidance and navigation software for the Saturn moon shot, Intergraph created a system of design graphics that allowed us to "see" what was happening on screen. As well as by NASA, the system was being used by construction giant Bechtel for complex projects, as well as other heavy-weight clients including Porsche and the U.S. Navy. CAD quickly became invaluable for us and for everybody involved in the creation of this new generation of very big yachts.

In the middle of all this I was coincidentally invited to talk with Nautor, builder of Noel's current *Whirlwind*, about a production version of *Imp,* the yacht that had gotten Noel interested in our studio in the first place.

The meeting was to take place at Porto Cervo in Sardinia, where the Finnish company was staging one of its regattas. For me the starting point was to be Monaco, where I met up with two of Swan's most successful agents, Mike Hurrell, who was selling my designs in Italy, Monaco and France, and Dave Johnson from Swan's U.K. agency. Both racing yachts-men, they had been making frequent mention to Nautor of how yachts that win races boost the sales of their production versions, and they wanted me to come along to hammer home the point to the Nautor managers. So this looked like an exciting opportunity.

When I arrived in Monaco it was too late to set out aboard Mike's high-powered motorboat, so we ended up drinking and dancing at the Siesta nightclub on the beach near Antibes. Next morning, somewhat the worse for wear, we clambered into Mike's rocket-ship and fueled up for a high-speed trip past Corsica to Porto Cervo on Sardinia. We embarked on what we estimated would be a six or seven hour trip. But three hours later, the mountains of Corsica weren't even on the horizon.

How could this be? We'd been flying along at 30 knots, hair streaming in the wind. All experienced yachtsmen, we finally decided to do what we should have done in the first place: namely, consult the chart. Remember, this was in the days before GPS.

So we unfolded the map to see exactly where we were, but just when we were about to pinpoint our position, the wind whipped the chart over the side. Mike, who was at the wheel, turned back to retrieve it before it sank forever below the surface of the Mediterranean. But by the time we'd fished the chart out of the water, it was so soaked we had to spread it out in the cockpit to dry.

Now we were late and Mike gunned the motor again, maintaining our original course.

After a while I took another look at the chart. "Mike, we're heading in the wrong direction," I yelled.

"Which way?" he replied. I pointed in the general direction of where Corsica should have appeared. Mike spun the wheel and we shot off once again. An hour later, still no Corsica. No land in sight anywhere.

"We're lost," somebody admitted.

This was embarrassing to put it mildly. Fortunately we spotted a small sailboat heading in exactly the opposite direction to ours and, swallowing our pride, we headed over to ask for help. To our surprise the yacht had several naked people aboard – a teenage daughter, Mum, Dad, and Grandma. They didn't seem in the least embarrassed as we approached.

"*Où est Corse*?" Mike yelled in his best French.

They pointed 90 degrees to the direction we'd been heading at 30 knots. We could hardly have been more wrong. Red-faced, we fired up the motorboat again and soon left the sun-worshippers in our wake. But we had lost hours, and we had to navigate the Strait of Bonifacio, and the treacherous northwest coast of Sardinia with its jagged rocks, in almost complete darkness.

When we finally made the narrow entrance of Porto Cervo harbor, hungry and thirsty, we were each met with a much-appreciated bottle of Peroni beer.

"Where have you been?" asked our perplexed host, John Griffis, one of the Aga Khan's architects for the original Porto Cervo development, which had become one of the most exclusive locations in the world, especially if you owned a yacht. I had been first in Porto Cervo in 1973, racing aboard *Ganbare* with Doug Peterson, before the location became fashionable.

There was no way out of it. We had to explain that we highly experienced yachtsmen had gotten ourselves completely lost in a fizz boat, almost as soon as we'd left sight of land. The story quickly traveled all around Porto Cervo.

Meantime, after two years in construction *Whirlwind XII* was launched into the canal alongside the Huisman boatyard. We were all on board: Noel and Sylvia, Wolter puffing at his powerful European cigarettes, Mike, Jens and myself – all the people who'd put so much into this yacht.

Under engine the yacht motored down the channel and into the Ijsselmeer, a protected stretch of water that was originally farmland, for her first acquaintance with the Dutch-created artificial sea. Hardly an hour into a test of her sailing systems, somebody asked, "What about the spinnaker?"

We all looked at each other. The biggest spinnaker on the planet, it would have to be run up a 120-foot mast by a newly-hired crew who, although highly experienced, had never previously stepped aboard a yacht of this size. Sorely tempted to try it, we reasoned that the wind was light, blowing across the Ijsselmeer at around ten knots. It was Noel's decision. "Let's do it!" he said.

▲

Whirlwind XII and the world's biggest spinnaker. After procrastinating for over a year after the keel was laid, Noel decided to purchase the spinnaker. The first of day sailing we all agreed it must be set!

Captain Mike, project manager Jens, sailmaker John Channon, myself and everybody else jumped to it. With some trepidation and much enthusiasm, we hoisted the enormous sail and it filled with wind. Within seconds the mighty yacht sprang forward under a power that none of us had ever experienced in such light winds. There was a mighty cheer from all on board, including our happy client, as much from relief as from joy. It was a great moment and one I've always cherished. *Whirlwind XII* turned out to be a defining commission for us.

Within a few months of her launch, which was celebrated by photos in yachting publications all around the world, our studio fielded orders for three new yachts of over 100 feet in length, including *Gleam* for Texas yachtsman Tom Taylor, *Garuda* for Franz Burda of the German publishing house, and *Ladyhawke* for Californian owner Pascal Mahvi. These beautiful superyachts were under construction in New Zealand, France and Finland. All of them inherited what we'd learned from *Whirlwind* and our racing yachts, going right back to *Eygthene*. I believed that if done right, racing boat technology could have a profound and positive influence on cruising sailing yachts.

As for the Listers, they would eventually complete not one but two circumnavigations of the globe over a ten-year period, more than 75,000 miles. Mike skippered *Whirlwind* to the ends of the earth. In trade wind conditions she would fly along covering up to 300 miles a day on average. And she never let anybody down, not once missing through breakage any of the schedules that Noel liked to plan a year in advance. And, as Mike remembers, "She was easily sailed with a crew of four."

▶

Whirlwind XII racing in the Nantucket Bucket. The first of a new generation of large private sailing yachts: pushing the boundaries, she was over 100 feet in length yet carried only four permanent crew.

In the Roaring Forties, deep in the Southern Ocean, you are seriously relying on the integrity of your yacht's design and construction and the skill of the crew, especially the skill of the helmsman. Here *Drum* is surfing down a giant wave – a long way from any help if you need it.

The missing keel

LEADING UP TO THE 1985/86 WHITBREAD RACE, the success of *Kialoa IV* led to a string of maxi commissions. Within a year the studio was busy designing and supervising three new IOR ocean racing yachts of around 80 feet, as the word got around that we were developing a special expertise in IOR maxis. Although Jim Kilroy had no intention of mounting a Whitbread campaign – his commercial real estate business in Los Angeles kept him too busy to take out the full year that it would require – he was winning a lot of races including the World Ocean Racing Championship, often in the kind of conditions that round-the-world yachts had to endure day after day.

In consecutive order we received commissions from British insurance magnate Bob Bell, from a New Zealand organization which made it clear it intended to win the Whitbread, from the Colt Cars company, and from an experienced Detroit yachtsman. After Rob James died and Colt Cars canceled its Whitbread project, to my relief and pleasure Michael Orr's round-the-world project was revived, albeit in a different form and in a highly unexpected way. Simon Le Bon, lead singer in rock band Duran Duran, and his managers, Paul and Simon Berrow, bought the unfinished hull. Despite a busy touring schedule, Le Bon was prepared to step off the stage for a year, much to the annoyance of some of the others in the group who thought the Whitbread was a crazy and dangerous event, and couldn't understand why their lead singer wouldn't be available for a year's gigs.

261

"The Fastnet started in moderate conditions, and with Phil on the helm and most of the crew on deck, *Drum* soon found herself at the head of the entire fleet under full sail. Although it was early days in the proceedings, Simon Le Bon and the rest of the crew must have begun to hope for a famous victory."

Now in the construction phase, so far *Colt Cars GB* had been built using unusual and even radical methods compared with our earlier maxis, before work had stopped and the entire project stalled. The materials basically came from the aviation industry, the same ones that Boeing was employing in its latest 767 commercial aircraft. We were looking for the lightest possible yacht but without sacrificing any strength. Our brains trust, including the much-missed Rob James, had carefully considered all the implications and decided that these materials justified the risks, although we didn't see the latter as being particularly high.

The new maxi wasn't being built by an established yard but by a team originally put together by Michael Orr and Rob James near an assembly line for Mitsubishi vans in Cornwall, near Plymouth. Mainly because Rob had been the original project manager our studio had always enjoyed a good relationship with the builders, and we had every confidence that *Colt Cars GB* was being constructed exactly along the agreed lines. In short, she would be bulletproof. But when the new owners took over the project, their new project manager made it clear he would finish the boat their way, and we were excluded from the rest of the construction project. I couldn't help but be concerned in case the hull failed to meet our original criteria for integrity and robustness. After all, the yacht – to be renamed *Drum* – still bore the Ron Holland imprint and everybody knew it. But we'd been sidelined and there was nothing we could do about it.

It was some comfort that Phil was invited to be involved as a member of the crew that was being put together by veteran American ocean racer Skip Novak. Since his initiation into ocean crossings so many years ago, my brother had become a highly experienced deep water sailor – one of the best – and his feedback would be useful before *Drum* was put to the test in the rigors of the Whitbread. The maxi's warm-up racing was to be Cowes Maxi Racing Week, the first time a maxi series had been staged in England. This would culminate in the 600-mile Fastnet Race, an event which most of the Round-The-World Race crews were using as an opening act for the real thing.

The Fastnet started in moderate conditions, and with Phil on the helm and most of the crew on deck, *Drum* soon found herself at the head of the entire fleet under full sail. Although it was early days in the proceedings, Simon Le Bon and the rest of the crew must have begun to hope for a famous victory. Then, without warning, there was a loud bang.

The steering went soft in Phil's hands and the 25-ton yacht veered wildly out of control. Phil fought violently to bring her back on track, but the wheel just turned uselessly. Next, a second loud bang rang right through the boat, followed seconds later by another even bigger one. To my brother's dismay, *Drum* rounded right up into the wind, sails flapping, and rolled over on her side, her mast and sails hitting the water. It all happened within seconds.

Caught completely unaware, the crew trimming the genoa on the leeward rail were dumped into an cold English Channel. The rest followed immediately afterwards, falling into the water straight off the deck and crashing past winches, ropes and lifelines. Within moments, *Drum* had capsized on top of all of them.

Phil's childhood training clicked in. Remembering what he'd been taught in the little P Class dinghies back at the Torbay Boating Club, he managed to scramble out of the cockpit and scurry up the side of the hull as it turned turtle, while holding onto the mainsheet. He clambered into a precarious position sitting on top of the boat where he hung grimly onto the rudder, which was flapping in the breeze. He didn't even get his feet wet.

Looking around, Phil saw immediately why *Drum* had overturned. The entire keel was missing, shorn clean off the hull. He faced a full-scale emergency. He was the only one up on the boat: most of the crew were floundering around in the water in heavy oilskins, struggling to keep their heads above water. With so many ropes, rigging and sails sloshing around in choppy seas, there was a serious danger they could be tangled up in them and drowned.

▲

Duran Duran are playing in Vancouver during their Paper Gods Tour 2017, so I invite Simon to come sailing. He has not lost his touch on the helm sailing to windward. Band members Anna Ross and Erin Stevenson show appreciation for a day on the water.

Thinking fast, Phil threw the mainsheet over the side – it had become a lifeline – and using all his strength, half-dragged, half-hauled a crew-member all the way up and onto the upturned hull. With two aboard it became easier, and between them they dragged the other guys, one by one, onto the precarious safety of the upside-down hull.

But the rest of the crew were still trapped inside. Six men including Simon Le Bon were caught in a cabin half full of water, like a dark cave. Any exits were blocked by loose sails, ropes and other gear that were floating freely. Already, one man had nearly drowned. Knocked unconscious by a heavy sailbag that had crashed on top of him and pinned him to the cabin roof, which was now the bottom of the yacht, he'd only been saved by a quick-thinking mate who had dived down and dragged him free.

But now there was the grave danger that the yacht would sink and take them down with her. Because they'd been lying in their bunks when the boat rolled, most of them were wearing light clothing and began to suffer from hypothermia. Breathing became difficult as the air condition deteriorated, and acid began to leak from the batteries, burning their skins. They were only able to communicate their plight from the heads, shouting through tubes leading to the outside of the hull. But to the frustration of the rest of the crew up top, there was no way of extricating their six mates. The only exit was through hatches, and these were deep under water. The danger was mounting by the minute.

It was the air-sea rescue services that saved the day. By a stroke of luck, an off-duty member of Her Majesty's Coastguard had been watching *Drum* through binoculars from the top of a cliff in Devon. To his amazement, one minute she was sailing majestically down the Channel ahead of the Fastnet fleet, and the next minute she'd all but disappeared. It was only when the bottom of her hull appeared on the surface that he realized what had happened, and he immediately called in the rescue.

It came in the nick of time. The air down below had turned nearly poisonous when the Royal Navy chopper turned up. A diver swam inside the upturned hull and took stock of the situation: "You've all got to get out of here urgently," he yelled.

But with all kinds of flotsam blocking the exit, he first had to clear a passage. Even so, Simon Le Bon nearly drowned. As he was trying to swim clear, his clothing got caught in the rigging and he had to fight his way out, eventually breaking the surface wearing only his underpants, fighting for breath.

Once safely aboard a lifeboat, the crew were dropped off at the nearest accommodation, the Falmouth Hotel in Cornwall. Here they proceeded

Drum capsized

I first saw *Drum* capsized from Johnny McWilliams' Piper twin-engine plane as we arrived over the English Channel after flying across from Ireland. It was a shocking sight to me. When we arrived the *Drum* crew had already been rescued by Royal Navy divers and the lifeboat crew, and were on their way to the Falmouth Hotel. It's very lucky everyone aboard was still alive.

Brother Phil was the first crew member to clamber up on to the top of the upturned hull, with the only dry pack of cigarettes among the crew.

This photo was taken from the Swedish Admiral's Cup yacht *Carat*, the first yacht to arrive at *Drum* after the capsize.

▲

David Barker painting of the IOR maxi yacht *Drum*. She completed the 1989/90 Whitbread Round The World Race in third place.Her crew included owners Simon Le Bon and Paul and Michael Berrow.

to drink the bar dry to the amazement of the mainly elderly guests, while reporters, having been alerted by radio, gathered outside. The dramatic headlines in the next day's newspapers were predictable: Simon Le Bon's involvement in the Whitbread had attracted a much wider interest in the race than ever before.

I received a call – I can't remember from whom – back in our holiday home in West Cork, the now restored cottage that Laurel and I had bought from Dinny McCarthy, it seemed so many years earlier. From the nearby shore I was planning to watch my yachts turn around the Rock. I was shocked to learn that *Drum* wouldn't be among them.

Drum had capsized! It seemed utterly impossible.

Worried for Phil and the rest of the crew, I hastily called Johnny Mac and asked him to fly me to the scene. I raced back to Crosshaven in the car and we took off in Johnny's new twin-engined Piper aircraft. Two hours later, after crossing the Irish Sea and Cornwall, we buzzed over the abandoned hull. Looking down, it was even more of a shock to see a beautiful yacht, one I still saw as very much Rob's project, floating upside down without her keel.

"How can that happen?" Johnny Mac yelled to me.

I didn't have the faintest idea. Although we'd had no role in the completion of *Drum*, and some of the techniques used in her lightweight construction were different from our earlier maxis, we'd never wavered from the specifications laid down for the way the keel is attached to the hull, perhaps the most critical aspect of the entire construction process. *Kialoa, Condor* and the others had been raced hard for many hundreds of miles without any problems – and *Drum*'s keel was basically designed to the same well-proven standards as theirs.

The official explanation for *Drum*'s capsize emerged soon enough in the inevitable inquest. But long before I gave evidence, I knew what the problem was. After *Drum* was lifted out of the water I had gone immediately to inspect her. I was shocked when I looked at what was left of the keel, still bolted to the hull. The welding of the top plate of the keel, which connected it to the rest of the yacht, looked as though it had been done in the rain, so porous was it. I could even see air bubbles throughout the weld beading. This weld was an absolutely critical element in the whole design. Bolted to the bottom of the hull, the plate totally supports the keel skin and internal frames.

How had this gone undetected? Once again, it was a lesson about how every step in the creation of a yacht, especially a racing one, where safety margins are reduced to a minimum to save weight, must be conducted

"The official explanation for *Drum's* capsize emerged soon enough in the inevitable inquest. But long before I gave evidence, I knew what the problem was. After *Drum* was lifted out of the water I had gone immediately to inspect her. I was shocked when I looked at what was left of the keel, still bolted to the hull."

with the integrity, demanded by reason, that lives can be put at risk. This is especially true of the construction process, as I'd already learned to my cost: another design of mine, a 77-footer named *Charley*, commissioned by one of the pioneers of electronic games, Nolan Bushnell of Atari, had lost her keel while returning from her victory in the Transpac Race between Los Angles and Honolulu. The keel had not been attached using my well-tested standard design details. The boat was designed as a "sled", a downwind machine made especially for the race to Honolulu with a minimum of form stability, but miraculously she didn't capsize when the keel separated. Her very competent captain and delivery crew kept *Charley* upright and nursed her safely back to Honolulu, so fortunately there was no loss of life in this incident either, but I worried that one day somebody's luck was going to run out.

The insurance company involved was suing everyone connected to the design and construction of *Drum*, so Butch and I had to defend our position in the one and only time Ron Holland Design appeared in the courts. The case, which took place in central London, turned into a shouting match with lawyers trying to score points off each other. At least I could face them in total confidence that we were in the clear.

Knowing we would be subjected to an interrogation I had sent our drawings, calculations and specifications to Wolter Huisman. Long acknowledged as the world leader in aluminum construction, Wolter took

▲

Californian serial entrepreneur
Nolan Bushnell commissioned me
to design *Charley* to win the Los
Angeles to Honolulu TransPac
Race. A new design approach was
required, a design that could get
to Honolulu fast enough to finish
first across the line, but could
also win the race on handicap. A
target not often achieved .

a hard look at the documents and reassured us that we had built in more than enough of a safety margin. His judgment gave me a lot of comfort. Still, lawyers being lawyers, it took over £30,000 in legal fees to clear our name and reputation. I came away knowing we'd won, but feeling we'd lost.

Rebuilt and repaired, *Drum* was ready in time for the 1985/86 Whitbread, but only after I insisted that fully qualified welders were employed to build a new keel. With Phil jumping aboard for just one leg, from Cape Town to Auckland through the icebergs of the Southern Ocean, she finished a highly creditable third. Although the bottom of the hull needed strengthening at Cape Town, making her a little heavier and slower, *Drum* came through the rigors of the Whitbread without any more dramas. After the fiasco of the lost keel, I was relieved and pleased.

Our studio had another maxi in this Whitbread Race. We'd been given the commission for *Lion New Zealand,* which would be skippered by the legendary Peter Blake, a veteran of round-the-world races and a star of deep water sailing. Not only was the yacht sponsored by New Zealand's biggest brewery, she bore the hopes and ambitions of a sailing-crazed and deeply patriotic nation. If this wasn't responsibility enough for our studio, we'd been told in no uncertain terms that "This yacht must not break."

Burned into Peter Blake's memory – and that of half the nation – was his failure, at least in New Zealand's eyes, in the previous Whitbread Race. Driven to the limit by her hard-charging crew, the Blake-skippered *Ceramco* finished second overall, but could have won if her mast hadn't collapsed during the first leg to Cape Town. She'd limped across the line under a hastily improvised jury rig: this was a misfortune which must not happen again, as the boss of the campaign, businessman Sir Tom Clark, often reminded us and everybody else involved in our project, including Tim Gurr who was heading up the construction team.

The conflict between safety and speed presents a yacht designer with a constant dilemma. Obviously, I didn't want my Whitbread designs breaking under the extreme conditions of a race in which the yachts are flogged day and night through the world's stormiest and most remote regions. But there's another side of the coin: the yacht is expected to win as well as survive the worst that the oceans can throw at her. Thus the two essential requirements of *Lion New Zealand*, like any racing yacht, were intrinsically antagonistic. *Lion New Zealand* wouldn't be fast enough if she were built heavier than her competitors, but she also had to get around the course, and Whitbread yachts often suffered damage. You can't win if you don't finish. This is a dilemma that I was very conscious of. Winning is nice, but finishing with everyone alive is better.

"Despite being overweight, *Lion New Zealand* started her racing life impressively by winning the 1984 Sydney-Hobart by a street. The victory made the headlines in New Zealand, with the newspapers and television running pictures of the metallic gray-hulled 78-footer flying up the Derwent to the finishing line."

As the boat took shape I regularly visited Auckland to check on her construction, and was impressed with the integrity of the build. This yacht certainly wasn't going to break.

But when *Lion New Zealand* was launched in Auckland with considerable fanfare at a public ceremony, I became a little concerned. Even before the rig and the rest of the hardware was installed, I could see she was floating lower in the water than I'd expected. By then it was too late. There was nothing that could be done except pray for heavy weather in the Whitbread.

Despite being overweight, *Lion New Zealand* started her racing life impressively by winning the 1984 Sydney-Hobart by a street. The victory made the headlines in New Zealand, with the newspapers and television running pictures of the metallic gray-hulled 78-footer flying up the Derwent to the finishing line. I began to breathe more easily.

During a variety of conditions in the Cowes Week Maxi Series, *Lion New Zealand* couldn't match *Kialoa* or *Condor* which weren't entered in the Whitbread. Still, this didn't worry me. Compared to racing around the Solent, the Whitbread is chalk and cheese. But then, as it usually does, the weather intervened. It was a relatively soft Whitbread. Although Peter Blake and the crew flogged *Lion New Zealand* as hard as they could, she simply lacked the speed of some of her rivals, especially Switzerland's *UBS* designed by fellow-New Zealanders, Annapolis-based Bruce Farr and

Russell Bowler. Brilliant sailing kept her in the race. Eventually *Lion New Zealand* finished second, and once again Peter Blake missed winning. He would make up for this in later round-the-world races.

Back in Currabinny we weren't completely disappointed. In my view a second and a third (by *Drum*) wasn't too shabby a result for our design. But New Zealand felt differently. The nation had expected nothing less than victory and Ron Holland Design got the blame. In his subsequent book, *Lion*, co-written with yachting journalist Alan Sefton, Peter (later Sir Peter) referred to the yacht being overweight and described her as "the right boat for the wrong race." That is, apart from the opening leg, the expected storms never turned up.

My own view is that *Lion New Zealand*'s extra pounds were nobody's direct fault. With Sir Tom, a larger-than-life character with a parade-ground voice, telling everybody to put a little "insurance," as he liked to say, into her construction, the inevitable happened. She just got a bit too much insurance, if you like.

At least the boat didn't break, and at the end of the day that was my principal concern. I could live with not winning, but not with deaths at sea that could be attributed to flaws in my design. And 30 years and thousands of sailing miles later, *Lion New Zealand* still hasn't broken. Nor has the keel fallen off.

After all the negative publicity, most of it misinformed, that followed *Drum*'s capsize and *Lion*'s second place, I was looking forward to returning to the slow lane for a while. That's exactly what I got with an unexpected commission for a cruising yacht from somebody I'd only read about in the newspapers.

And this was no ordinary cruising yacht.

▲

Lion New Zealand was designed and built for the 1985 Whitbread Round the World Race. She finished second in the Whitbread after finishing first in the 1984 Sydney Hobart Race. *Lion NZ* is still going strong, taking thousands of guests sailing in New Zealand and Australian waters.

Stalca was designed for safe
and comfortable cruising for
Prince Rainier and his family.

PART THREE *Just say yes*

The Monsignor's yacht

WHEN PRINCE RAINIER'S BODYGUARD removed a 9mm gun from his holster and placed it on the table at the first meeting to discuss his boss's new yacht, my brother Philip was a little surprised, to put it mildly. The gun stayed there during the entire discussion while my brother tried to ignore it.

The meeting took place in the prince's private office at the Palace of Monaco, whose windows overlook the harbor where some of the world's finest yachts are often moored. Servants brought coffee and food as they talked. Although Phil made sure to address the head of the Grimaldis, Monaco's ancient royal family, as Monsignor, which we'd been told was the correct protocol, Prince Rainier proved to be charming, relaxed and open with a ready sense of humor. Hoping to bring his family together more frequently, the prince wanted us to design him a new yacht with some personal features.

The meeting took place eight years after the passing of Grace Kelly. The former actress had died in 1982 when she suffered a stroke, and her car, also carrying daughter Stephanie, plunged down a 120-foot cliff. Prince Rainier hoped the new yacht would provide his family with a respite from the constant attention that had engulfed the children since the tragedy. But also he just liked to tinker with boats. I've got a photograph of him taken around the same time as the meeting. It shows the prince wearing nothing but old shorts and a shirt, a cigarette dangling from his lips, while he works on a wooden speedboat with three tradesmen. He looks happy and relaxed.

"Prince Rainier's commission had come through Gianfranco Padoan, an Italian engineer who had created the CCYD boatyard near Venice where he'd built several of my designs of between 75 and 120 feet. And it came out of the blue."

It was at Prince Rainier's specific request that Phil had flown to the principality. He wanted an experienced yachtsman involved who could deal with the technicalities during the construction and talk on level terms with the builders. After all these years as the studio's troubleshooter, this was right up Phil's alley. We were also getting used to dealing with royalty. Butch, who raced on my *Kialoa IV* design with Spanish monarch Juan Carlos, and at times with other members of European royalty and aristocracy, once joked, "Some of my best friends are kings."

Contrary to the way royalty are often presented in the media, we've found them to be modest people who like to be one of the boys or girls, especially when they're around boats. When Butch was aboard with Juan Carlos on one occasion, the king was fascinated by the power of a "grinder," the burly guy working the winches. Leaning across, an impressed Juan Carlos said loudly in Butch's ear, "My god, that man's got big balls."

Prince Rainier's commission had come through Gianfranco Padoan, an Italian engineer who had created the CCYD boatyard near Venice where he'd built several of my designs of between 75 and 120 feet. And it came out of the blue.

At the inaugural Monaco Boat Show in 1990, a modest affair compared with the glittering occasion it has since become, the prince had stepped aboard one of my CCYD-built designs, and as Franco told it, was impressed by what he saw. Franco being a persuasive and entertaining personality, the Venetian took the opportunity to regale the prince with the attractions of a new 85-foot motor-sailing schooner that I had designed for the shipyard, and which he was planning to start building immediately after the show. Franco must have made a great sales pitch because the head of the Grimaldis agreed right then and there to buy the boat, sight unseen.

Obviously he didn't have to ask the Monéguasque finance minister for permission.

I first heard the news from Franco. He went looking for me at the show, and with much gesticulation announced that CCYD would soon be starting work on another of my designs, and that the owner would be none other than Prince Rainier. All I had to do was make a few adjustments to the design to fit the royal requirements. Normally with a twinkle in his eye, Franco was excited to say the least. I've got to say I was pretty excited myself. I was proud of the motor-sailer schooner, which took us in a different direction from our racing and fast cruising boats. She was designed to be as simple to sail as was possible for an 85-footer, but she was also easily driven by engine when the wind dropped. The prince's hectic schedule did not allow him to be becalmed overnight at sea, which often happens on the Mediterranean.

In short order (you don't wait around when the client is a prince), our studio came up with a steel-hulled 85-footer that boasted an unusual amount of internal space so the Grimaldi family and their guests would enjoy plenty of room. Most important, because this was an essential element of the prince's brief, we gave the boat small sails that would be easy to control. This became the main philosophy of the entire project: "She must be very easy to sail," Prince Rainier would say. I suspect he didn't want to frighten off his daughters who weren't as comfortable in a boat as his son and heir, Prince Albert, an experienced sailor who would attend some of the meetings with his father.

A decisive man who clearly knew what he wanted, Prince Rainier soon approved the plans and construction began. Almost immediately I became a frequent flyer aboard British Airways links between Venice and London, standing in for Phil when his sailing schedule kept him away. It wasn't particularly hard work, I have to admit, because the commission gave me an excuse to spend more time in Venice.

If you love boats, you love Venice with its 118 islands. The only way to get around this fabled city is by boat or on foot. The schooner was taking shape in the CCYD yard at Mestre, a polluted industrial area outside Venice. And, contrary to what you often hear about Italian timekeeping, Franco

I enjoyed the diverse detailing for our designs that resulted from our clients inviting various interior designers to contribute their styling and detailing ideas to my overall interior space planning.

RIGHT: Here for the 106-foot sloop *Shanakee*, Pieter Beeldsnijder of PB Design, Edam, Holland, created an elegant, fine teak joinery solution.

BELOW LEFT: Andrew Winch proposed blond oak joinery and contemporary detailing for *Sensation*, one of his first design projects after creating Andrew Winch Design in London.

BELOW RIGHT: Combining classic design detailing with high quality materials for the modern 150-foot sailing yacht *Christopher*, Courtney Walker and Angela Goldsbury created an elegant interior design environment for world voyaging.

BOTTOM: For *Ethereal*, following our clients' suggestion PB Design found a way to include a bath in this modern, energy-efficient sailing yacht.

Interiors

was usually right on schedule. Managed by Franco and his three daughters, CCYD wasn't a big yard and he took on only one project at a time, which gave him plenty of time for socializing, an important part of doing business in Italy. So, after the obligatory inspection and review of the next stage of the construction program with his production team, we'd leave Mestre behind, driving across the causeway to beautiful Venice for dinner.

Franco knew everybody in Venice and it seemed like everybody knew him. Before opening the shipyard he had manufactured wheels for Formula One racing cars, and had developed a wide and influential network of friends and acquaintances in Italian industry. One of them was Arrigo Cipriani, son of Giuseppe who had founded the original Harry's Bar in 1931, and who could always find a table for Franco. In the quiet tourist season we'd sit there on a misty evening overlooking the canal, and drink too many of the bar's Bellini cocktails while discussing boats and racing cars long into the night.

They were some of the best nights I've ever had.

It was after one of these occasions that I got into trouble with British Airways. Because I was traveling so much, every week in fact, I always made a point of arriving at airports at the last possible minute so I didn't have to spend too much time hanging around. I usually got away with it and would be the last passenger hustled aboard. This time I turned up at Marco Polo Airport not only late but without my New Zealand passport. It had been confiscated by the hotel on check-in, probably as a safety measure against one of its guests being kidnapped by the paramilitary Brigate Rosse, the "Red Brigades" cell who around that time had several assassinations to their credit, including former prime minister Aldo Moro. I'd just forgotten to collect the passport, so it was probably sitting in a drawer in the hotel office, which wasn't much use.

There was no time to go back for it or have it forwarded to the airport, so I had to do some fast talking with British Airways' manager at the airport. "The hotel confiscated my passport," I explained. "But I can't take a later flight because I've got an important client waiting for me in London."

Recognizing me from previous visits, he reluctantly agreed to let me aboard.

"Your real problem though will be when you land at Heathrow. They might not let you through."

"I'll take the risk," I assured him, confident I could talk my way through passport control in Britain.

How wrong I was! When I arrived at the Heathrow desk, U.K Immigration Service officials were most displeased. "Nobody is admitted to Brit-

◄

Seahawk racing during the St. Barths Bucket. The first example of the Perini Navi/Ron Holland 60-meter design collaboration, *Seahawk* was honored with a feature article in *Architectural Digest* magazine.

ain without a passport," they said. In mitigation I explained that I would only be in the country for the one day, but with the IRA terror campaign being at its height this didn't help much. Well, actually not at all.

"You can't enter Britain." They were firm.

"Can't enter Britain! But I'm designing a new *Morning Cloud* for Mr. Edward Heath, your former Prime Minister," I protested. "We know who he is," they said.

"Right, well, he's expecting me at his residence in Wilton Street and I'm running late. I've just come from Venice, where I'm designing a yacht for Prince Rainier of Monaco." I was really laying it on. Still, Immigration officers were unmoved. They don't believe me, I suddenly realized. They think I'm telling lies. So I pulled out a stack of photos of my designs that were under construction, plus others of me with my high-profile clients. By now, there was quite a gathering of immigration officials around me. I could see they were relenting so I came up with what I hoped was the clincher.

"Please call Mr. Heath's office," I said. "They will confirm who I am."

"Sit over there," I was told sternly, "while we check."

I did as I was ordered, wondering if I'd soon be put back on a plane to Italy, but after a while an officer came over and said I was permitted to enter the U.K. while warning me never to repeat the offence or there'd be trouble. I was also given a time limit for staying in the country, which didn't concern me greatly because I was passing through anyway. Much

▲

It looks like I'm being restrained but I had a very nice relationship with the Grimaldi family during the design and building of *Stalca*.

relieved, I was admitted into Britain, had a successful meeting with Mr. Heath, and later that evening boarded my plane for Cork.

I'd got away with it, but the incident had an unhappy sequel. On my next visit to Marco Polo Airport I made a point of looking out for British Airways' airport manager to thank him for bending the rules. To my surprise he wasn't at all pleased to see me.

"British Airways was fined over £1,000 for letting you on that flight," he told me tersely. "And I got into trouble too."

Apologizing, I made myself scarce.

While Venice is always a special place to visit, I also liked going to Monaco whenever I could. My acquaintance with the Principality had started in the mid-1970s after I received a letter out of the blue from Ireland's tax authorities. Most days I got a stack of mail, much of which was irrelevant, and I gave this particular letter a cursory glance and nearly threw it away. After all, it wasn't about boats and my interest in tax matters was, shall we say, relaxed. As far as I was concerned, money was to be spent on business travel to boatbuilders, clients or the next yacht race. None of us at the studio really bothered too much about money.

I'd not even given any thought to hiring an accountant. When I'd arrived in Ireland, my entire preoccupation was yachts, and anyway it had taken a while to build up an income big enough to create any tax obligations.

But for some reason, this time I decided to open the letter. I hastily read it, and spotted something about back taxes. Remember, my reading was never exactly brilliant. I re-read the letter, trying to take it all in. £2,000 in back taxes! It seemed like a lot of money.

Startled, I went through it again. No, back taxes of £20,000! What?!

That certainly got my attention. And as the letter warned sternly, I had to find this enormous sum quickly. That cured me of my disinterest in the finances of the studio. I promptly sought help from wealthy clients, and one of them recommended that I talk with a financial adviser in London. He recommended John Hemmingway.

I contacted John immediately. He suggested that he design a tax-compliant structure that reflected the fact that, although I was based in Ireland, my income originated from just about everywhere else. Within a few days I found myself speaking with a Monaco-based firm specializing in international business affairs. The demand for back taxes was weighing heavily on my mind: I didn't have £20,000 or anything like it. Now as it happened the Monaco firm's founding partner was an Irishman named Eamonn McGregor, and we struck up an immediate rapport. Eamonn, who now owns his own firm, Monaco-based Moores Rowland, designed

"The construction of the Monsignor's yacht took two years. Typical of Prince Rainier's desire for the quiet life when he was off duty, the launch was a low-key affair with just a few friends present, much different from the extravaganzas some of my other clients have organized over the years."

an appropriate international structure that helped keep the firm legal. At first Ron Holland Design was incorporated in Bermuda, then in Panama, and finally in the Seychelles along with many other companies which have registered there. So the firm remained tax-compliant thereafter and I got no more demands for back taxes.

Whenever I could, I liked to visit for the Monaco Grand Prix, watching the race from the office of a good friend, Nautor Swan agent Mike Hurrell. He ran the business from his own private grandstand – a building overlooking the first right-hand corner where drivers fought for a clear run up the hill. But I'm a sailor who loves the sound of the wind and the waves, and although the technology of design and construction of these amazing machines bore an obvious relevance to racing yachts, after a few years I was turned off by the crowds, traffic and deafening noise.

But the Monaco Yacht Show was different.

After the debut show in 1990, it became a highlight of my year and gave me another excuse to visit the Principality. In spite of the misgivings of much of the yachting industry, who said the Monaco show would never compete with the more established ones because the port lacked the facilities, it went from strength to strength. In time the yachting industry came to see that the original Old Port beneath Monte Carlo was a natural amphitheater for an on-water display of boats. Thanks largely to Prince Rainier's enthusiasm and drive, over the years Monaco became the industry's main showcase, eclipsing competing events in Nice, Cannes, Hamburg, London and Genoa.

The construction of the Monsignor's yacht took two years. Typical of Prince Rainier's desire for the quiet life when he was off duty, the launch was a low-key affair with just a few friends present, much different from the extravaganzas some of my other clients have organized over the years. The prince was clearly excited though. The schooner was beautifully built, a credit to Franco and the team at CCYD.

Because he was racing one of our new designs on the Great Lakes Phil couldn't attend the launch, but the prince specifically requested that he join the boat for her maiden voyage from Venice to her home berth in Monaco.

"Of course, he'll be delighted," I said.

Privately, I wasn't at all sure how we could pull this off. As soon as Phil would finish one race in the Great Lakes, he was engaged to crew aboard my latest maxi called *Sassy* in the local classic between Chicago and Mackinac, which at 290 nautical miles was the longest freshwater race in the world. The owner hoped to break the record, an ambition in which Phil's involvement was crucial. After all, he probably knew more about racing maxi yachts than I did. I called Phil and relayed the request.

"Can you get to Venice and back to Chicago in time?" I asked. "I'll see but it'll be tight," he said. Eventually we worked out that, if everything went to plan, he could join the prince's yacht for her maiden voyage, provided he was dropped off the boat as they passed Corsica.

Although the prince had owned other boats over the years, this one was clearly his pride and joy, as her name attested. He christened her *Stalca* after the first two letters of his three children's names in order of age – Stephanie, Albert and Caroline.

Phil joined the prince for the three-day trip from Italy to Corsica, all the way from Venice down the Adriatic Sea, around the bottom of the Italian mainland and through the Messina Strait, then up the Tyrrhenian Sea along Italy's other coast, past Rome, and finally back into the Mediterranean and her home berth. On the maiden voyage everybody took a turn on the helm, but it was hard to pry the Prince's hands off the wheel. He had the wind in his hair and he loved it. One of Phil's most prized photographs is of him standing beside a smiling Prince Rainier with the royal arm thrown around his shoulders. And the Monsignor is steering.

As scheduled, Phil got put ashore as *Stalca* sailed past Corsica, and eventually made it back to Chicago just in time to jump aboard *Sassy*.

▲

Philip joined Prince Rainier aboard *Stalca* for the delivery from Venice down the Adratic and into the Mediterranean. The prince was happy to have him aboard.

◀

I couldn't resist capturing the Optis in the harbor during the Monaco Yacht Show. I love the contrast to the surrounding superyachts. You can't start sailing too young!

The Pacific Islands beckoned.
I designed *Golden Opus* to
take my family to these special
locations.

A boat of my own

FOR YEARS I'D YEARNED FOR MY OWN YACHT. Not since *Eygthene* could I say I'd owned a boat I could call mine, if you discount a couple of Laser dinghies in which I liked to go for a spin and get wet. And I hadn't even had *Eygthene* for long: I'd sold my world champion yacht soon after Laurel and I moved to Ireland.

Yes, I could step aboard literally dozens of yachts from my drawing board and go sailing, but none of them belonged to me and they were all designed to the requirements of others. In a contradictory way, the more yachts I designed and sailed, the more I wanted a sailboat that reflected exactly what I wanted. The thinking I'd put into *Stalca* among other yachts often made me realize what a wonderful thing it is to come up with a boat that fulfills the individual requirements of the owners. And I had a lot of ideas of my own. This yacht would be special, about as easy to sail as anybody could imagine. And fast.

One evening in Kinsale while we were having a drink after dinner, I broached the subject to Joanna, the more realistic member of this partnership. "Absolutely not." Those were not her exact words but I could tell that's what she meant and she proceeded to mount some convincing arguments, including the pretty much unanswerable one that I'd never have time to enjoy a yacht of my own because I would still be too busy with my clients' yachts.

As the person who kept her eye on the accounts, she also pointed out

285

▲

Confirming Ireland's first Round
the World Race entry *NCB Ireland*.
Meetings in Dublin with Ireland
Premier Charles Haughey and
Jefferson Smurfit boss (later
Governor of the Bank of Ireland)
Howard Kilroy. We invited Californian Jim Kilroy to meet us to
take advantage of his experience
campaigning *Kialoa IV* in many
regattas around the world.

that business was slowing down. This was around the time of the 1987
crash when stock markets plunged around the world and wiped out a lot
of wealth. The phone wasn't ringing nearly as much as before, and even
clients who could afford to commission a new yacht didn't want to be seen
doing so. It wasn't just me and the custom yacht business that was suffering in the aftermath of the financial turmoil: on both sides of the Atlantic
builders of series production yachts were struggling as orders dried up.

It had come to a position where I had no idea when, or if, my next commission would turn up. This was the first time since I'd arrived in Ireland
that I'd run short of work, and it came as something of a shock. Unfortunately our overhead costs were still the same. With 14 people on the payroll,
all of them being paid out of the studio's collapsing income, I was bleeding
cash. The correct commercial thing to do, as I knew deep down, was to cut
operating costs by laying off staff and just sit and wait for things to pick
up. But I felt unable to do so, partly out of loyalty and partly out of a desire
to keep this talented team together.

In a more personal sense it was an unhappy time for me because my
mother Gwen had died suddenly in her home in New Zealand, a few years
after my father Phil had passed away. Mum had never left the area where
she had raised their children, and where Mum and Dad had introduced
us to a sport that would define our entire lives. I always stayed with her
whenever I returned to New Zealand, and she liked to show me the scrap-
books she faithfully kept about her sons' worldwide activities. Sometimes
I think she could never quite believe what her sons had achieved, especially
Ron the school dunce.

But I knew why. It was because she'd loved us, and although she must
have despaired of me during my school years, she'd never lost her faith
in us. Even now I remember her constant warning: "Wear your lifejacket,
Ronnie. And come back safe."

For many months on end, while still nursing the idea of having a boat
of my own, I dug deep into my savings to keep the business afloat. "How
are you going to keep paying the bills?" Joanna persisted. "And still find
the money for your dream yacht? You're risking everything you've worked
for all these years." I had no good answer except that this was a lifelong
ambition. In addition an opportunity to have the yacht built in New Zealand
had arisen and I didn't want to miss it. And, as a natural optimist, I was
sure business would pick up before the construction bills started arriving.
At least, I thought, I wouldn't have to pay the designer.

I did produce an ace or two from up my sleeve in my conversations
with Joanna. My yacht would be available for charter, which would cover

the cost of maintaining her and contribute an income. I knew people in the charter business, and they assured me there would be a good demand for a comfortable yacht that could be easily handled by a small crew. (I still hadn't forgotten the lessons of *Whirlwind XII*.) Encouragingly my friend, the Governor of the Bank of Ireland, Howard Kilroy, had joined me as a partner in the venture and arranged a loan to build the yacht.

So, feeling a little guilty, I took a deep breath and went ahead with the planning.

My dream yacht would be a 72-footer that just two people could sail anywhere in the world. Yes, just two. I was halving Noel Lister's stipulation. Not bound by any racing rules, I would be free to design her exactly the way I wanted. She would have a raised saloon and pilothouse to provide 360-degree visibility protected from the elements. Her stern would be of a classic shape rather than a reversed one that reduced the useful deck area aft: although the reverse transom was originally an influence of the IOR racing rules, it had become a fashionable approach to modern yacht design. She would have the maximum interior volume, and a lot of free and uncluttered deck space for lounging around.

And she would be beautiful. Although beauty may be in the eye of the beholder, I firmly believe there are rules of aesthetics that should never be broken. Some of today's yachts incorporate what might be called shock features in their design, mainly to attract attention rather than serve any

▲

The opportunity to build a boat of my own arose when my Dublin businessman friend, Howard Kilroy, agreed to join me in a new cruising yacht venture. We built *Golden Opus* at Sensation Yachts in New Zealand, and sailed her across the oceans from New Guinea in the west to Palma, Majorca in the east. En route I took her through the Panama Canal.

▲

With interior design detailing by Andrew Winch, *Golden Opus* featured a protected interior control station with good external visibility. This was the design arrangement I chose for my family ocean-cruising yacht.

practical advantage, but I wanted my 72-foot ocean cruiser to have a timeless quality.

So I chose a classic sheerline style with moderate overhangs at the bow and stern in which the amount of freeboard would be critical. A juggling act that affects a lot of factors – internal volume and headroom, the amount of sea water that breaks over the deck in rough weather, and especially aesthetics – the calculation of freeboard and sheerline is one of the trickiest elements in all yacht design. To put it plainly, high-sided yachts look ugly and low-sided yachts are wet.

I also had female passengers in mind because I was targeting renting out the yacht to help cover our operating costs. A raised pilothouse and saloon makes for easy access down below into the cabin with just a few steps. By contrast, flush-deck yachts may look sleek and racy, but women had often told me that they feel as though they're entering a cave when they descend to the cabin. Another huge advantage of a raised pilothouse, which is often the main gathering place, is that it allows for panoramic windows and, more practically, space below the floor for a real engine room.

There are technical advantages too. In my yacht's pilothouse I planned to install duplicate engine controls and autopilot controls, the primary controls being located at the helm station on deck. I could also install a big chart table with navigation instruments arranged around it, with clear forward visibility. None of this is possible in a flush-decked yacht.

Going several steps further than Noel Lister, I set her up to be sailed by just one person if necessary. The sheet control and mainsail reefing winches would be located directly within reach of the on-deck helm station, while the captive winch for the main halyard would be placed below deck – that is, under the cabin floor near the foot of the mast. My thinking here was that the lone sailor could control the mainsail halyard and the mainsheet from the helm station. In other words, he or she could hoist, trim, reef and lower the mainsail, all without getting wet.

I already had a name for her. She would be called *Golden Opus* as a tribute to Hugh Coveney. It was Hugh, the man who started it all for me, who came up with the "golden" name for Ireland's first serious venture into international yacht racing. Hugh had died in an accident and I wanted to commemorate him in some way. The opus related to music and composition.

By the time I'd finished all this thinking, planning and designing, I was getting more than excited by the prospect of taking my family cruising. I gave the construction contract to a New Zealand firm, Auckland-based Sensation Yachts, which had a lot of experience in big aluminum sailboats.

With Joanna increasingly nervous about the business, it was a big decision to go ahead with the project.

The financial side of the business had continued to deteriorate. The hoped-for commissions hadn't arrived but I was still paying the wages of a reduced staff, who had less and less work to do. Still, I kept thinking, things have to pick up soon. But there were times when even I was beginning to feel my optimism was misplaced. I had certainly put myself – and Joanna – under pressure.

Towards Christmas in 1995 the construction of my yacht was well advanced and I'd somehow been able to scrape up payments for the studio's financial obligations. And, fulfilling the promise of my yacht-chartering friends, I was getting interest from people in chartering *Golden Opus*. Interior designer Andrew Winch, with whom I'd done a number of important projects, contributed interior design details in return for the right to take his family sailing on her. I wouldn't say I was comfortable with the overall situation of my studio but I certainly wasn't depressed about it. I was convinced things would soon change for the better.

But one day Joanna sat me down and told me a few facts. The revenues of the business had deteriorated further. No substantial new commissions were coming in, and the overheads had hardly budged. Fortunately, although in a deteriorating market for aircraft, I had managed to sell the twin-engined Cessna. In the circumstances, I was simultaneously relieved and sad to see the aircraft go.

"After all the exciting and high-flying years, it seemed inconceivable that Ron Holland Design had come to this. Once they'd got over the initial disbelief, I was relieved that they promised to stay on to finish any work in hand. Although I didn't discuss it with the team, I was also on the hook for the sails, mast, rigging and other equipment ordered for *Golden Opus*."

"You've got to arrange a meeting with Noel McCarthy," Joanna ordered. He was our accountant, a capable professional who'd done the books of the studio for years.

"OK," I agreed, "let's arrange an appointment."

Before we met Noel, he asked to see all the documents relating to the current financial situation. When Joanna and I turned up, I could see from his grim expression that this wasn't going to be much fun. Noel sat me down and gave it to me straight.

"You are legally obliged to stop trading," he said. "The law requires that you put the business into voluntary liquidation."

Voluntary liquidation! I was no accountant but I certainly knew what that meant. Ron Holland Design was finished. I'd taken it over the cliff. Everything I had dreamed and worked for was gone. I was shocked to the core.

I can't remember exactly what happened after that. I think I managed to ask Noel what the procedure was for going into voluntary liquidation and what it would mean. Then I got to my feet and left, feeling numb.

As soon as I was outside, I collapsed on the pavement like a sack of potatoes. Everything was whirling around me. I couldn't get to my feet. Helping me up, Joanna bundled me into the car and drove me to our doctor's surgery nearby where I was given an examination. After declaring me to be more or less OK, albeit shocked, they sent me home with orders to rest. On the drive back to Kinsale I felt the dread of having to tell my team, just before Christmas, that not only would there be no usual end-of-year bonus, there would be no job either. These were people who had learned to turn their hands to practically anything. If something big was on, they'd work long hours without complaining. We were so proud of what we'd achieved together. It was one of the worst hours of my life as I contemplated what I would say.

Next day I called them all together in the office and explained the situation as best I could. "There was nothing else I could do," I told them, "The law does not permit a company to continue trading while insolvent." Appalling though it was, at least the decision had been made for me. Taken out of my hands. They listened pretty much in silence until I'd finished.

"Any questions?" I asked when I was finally done. I felt dreadful. There was a stunned silence before the penny dropped. Some were nearly as shocked as I'd been at Noel McCarthy's office, although they all knew things hadn't been going well. One or two were angry that they'd not been given more notice. And I couldn't really argue with them. At least I didn't have to break the news to Butch, who had fallen in love with a French woman, Elisabeth, and gone to live in the South of France a few years earlier.

After all the exciting and high-flying years, it seemed inconceivable that Ron Holland Design had come to this. Once they'd got over the initial disbelief, I was relieved that they promised to stay on to finish any work in hand. Although I didn't discuss it with the team, I was also on the hook for the sails, mast, rigging and other equipment ordered for *Golden Opus*. More bills were coming in, and many of these suppliers were long-term friends of mine who had given me hefty discounts to be part of creating *Golden Opus*. It was the lowest time of my life. Then it got worse.

Noel called in a professional liquidator who proceeded to put everything up for sale: every bit of furniture, every memento, every book – even the personal ones that had been signed by their authors – and my prized collection of vinyl records. That really hurt.

After having lived through this difficult experience I can now recall reflecting on "what doesn't kill you makes you stronger." In fact, now I see these types of dramatic events always create positive opportunities. At the time I couldn't see this, but looking back at what happened and what followed, I see the benefit.

▲

Taylor Holland doing the honors launching *Golden Opus*. I was conscious of the huge responsibility I was taking on by building a 72-foot ocean sailing yacht. A yacht designer can't afford to own a yacht like this. But the opportunity presented itself, and I said yes!

Over 70 years after being shot
down during the Second World War,
Dave Allen sailed my *Golden Opus*
to Papua New Guinea to find his
lost pilot friend. The fighter plane
was right where he remembered
last seeing it all those years ago.

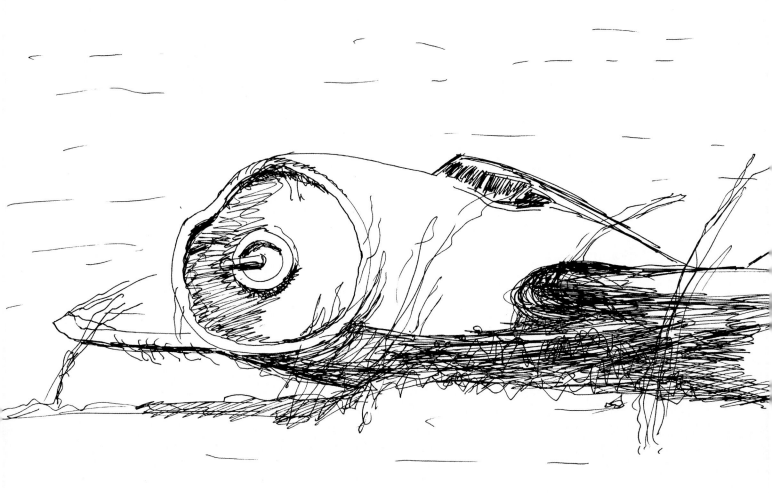

Transitions

DAVE ALLEN WASN'T WELL. Typically he was putting on a brave face but it was obvious, following his extensive diving looking for a crashed WWII fighter, that he was slowing down. As a devout Christian Scientist he normally wouldn't go near a doctor, but when he realized he was suffering from pneumonia he agreed to go ashore to the very basic hospital in Madang.

"I'm OK," he kept on saying. "I just want to finish the voyage." He was 82 years old.

The voyage, one of so many he'd made in his long and eventful life, was due to end in a secluded bay in the Pacific Ocean lying just off a remote island on the north coast of Papua New Guinea. His family did not realize Dave was actually on a mission rather than a cruise. He wanted to find something that was important to him and he insisted he knew exactly where it was, on that rarely visited coast.

With several members of his family, Dave was aboard *Golden Opus*. He'd flown all the way from San Francisco to join up with the yacht in Fiji. In fact, he'd been the first person to book her. While she'd been under construction in Auckland, he'd called me out of the blue and announced that he'd like to charter her for several weeks. He wanted to sail with his family and friends to a part of the world he hadn't visited for many years, indeed not since he was a young fighter pilot defending the skies above the Pacific islands from Japanese invaders.

Dave hadn't done much hard sailing in the last few years. I suspect that

293

"Dave had gone back to the Pacific because of a buddy. In the war he'd lost his great friend, shot down during combat over the coast of Papua New Guinea. In all the years since, while building a successful property development business, fathering a large family and racing his yachts, Dave had never forgotten the young man whose life had been cut short."

he'd lost his old enthusiasm for racing after the glory years of *Imp*. I mean, how could you beat that? But he'd never lost his love of the sea, and for this family voyage he liked the idea of an easily-handled fast cruising yacht like my 72-foot *Golden Opus*.

I felt this voyage was more of a quest than anything else. An impossible quest. While more than happy to humor their father, I got the impression that Dave's extensive family just saw it as another adventure that he had to do, rather than a last quest.

Dave had gone back to the Pacific because of a buddy.

In the war he'd lost his great friend, shot down during combat over the coast of Papua New Guinea. In all the years since, while building a successful property development business, fathering a large family and racing his yachts, Dave had never forgotten the young man whose life had been cut short. And now, in the twilight of a long life, one that his buddy had never enjoyed, he wanted to say goodbye to him. And the only proper way to do that, Dave felt, was to visit the spot where his buddy's fighter plane had gone down 60 years earlier.

I had been told this story many times. It was burned into Dave's memory, and he was darned if he wasn't going to succeed in his last mission.

Yes, I'd paid all the bills and taken delivery of my dream yacht. During the two years of her construction at Sensation Yachts in New Zealand, the yacht design business had picked up steadily.

Starting with a commission for a fast 130-foot ketch for English yachtsman and helicopter tycoon Alan Bristow, I was booking commissions for bigger and more exciting design projects.

It was almost like the old days.

I'd been able to hire new, highly capable staff like Rob Doyle, a graduate of the University of Southampton and an experienced racing yachtsman, as well as sub-contracting design work to some of my former design team, so things were returning to normal at the studio. Tragically, my long-time assistant, Michelle Dunne, who had hung in with me during the slow period, had her life cut short by an aneurysm, at way too young an age, after the business was rolling again.

But bit by bit the business had recovered along with the rest of the yachting industry around the world. Ron Holland Design wasn't the only victim of the recession by any means – too many marine sector businesses had gone under – but this uncertain period had been a searing experience that's still burned into my memory.

Golden Opus had turned out to be exactly what I'd planned and hoped for – quick, comfortable, manageable and good looking. Many a time I'd been able to hoist or lower the big mainsail directly from the helm station on my own, and her relatively small self-tacking headsails gave me pleasure every time I threw the wheel over. There's something very satisfying about tacking a 72-foot yacht when you're completely alone on deck. I used to like watching it all happen as the jib swung across just forward of the mast, the jibsheet car sliding smoothly across the track. To complete the tack, I had to trim just one winch to control the tension on the sheet. She was a wonderful sailing boat.

It's not just me who said that – in 1997, *Golden Opus* was presented with an International Superyacht Design Award for sailboats of between 23 and 36 meters, one of the many prizes I've won that I value most. She had a sister named *Volare*, launched six months after *Golden Opus* hit the water.

And as I'd dreamed, I'd taken my family cruising into the Pacific. On one magical voyage I had sailed with friends over 1,000 miles from New Zealand to meet Joanna and the girls in the Fiji Islands. And we'd do a lot more in the years to come – visiting Vanuatu being one highlight. I also sailed *Golden Opus* from New Guinea to New Zealand and on to other Pacific areas: Tonga, Tahiti, then through the Panama Canal and up to the northern Caribbean; spending an evening in St. Barths, consuming "Cheese burgers in Paradise" and a few beers at Le Select, on our way to Bermuda. Then *Golden Opus* sailed across the Atlantic to Palma de Mallorca and the

▲

Recalling the experience I had gained from paddling Chief Benny's canoe in Fiji, I tried again during our *Golden Opus* visit to the remote Trobriand Islands in the Western Pacific. It's not as easy as it looks!

French Riviera. In the Pacific we'd explored Vanuatu's active volcanos, and in the Fiji Islands, at various chiefs' invitations, visited remote churches on Sunday mornings to hear beautiful singing from the village school children. It meant a lot to me that my daughters were able to experience this.

It had not all been fun and games though. On one voyage out of Opua, a little port in the Northland of New Zealand, we'd lost the mast.

We were making good time on a beautiful day, close reaching at over nine knots, full and by in a 15-knot wind and moderate ocean swell left over from a few days of gales. I'd flown in from Florida with my friend Steve Anderson and we'd set a course due north for the Fiji Islands. The wind was in my face and the New Zealand coastline was fast disappearing over the horizon. Happy to be back at sea, I went forward to trim the outboard jibsheet barber hauler, to squeeze out an extra tenth of a knot or so of speed. *Golden Opus*, thoroughbred that she was, responded immediately.

"This is going to be a fast passage," I told Steve. Although an accomplished and experienced powerboating hand, he'd not had the helm of a 72-foot sailing yacht before. He had a grin on his face as wide as the yacht's beam as *Golden Opus* smoked along, bow wave creaming under the hull and her wake carving a white line through the blue Pacific Ocean.

Then without warning, not even a creak or a groan, there was a loud bang and the mast basically exploded. One minute the stick was standing upright, the next most of it had collapsed into the sea to leeward, dumping bits of carbon fiber and twisted stainless steel rod rigging everywhere. The top of the mast and destroyed sails were sinking rapidly into the Pacific while the wreckage was heaving to and fro in the swells and threatening to damage the hull.

A long way to come for nothing, I thought.

But we had to clear up the mess, and skipper John Matla leapt into action with an electrically-powered angle cutter, an essential tool for emergencies at sea in big sailing yachts, and sliced through what was left of the windward side rigging that was supporting the still standing bottom of the broken mast and boom. After he made his final cut, the whole lot went over the side and sank. Dismayed, I watched our beautiful sails and rigging disappear beneath the ocean surface.

What do we do now? we asked ourselves.

There wasn't much of a choice, so we turned on the engine and headed disconsolately back to the New Zealand coast, accompanied by a school of porpoises. If they're heading for New Zealand, I thought, they'll be there long before us.

▲

The deserted north coast of Papua New Guinea, near where Dave Allen navigated *Golden Opus* towards his friend's downed fighter plane.

"It was beautiful and clear weather when Dave sailed down the Papua New Guinea coast. He wouldn't leave the deck, eyes glued to the headlands and bays the yacht was passing. Bush and trees tumbled in profusion right down to the water. The coastline was deserted with no other boats in sight."

As I've earlier pointed out, it's no great shame to lose a mast on a racing yacht because they're built "on the edge" to save weight. My boat-builder/sailing buddy Killian Bushe once pointed out, after we'd lost our Quarter-Tonner rig while racing in the Solent, that in one race during the 1978 Quarter Ton Cup in Japan six masts had come to grief on yachts I'd designed. Thanks for reminding me, Killian! But you're not supposed to lose the stick on a cruising yacht that doesn't get subjected to anything like such harsh treatment.

After a months-long wrangle the insurance company agreed with me, and *Golden Opus* acquired a new rig just in time for Dave's charter.

With the Allen family and friends aboard, *Golden Opus* sailed west from Fiji towards Papua New Guinea. After arriving in Papua, Dave and his family were ashore visiting one of the small villages when a group of locals heard that Dave had been there before as a young American pilot. They applauded him on the spot, a very moving moment for Dave and his family.

It was beautiful and clear weather when Dave sailed down the Papua New Guinea coast. He wouldn't leave the deck, eyes glued to the headlands and bays the yacht was passing. Bush and trees tumbled in profusion right down to the water. The coastline was deserted with no other boats in sight. A hot sun made the sea sparkle and visibility was perfect: from the deck it was possible to see the sandy bottom.

▲

Anchored in the Fiji Islands, *Golden Opus*'s on-deck dining table is arranged for breakfast. Another feature I insisted on during the design process was to locate the steering wheel and sailing control lines in close proximity to family and guests, who would be comfortably lounging on the yellow striped cushions.

▶

Early in the design process I decided that *Golden Opus* should have a spinnaker. We did not set it very often, but it was fast.

"I think it's here in the next bay," David suddenly announced, pointing at a bay just around the corner.

Perhaps Dad's right, some of his family were beginning to wonder. On his command they dropped the sails and started up the engine, motoring into the secluded little bay. There was nothing – no houses, no boats, not even a jetty.

"Drop the anchor here," ordered Dave. As soon as *Golden Opus* stopped, he got himself into the tender with the help of the family and skipper John.

"I think this is the spot," Dave said to John. "This is where my buddy went down."

Obediently John steered the tender as Dave directed, until they were over the exact place where Dave was pointing. Local fishermen were waving and pointing to a location a few yards away, John and Dave motored over and jumped into the water.

There it was, a fighter plane sitting on the bottom exactly where it had crash landed, the twisted metal clearly visible. Some areas were covered in weed and grass but other areas shiny metal. John was shocked. After diving they stayed there in the tender for a long time, Dave looking down in silence and the rest of the family watching from *Golden Opus* on the other side of the bay, in awe and respect.

After Dave and John returned to *Golden Opus*, Dave went to his cabin to rest. He was not feeling well. John and the family motored the yacht to Madang Harbour and managed to get Dave ashore to a very basic open air hospital, where he died the next day. How improbable.

When I heard of Dave's death, I was deeply saddened. I'd known him for so long and he'd been so important in my life, and I owed him so much. And yet at the same time I was thrilled for him. Dave died exactly as he would have wanted – totally on his own terms, on a sailing yacht with his family. On my yacht and saying goodbye to his buddy.

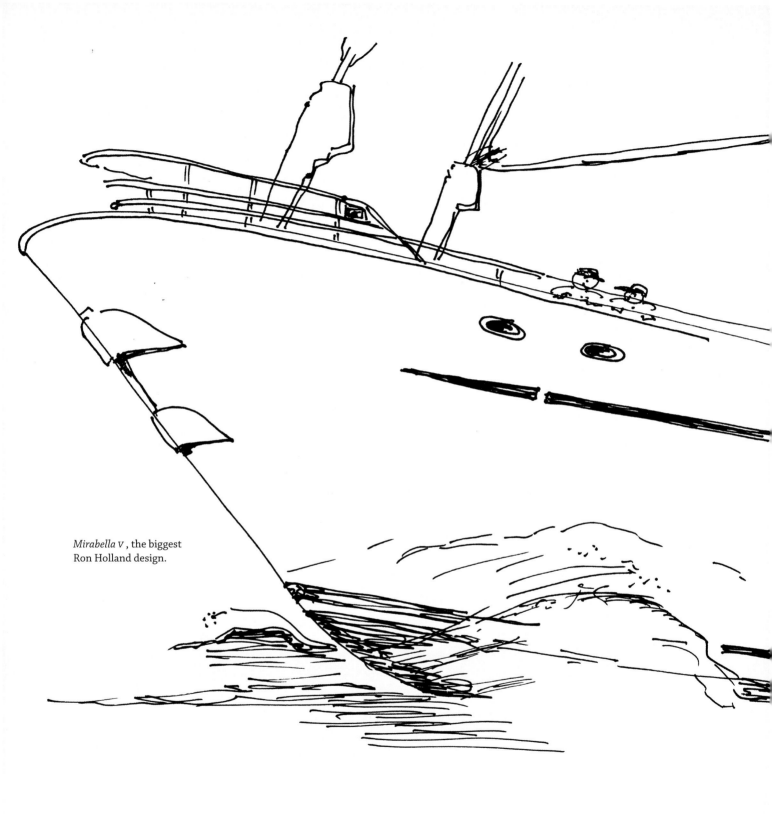

Mirabella v , the biggest
Ron Holland design.

Mirabella gigantissima

OF ALL THE LAUNCHES OF MY DESIGNS, none had attracted as impressive an audience as *Mirabella V*. Among the official attendance at the Vosper Thorneycroft shipyard in Southampton, England, were the American owners Joseph and Luciana Vittoria with their family and friends, numerous dignitaries including Queen Elizabeth's nephew Viscount Linley, whose company had done an exquisite piece of interior joinery in the saloon, and around 200 workers plus their families. The shipyard's employees had toiled on the yacht's construction for over two years. There was also a big media presence – journalists and photographers, television channels, ITV and the BBC, as well as a contingent from American and European newspapers, magazines and television. There were numerous other interested spectators from the Royal Navy, which had a long and special relationship with the VT yard, as it's usually called, and from the British yachting world which had followed the progress of the yacht all the way through from her conception and construction to this, her most public moment.

A nautical audience had even assembled on the River Itchen that flows down into Southampton Water. Bobbing up and down in the waters just off the shipyard were about 50 boats, some of which had sailed across the Irish Sea for the occasion. And finally, another crowd of spectators had jammed the footpath on the bridge over the river because it conveniently overlooked the launch area. Up there it was standing room only. All of us were waiting to see an event of special significance in yachting – the world's biggest-ever single-masted sailing boat was about to hit the water.

Biased as I was, the interest in *Mirabella* was understandable to me. Even before her launch she had broken a string of records. Besides being the world's biggest single-masted yacht, this 247-foot sloop had rewritten the rules of sailboat design and construction in a number of ways. First, she was the largest yacht ever to be built in composite materials. Once fully rigged, *Mirabella V* would boast the tallest mast in the world – a technological marvel of carbon fiber that would tower nearly 300 feet into the sky, or roughly 25 stories high; so high that she would not be able to pass under any bridge in the world, including the one over the Panama Canal. Second, she would carry the biggest sails – one of her headsails had already been certified by the Guinness Book of Records as the largest in the world – and her mainsail alone was roughly the area of half a dozen tennis courts.

To accommodate all this power, all her on-deck equipment and sail-handling hardware had been custom made. Her captive winches, for example, were gigantic hydraulic powerhouses that had tested to the limit the expertise of their German designers and manufacturers. (Unfortunately, it would soon turn out that the cost of their development caused at least one of them to go broke.)

Practically nothing on this boat had come off-the-shelf, simply because there was so little available equipment on the shelf that was good enough or big enough. The American company Harken had designed and manufactured gigantic new winches specifically for *Mirabella*. She was just too large and powerful for any standard gear. And at around US $60 million, *Mirabella V* certainly had the benefit of one of the biggest ever sailboat budgets.

But now she was stuck on the slipway, refusing to enter the water. I'm often a little nervous on these occasions. It doesn't matter how carefully the calculations have been checked and re-checked, there's always an element of uncertainty in yacht design. Together with VT's engineers, our design team had pored over the weight calculations, spending hour upon hour trying to ensure their total accuracy. But you can never be fully confident that a new, one-off yacht – and especially one as huge as *Mirabella V* – will float precisely on her designed lines until that moment of truth when she finally reaches the element that will be her home.

We all held our breath as the giant sailboat refused to budge. The slipway had taken a long time to construct. It was made of timber in the traditional manner, and VT had done a lot of calculations to ensure *Mirabella* would slip into the water without putting undue stress on the hull: work-

approaching ten knots

men had spent days rubbing tallow into the wood. Unfortunately, it had been a cold night and the tallow had become too sticky. This was an old-fashioned way of launching a yacht – most of them are lifted into the water by cranes these days – but Joe Vittoria had a sense of theater.

Up on the VIP platform his wife Luciana, who had broken the traditional bottle of champagne on *Mirabella*'s bow, joked: "Have you paid all the bills, Joe?"

"Every single one," he said with a grin.

Finally, the seconds stretching into minutes, the grease warmed up. With a helping hand from the VT construction crew who gave the boat a shove with a tractor, the immense hull began to move. It had taken an anxious 15 minutes, but now she was sliding an inch or two at a time. Soon she gathered speed until she hit the water, scattering spectator boats in all directions.

Joe, an American who had been chief executive and president of the Avis car rental company, is a keen and experienced yachtsman who had owned a string of sailboats. These included, during the 1970s, a Nicholson 33, a successful production cruiser-racer that was one of the first designs to come off my drawing board. I had known Joe for years, having first met him after *Eygthene* won the Quarter Ton world championship in 1973. At that time he was, among other commercial activities, the Italian representative for Camper and Nicholson, the British yacht builder. Joe had

▲

I'm standing on the edge of the River Itchen at the bottom of the Vosper Thornycroft slipway to watch *Mirabella V* hit the water. Down the greasy ways, just like Admiral Nelson's ships, in days when Napoleon's navy challenged England's maritime supremacy. She floats exactly as I had hoped.

Most yacht owners find they need more storage space, but not so with *M5*. I always found it amusing to show visitors her boat garage, with space for a Hinckley Center Console 29 tender below deck and the Carbon Cub float plane above deck. This is a real garage!

When Joe Vittoria asked me to design his new yacht's lazarette to store his Hinkley 29-foot tender, I had to increase the yacht's length to over 250 feet. Our biggest design, and the biggest sailing yacht lazarette in the world.

raced his Nicholson 33, which he'd named *Catch 22*, on the Mediterranean circuit and won a lot of events.

My brother Phil often crewed for Joe, and they pushed what was only a production yacht so hard that they kept blowing out spinnakers. Joe didn't mind: he loved winning, and a few ripped spinnakers were neither here nor there. And nor did Camper and Nicholson mind because the success of *Catch 22* helped sell a lot of these designs in Italy. After *Catch 22* had won a regatta Joe would sometimes find himself dealing with a line-up of potential buyers.

I wasn't Joe's automatic choice as *Mirabella V*'s designer. He'd been in discussions with Bob Derecktor, the American boat designer and builder whose yard near New York was then constructing the fine 112-foot Sparkman and Stephens-designed *Zingaro*. But the Vittorias had not finally made up their mind, and they invited me to fly over from Ireland and meet with them at their house in Palm Beach. As I always do with prospective clients, I invited the couple to explain in their own words what kind of yacht they wanted and how they intended to use it. Describing his vision of a sailboat that would set new standards in yacht chartering, Joe said: "I'm thinking bigger than 150 feet." OK, I saw that as a promising start.

This was exactly the kind of commission I liked best: challenging but not impossible. After all, my 103-foot *Whirlwind XII* had broken all records in the mid-1980s, and I had gone on to design much bigger yachts such as the 220-foot *Felicita West*, the world's biggest aluminum sailboat at that time. Most of these boats had taken the industry into unchartered technological waters, so Joe's concept sounded OK to me.

By any standards 150 feet was still a lot of yacht. She would dwarf the once-mighty early America's Cup yachts as well as the J-Class boats that had contested the 1930s America's Cup races. "Tell me more," I said.

Over the following hours that's exactly what he did in discussions with me. Suddenly, the vision began to grow. Instead of spreading what would obviously be a vast sail area over two or three masts, as would be expected for such a big yacht, Joe told me he wanted just one mast. This was something of a shock, but as he explained, all of his yachts to that point had been single-masters and he intended to continue the tradition. Yet even at 150 feet a single-masted sloop would require the largest sails ever made, by a big margin.

But Joe was only warming up.

Out of the blue, one day soon afterwards, he expressed a wish to boost the yacht's length to 250 feet. Wow! This really got my adrenalin flowing.

"My potential clients weren't setting out to be difficult or to impress. They didn't want the world's biggest sailboat for its own sake but for a reason that Joe, a true lover of sailing and the sea, had originally explained. His primary goal was to create a sailing yacht that would attract charter passengers and would be as comfortable as any large motor yacht."

Suddenly, all records would be broken. The biggest this, the biggest that. So many daunting issues would flow from such a leviathan of a yacht.

Take for example the keel, that part of a yacht which nobody sees but which is so crucial to her performance. Joe stipulated a lifting keel rather than a fixed one. The reason was a sound one: with the keel retracted, the yacht's draft (its underwater depth) would be reduced from a fully extended 30 feet to 15 feet, shallow enough to allow his yacht to enter the port at Palm Beach on the east coast of Florida, the Vittorias' home base, as well as other favorite cruising locations around the world. I mentally calculated that a keel for a yacht of this size would come in at around 150 tons, an immense weight to hoist and lower. Now here's a challenge, I thought. Things were heating up.

And because such a charter yacht would often have to drop anchor offshore rather than lie alongside a wharf, Joe said he would want underdeck stowage for his 29-foot tender, a classic-style powerboat built by the 80-year-old American company Hinkley, that would take crew and passengers ashore. But a 29-footer takes up a lot of room and she would require an opening transom, in effect a giant garage in the stern. Wow! A 29-footer! That meant the opening transom would be easily big enough to swallow a yacht like my old Quarter-Tonner *Eygthene*.

Now, with all this weight inside the boat, she would need a lot of sail power, even more than we'd originally envisaged.

"So we might be talking about a 300-foot mast," I said. "No problem there." I wasn't nearly as certain as I hoped I sounded.

It was Joe's final stipulation that really got my head spinning: he wanted his boat built in fiberglass composite materials. Most of my big sailboats had been constructed in marine grade aluminum, and so were most of the recently launched superyachts. Aluminum had become the way to go, and a composite yacht of this length was a daring proposition that posed all kinds of technical challenges.

My potential clients weren't setting out to be difficult or to impress. They didn't want the world's biggest sailboat for its own sake but for a reason that Joe, a true lover of sailing and the sea, had originally explained. His primary goal was to create a sailing yacht that would attract charter passengers and would be as comfortable as any large motor yacht. It would boast generous on-deck and below-deck spaces where passengers could walk around and relax in comfort and luxury. At charter rates of over $200,000 a week for such a unique boat, this would be a serious commercial proposition.

As Joe put it, the vision had come to him when he was cruising off the southern Italian coast near Naples with family and friends. He had noticed some friends from Florida standing on the quay, nervous about getting back to their charter yacht in a small dinghy because the seas were growing choppy in the afternoon breeze. He offered to give them a lift in his bigger tender and, as they cleared the harbor breakwater, Joe asked, "Which is your yacht?" "We don't know," they said. "They all look the same to us." Something clicked in Joe's brain. Nobody will ever be able to say that about the next yacht I build, he thought to himself. And that, as I understand it, is how it all started. His next yacht would be unique and unmistakable.

After a period of due consideration the Vittorias handed me the commission, and I fully briefed my design team as well as doing some hard thinking. The original design brief had now changed dramatically. It had gone from a more or less routine big project to one that verged on the preposterous. I knew I would have to bring extra talent into my team to get the job done. No doubt about it, this was the most daunting commission that had ever been entrusted to me. It was like *Whirlwind XII,* only multiplied by two and a half times. A big step into the unknown.

The biggest sailing yacht in the world, no problem! I tried to convince myself.

I had to admire Joe's sense of adventure, but such a project demanded heavyweight research before I even put pen to paper. A couple of weeks

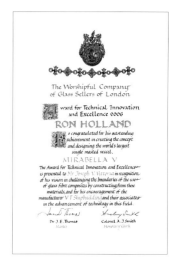

▲

All involved in the creation of *Mirabella V* received several unique honors, including an invitation to a Lord Mayor of London event at the Mansion House. The most unusual however was this award bestowed by the Worshipful Company of Glass Sellers of London. They honored her because she had been built using fiberglass! Lots of fiberglass!

later I returned to the Vittoria residence in Palm Beach to present my initial ideas. The entire family, including their daughter and three sons, showed up for the meeting. I had taken a lot of trouble and prepared drawings of six different design concepts for their new *Mirabella*. One by one I laid them out on a large table in the living room before this knowledgeable selection committee. All of the Vittorias had grown up sailing and knew about yachts, and there was a lot of debate as each concept was presented to them.

But then, to my horror, each of the six members of the family chose a different design.

A stalemate? Would I have to go back to Ireland and produce another six designs? But this is America, home of democracy, and after some more debate the family abdicated the decision to Luciana. They agreed that the concept that Mom preferred would be the new *Mirabella* – and that's exactly what happened.

I returned to Ireland and got down to work on the long and demanding process of converting preliminary one-dimensional lines on paper into a three-dimensional living vessel, the biggest of its kind on the planet. I would be lying if I didn't say I had a few qualms about whether we could pull this project off.

At least I was philosophically prepared. I might have launched my reputation as a designer in a little Quarter-Tonner and consolidated it in relatively small racing yachts before going on to bigger ones, but I had always been fascinated by the big yachts and great sailing ships of the past. I had devoured books about them, their crews and their designers. Of the huge collection of books I had acquired over the years – a habit that would have amazed my early teachers who considered me barely literate – many of my favorites were about these historic vessels. I often delved into my library for inspiration, knowledge and entertainment. And I still do.

So many times had I read *The Last of the Wind Ships* by the writer and photographer Alan Villiers, a classic about the demise of the sail-powered merchant vessels, that its pages had become dog-eared. Many of these books held memories for me. In my teens I had the temerity to send a letter to Captain Villiers in England, asking if he would be kind enough to include me among the crew of his planned replica of Captain Cook's *Endeavour*, the boat in which he intended to retrace the great navigator's voyages. With astonishing courtesy considering the volume of mail he must have had to deal with, he wrote back explaining that the project may not happen but; if it did, an apprentice boatbuilder like me could be useful.

And I often dipped into *The Best of Sail*, about the wild days of the clipper ships. Written by Basil Lubbock and illustrated by Jack Spurling,

▶

I wrote to Captain Alan Villiers in England, hoping to join his crew re-enacting the Captain Cook voyage to New Zealand. I was thrilled to receive a reply from him. Unfortunately the project never happened.

Oxford
Oct. 3 1966

Dear Mr Holland,

Thanks for your letter, with picture of ship. The position on the <u>Endeavour</u> project is unchanged; until it is sure there is to be a ship, there obviously isn't anything further I can do about it. We are ready on this side.

Interested about the <u>Esmeralda</u>.

Sincerely yours,

Alan Villiers

"When I was hardly in my teens, I had come across an illustration of the sail plan of the schooner *Varua*, the 70-foot yacht designed by the legendary American W. Starling Burgess. Unable to resist the temptation, I have to confess, I liberated the page and pasted it into my treasured, signed copy of Eric Hiscock's classic *Voyaging Under Sail*. The illustration is still there today."

the stories of the hardships and dangers these sailors routinely faced as they dashed around the world with their precious cargoes still thrill me. These boats had captured my imagination from an early age. When I was hardly in my teens, I had come across an illustration of the sail plan of the schooner *Varua*, the 70-foot yacht designed by the legendary American W. Starling Burgess. Unable to resist the temptation, I have to confess, I liberated the page and pasted it into my treasured, signed copy of Eric Hiscock's classic *Voyaging Under Sail*. The illustration is still there today.

You just couldn't help but be inspired by these people. Just like us at Ron Holland Design, they had been faced with daunting technological changes and challenges, often in the face of outright skepticism, and had managed to overcome them. Taking the schooner *Varua* as an example, she was a pioneer of composite construction just as *Mirabella* would be. In *Varua*'s case though, the materials were steel and wood, a daring combination at the time.

Another hero of mine was the great Scottish designer George Lennox Watson, one of Britain's original independent naval architects who also experimented successfully with new materials in the early 20th century. Never afraid to challenge conventional thinking, his company designed a 300-foot luxury yacht, the steam-powered *Nahlin* (meaning fleet of foot) launched from Glasgow's legendary John Brown yard in 1930. Originally commissioned by a member of the Scottish nobility, *Nahlin* was owned by King Carol of Romania before being converted consecutively into a museum, then into a floating restaurant. After many years languishing in this inappropriate state, she was acquired by a consortium headed by a friend of mine, British yacht broker Nicholas Edmiston, and painstakingly restored at Liverpool before being recommissioned under her original name. Today she's owned by inventor Sir James Dyson – and if anybody appreciates innovation, it's him.

As I worked on the design for *Mirabella V*, I often thought about these great vessels and genuinely thought of myself as following in the footsteps of innovative designers of yesteryear.

I was also prepared in a technical sense. Well, half-prepared. In the last few years my team had designed ever-bigger sailboats as owners saw what *Whirlwind XII* could do, romping around the world with just four professional crew. We'd done a 140-footer called *Juliet*, then a 160-footer called *Thalia*, a 174-footer called *Parsifal III* for Danish owner Kim Vibe-Petersen who invented a coffee brewing machine, then a few 184-footers, and then leapt the 200-foot barrier with a yacht that made the headlines.

She was *Felicita West*, which I'd designed to be built at the Italian yacht yard of Fabio Perini, a far-sighted industrialist who'd spotted an exclusive but valuable niche for big yachts with small crews. (Take a bow, Noel Lister.)

The largest aluminum sailing yacht ever built, *Felicita West* was also the first of my designs to receive the new MCA classification, effectively an industrial seal of approval that allowed her to be put out for charter. Her owner was British businessman Malcolm Healey, who'd built up an industrial empire on both sides of the Atlantic. Malcolm already owned a Perini-built yacht but wanted a bigger and faster one, and Fabio was happy to oblige.

Fabio Perini is a fascinating man. An engineer by qualification, he got into the yacht-building business by accident. All he wanted was a big yacht of his own, but the result was so unique and attracted so much attention that he launched into the slippery slope of yacht construction under the name of Perini Navi, and made a brilliant success out of it. Kim Vibe-Petersen once described Fabio as "the Prada of yacht builders," and I couldn't disagree. In my early association with Fabio and his team, they sold ten 185-foot aluminum yachts of my design at a price of around €30 million each, including one to media giant Rupert Murdoch.

Each of these yachts had broken technological barriers in one way or another. For instance, *Thalia* was the first big sailing yacht to step a carbon fiber mast, and *Felicita West* was the first Perini yacht to be constructed in aluminum alloy.

▲

My latest design collaboration with Perini Navi was for the Perini 60-meter. This was a development of the successful Perini 56-meter design, with larger internal volume and more sailing performance. Here *Perseus^3*, the first sloop-rigged version, is reaching under spinnaker during the 2017 St. Barths Bucket regatta.

▲

At the time of New Zealand's first America's Cup challenge these photos were carefully protected by the Team NZ design group. Here the tank model of KZ 7, with our latest keel and wings design, is being lowered into the test tank channel at the Wolfson Unit facility in Southampton, England, to check our design's performance.

From the outset, I knew one of the biggest challenges with *Mirabella V* would be Joe's insistence on fiberglass composite construction. The burning question was: Where would we find a builder prepared to take on such a giant commission in these materials? The best big-yacht builders were using steel for the hulls of motor yachts, and aluminum for sailing yachts. where light weight and high performance is more critical. In Europe, the boat- and ship-building yards had built their expertise and reputations on metal as the preferred material for the primary structure. I disliked steel. It's heavy, prone to rust and susceptible to galvanic corrosion over time.

For these and other reasons I strongly prefer aluminum. When it's correctly used, marine grade aluminum is lighter and more corrosion-resistant for starters.

I had no intention though of trying to divert Joe from his determination to have a composite yacht just because most of my big yachts were constructed in aluminum. Fiber composites are light and strong, and they display great resistance to marine corrosion. If handled by skilled boatbuilders, they are more versatile too. The skin and the structural members – the flesh and skeleton, if you like – of a boat such as *Mirabella V* can be more easily varied in thickness according to the strength requirements in various locations in the hull, deck and superstructure. This last virtue, the versatility of composites, has always been particularly important to me.

I firmly believe there's no point in adding strength – and by definition extra weight – where it's not needed.

If you can save weight without compromising strength, it adds up to a faster yacht. Starting with *Eygthene* I'd built my reputation on performance-oriented yachts, and had no intention of changing that. Also, Joe had made it very clear that he wanted his new *Mirabell*a to be fast when sailing to windward, another requirement that met my approval, but one that made accurate weight analysis absolutely vital.

My design team had a good record in composite-built yachts. Years earlier we had proven how effective composite construction was with our IOR maxi racing yachts, the now legendary *Kialoa IV* and the newer *Condor*. Also, my involvement with the first New Zealand America's Cup challenge related to the first fiberglass America's Cup yacht being built. The last thing I wanted to hang my reputation on was a giant sloop that was built like a Sherman tank – and sailed like one. I wanted the new *Mirabella* to be able to thunder along at over 20 knots in the right wind conditions.

We still had to find a builder who could do the composite job properly, and few boatbuilders or shipyards had both the experience and the necessary infrastructure capable of taking on a project as special as this one. So, while my studio got on with the research, I joined Joe's own newly formed team and launched a simultaneous worldwide quest for a suitable builder. To speed things up Joe chartered a corporate jet to visit potential builders around Europe. After running our eye over several candidates, we selected Vosper Thorneycroft in Southampton on England's south coast, later relocating to the historic Royal Navy dockyard at Portsmouth.

Whenever I went to the dockyard, which I would do a lot, I felt like I was walking back into the past. Founded in 1496, this was the port from which England had launched its wooden ships to fight Napoleon. As for Vosper Thorneycroft, it had made its modern reputation on motor torpedo boats, gun boats and minehunters, with a few famous exceptions. In 1939 the yard had built *Bluebird II*, the powerboat that Sir Donald Campbell piloted to a world water speed record of 142 mph. The Vosper part of Vosper Thorneycroft dates back to 1871 and has a history of turning its hand to anything. In the previous 30 years no fewer than 270 ships had been launched by the yard.

It wasn't of course the history that persuaded us, but the yard's special expertise in minesweepers, strange as that may seem. After all, you would be forgiven for thinking that nothing could be further from a minesweeper than a sleek private sailing yacht. The connection though is that minesweepers are built in composites, because the material negates

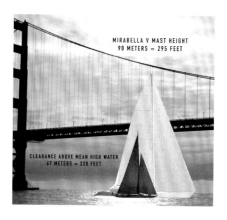

▲

My first public presentation of the *Mirabella V* design showed she could not pass under the Golden Gate. In fact she cannot pass under any bridge! Renamed *M5* she entered the Pacific Ocean in 2016 via Magellan Straight at the bottom of South America, thereby avoiding the Bridge of the Americas over the Panama Canal.

►

The first New Zealand challenge for the America's Cup took place in 1987, in the Indian Ocean off Western Australia. The Kiwis sprang on the sailing world the first fiberglass International 12-Meter Class yachts. NZ designer/engineer Russell Bowler gets credit for the detail design work necessary to meet the strict construction control requirements of Lloyds Classification. The Davidson/Farr/Holland design team was primarily trying to produce two duplicate yachts, so we could reliably test keel, rudder and rig variations at full size on the water. One of our competitors publicly stated that he thought we were cheating. Red flag to a bull! Never one to hold back, team leader Michael Fay agreed to a third design, *KZ 7*, that was a development incorporating all we had learned from our fiberglass twin yacht testing program. This was a fast design, and ensured that the first NZ challenge was a credible effort, only to be bettered by Dennis Conner's *Stars and Stripes*, the eventual winner of the America's Cup.

the magnetic influence that can trigger a mine explosion. Clearly we weren't worried about mines blowing up the new *Mirabella*, but we were concerned to ensure the structural integrity of the yacht as well as a high quality finish. After much discussion, Vosper Thorneycroft convinced Joe, me and his team that they had the capability to build his vision, and a contract was duly signed. So now we had a builder for the hull.

That left the other intimidating elements – the sails, mast, keel and all the on-deck hardware such as winches that would harness *Mirabella V*'s enormous forces, not to mention the engine and propellers, generators and other machinery that would keep her running smoothly during world-wide charter operations.

Joe nailed us to a tight schedule: he wanted the boat in the water by late 2003. That is, a two-year construction job. With the preliminary design work done, at my suggestion Joe decided to break the news about *Mirabella V* to the wider world. I felt it was better to make the project public rather than try and get it done under wraps, mainly because the news would inevitably leak out. In due course an invitation-only press conference was staged in Cowes, the most appropriate of all settings. We had created an impressive, color-rendered computer presentation including a large sail plan, something I knew would cause a stir. As expected, when Joe unveiled the illustrations of *Mirabella V*, there was an audible "Wow!" from the audience. Now that the word was out, it seemed that half the yachting industry argued it couldn't be done while the rest just didn't know.

The main topic of debate was the carbon fiber mast. A mast of 300 feet! Impossible, was the general opinion. It was thought that the loads and stresses on the equipment would be so great that in a decent breeze the giant rig would simply crumple like a tall building in an earthquake.

And I must admit I was running into a few nervous contractors, understandably so. They had to pull out all the stops to scale these technological heights. As a bemused *Yachting World* editor pointed out, "Some suppliers have invested seven-figure sums just to accommodate *Mirabella V*'s technology."

By any standard the numbers were off the scale. The winches would have to pull 40 tons without being ripped straight out of the hull. The mainsail alone would weigh 1.5 tons and yet must be winched to the head of the mast in under two minutes. The mast step alone – the base where the mast is seated – would have to take a load of 1,500 tons. All this in a fiberglass composite boat!

The tabloid newspapers had a field day. They pointed out that *Mirabella V*'s keel would weigh as much as a hundred family sedans. They discov-

▲

Following our original presentation for *Mirabella V* that compared her to the Golden Gate Bridge, we needed to follow this up. What better way than to show a London double-decker bus easily accommodated in the completed hull.

ered that the distance from the truck (top of the mast) to the bottom of the keel would make her twice as high as Nelson's Column in London's Trafalgar Square. And, as one of our original illustrations showed, more than one double-decker bus could be parked inside the hull. She had already been labeled the first "hyperyacht".

The media could also have mentioned *Mirabella*'s weight – at 750 tons, she would tip the scales at almost exactly the same deadweight as one of France's fabled fast trains, the 1,293-foot long, 300 km/h TGV TMST. Heavy as it may sound, a weight of 750 tons was extremely light for such a big yacht. It was difficult to explain to lay people but my design for the hull was closely related in principle to that of the Flying Dutchman, that sleek two-man dinghy that was for so many years an Olympic class. *Mirabella* was pretty much a giant dinghy.

While the press gasped over *Mirabella*'s dimensions we continued to tackle the technical challenges. Fortunately, Joe's hand-picked project manager was Englishman Paul Johnson, a calm operator who had already masterminded the construction of several big yachts, including two of Joe's earlier *Mirabellas*. Most importantly, he was familiar with composite construction techniques.

By early 2003 the yacht was starting to take shape in a huge hall where Vosper Thorneycroft had built its last minehunter. Highly skilled craftsmen were building the huge wooden mold for the hull into which the fiber and resin would be formed. We immediately ran into a problem. While they were perfectly at home with these materials, they weren't accustomed to the demands of yacht owners for smoothly faired glossy surfaces. As one of Vosper Thorneycroft's top managers would tell *Yachting World,* "Mine-hunters can have lumps and bumps but this finish has to be perfect."

Despite her immense size, *Mirabella V*'s hull was being built in one section, which would be joined later to the deck and superstructure that were being assembled in smaller sections in a VT hall nearby. Joe engaged a company called High Modulus to do the composite structural engineering. This wasn't engineering in steel or aluminum, but in these newer and exciting materials that had emerged mainly from the aerospace industry. I knew High Modulus well. It was a New Zealand company and over the years I had a lot to do with them. Their main preoccupation was that the boat needed, in effect, a strong spine. Because she would be so long relative to her depth (the dinghy shape), the yacht was rather like a tall person with an unusually long back that needed extra strengthening. To comply with new regulations issued by the international maritime authorities, a lot of time was required to prove this new construction concept. The outer skin would be only 7mm thick above the waterline out of a total hull thickness of 2.5 inches. The inside skin would be about 10mm thick. These numbers had aroused plenty of debate. Many said the yacht would not be strong enough and might break her back as soon as she started sailing.

But High Modulus, Vosper Thorneycroft, Paul and I knew how strong composite construction can be. The outer skin was being made of layers of Kevlar and stitched biaxial, resin-absorbing mat, materials that had already been well proven in racing yachts like *Kialoa IV* and in the VT minehunters. Altogether about 100 tons of this material would go into the "lay-up" process.

Unfortunately the new international regulations, which related to yachts intended for commercial purposes such as chartering, were slowing down progress. Because they stipulated that *Mirabella* was technically a ship, High Modulus had to be specially certified as suitable for the job. This turned into a complex and time-consuming process. Because nobody had ever designed or built such a large yacht using fiber composites, construction couldn't begin until High Modulus had jumped through a lot of hoops, some of them pure red tape that bore little relationship to the requirements of a sailing charter yacht. With everybody finding their way in an experimental project, there were numerous meetings and many hours of intense discussion between all of us working on *Mirabella* and the certification authorities, before we finally got the green light for High Modulus to start work.

But one important – and annoying – outcome of the regulations was that Vosper Thorneycroft was forced to add 40 tons of fire-resistant material to the composite surfaces, to bring the boat up to what was considered the flameproof properties of a steel hull. On top of this, she had to be fitted with a firefighting system that would spray water mist onto any outbreak of flames. While I could understand this is highly responsible for a multi-deck passenger cruise liner with hundreds or thousands of passengers, it made no sense for a sailing yacht with one single deck below. Moreover, a restriction of just twelve passengers was imposed on *Mirabella V* although she could accommodate considerably more.

Because Joe saw this as a commercial as well as a sailing venture, he wasn't at all happy about this restriction. It also gave the design team headaches because now *Mirabella* would be heavier than we had originally planned, and I worried it might compromise her sailing performance.

There were plenty of challenges going on above the deck too. Halmatic, a Vosper Thorneycroft-owned company, had inherited the responsibility for the carbon fiber mast and boom. With a chord length of about four

▲

Project manager Paul Johnson couldn't say no when his son insisted on testing the hull of *Mirabella V* as a giant skateboard park.

My favorite room in the world!
With Joe Vittoria, I presented
Mirabella V to members of
the New York Yacht Club in
Manhattan.

feet and a width of two feet, the mast was remarkably thin considering its length. When you looked at the sections during the construction process, you couldn't help but be struck by how insubstantial they seemed. Although this was also testimony to the strength of carbon fiber materials, many waterfront sages just could not believe the stick would actually stand up. The secret though was in how it would be supported, and that job fell to rigging specialist OYS based in Bournemouth, England, and another New Zealand-based company, that of mast designer Chris Mitchell with whom we had worked on our masts for racing yachts. VT had requested that Chris Mitchell check all the calculations by us and High Modulus, just to be on the safe side.

OYS produced extra high strength solid steel rods for the rigging. One of them, the forestay, would be nearly as long as the mast and would need connecting links. Like everybody else involved in this project, OYS strove to make things as light but as strong as possible. It's particularly important to keep down the weight above the deck because excess pounds aloft increase the tipping moment – the boat's propensity to heel in a breeze – and pose all kinds of strains and stresses on the rig and the hull. Also, an important consideration for Joe was that charter guests, some of whom might have never before stepped aboard a yacht, might get nervous when a yacht heels even though she's designed to do exactly that.

I haven't yet mentioned the boom. Also under construction at Halmatic, it was another marvel of carbon fiber. As it took shape, the boom was so big it reminded me of the entire hull of a 90-foot catamaran. Known as a "Park Avenue" type boom because of its width, it was designed to be more than six feet wide at the mid-point because the epic mainsail would fold down into it in "slabs", rather like a window blind going up but in reverse. The sides were four feet high to accommodate the stowed mainsail. If it were to fall onto the deck, it would require the manpower of 20 crew to tidy it up, and *Mirabella* would have only 15 in the crew.

Last but by no means least, the lifting keel pushed the boundaries perhaps more than any other element of the design and construction process. Because you couldn't see it, the keel largely escaped notice. This fin, which was made of high-grade steel, weighed 16 tons. But attached on its end, 30 feet below the waterline, was a streamlined bulb which a Cornwall firm, Henry Irons of Wadebridge, would fill with approximately one hundred tons of molten lead. By our calculations, that would be enough to keep *Mirabella V* sufficiently upright to be comfortable for her passengers. This immense weight would be raised and lowered by a giant hydraulic ram harnessed to its very own twin 15 kilowatt motors.

▲

When an experienced Texas yacht owner purchased *Mirabella V* and renamed her *M5* he asked me about the possibility of modifying her stern to increase the deck area aft. I decided to retain the original location of the backstays, which saved some cost and weight during the extensive refit, but most importantly allowed a Carbon Cub float plane to be safely stowed on the new after deck.

▲

Testing *M5* before she makes her transatlantic passage heading for the Pacific Ocean. I'm with Mike Carr of Pendennis Shipyard, sailing at 17 knots off Falmouth under the biggest mainsail in the world.

In my customary pursuit of lightness with strength, my original idea was to use just the one ram, but I wasn't sure if it would be powerful enough. At the suggestion of an engineering friend I ended up contacting a company in Aberdeen that specialized in manufacturing gigantic oil rigs for the North Sea. Somebody with a broad Scottish accent answered my call.

"I have a problem," I explained. "I want to lift a big yacht keel, 150 tons of it, with just one hydraulic ram."

There was a brief silence. "D'ye mean 1,500 tons?"

"No, just 150 tons," I answered.

"Och, 150 tons is nothin', man. We've lots o' them rams lyin' aroond the yard here. Eh, but 1,500 tons, that could be a challenge, richt enough."

On the basis of the advice of my unpaid Scottish consultant, we went ahead with the single ram. And the construction of the keel came together remarkably smoothly despite the challenges: among other record achievements the boys at VT had to execute the biggest steel weld in company history in order to join the bulb to the fin. The job took three days and nights to complete.

As I saw them at work, I had nothing but admiration for the craftsmen and engineers at VT. They loved their work, they were proud of what they were doing, and they had serious talent.

But the project took longer than necessary, primarily in my opinion, because VT kept changing project managers. Over the period of *Mirabella V*'s construction, no fewer than three managers took over, triggering inevitable delays as they were brought up to speed with the project. Apparently this was normal in the production of warships, but, compared with *Mirabella*, warships are relatively simple vessels to build.

As for the sails, that immense job went to Robbie Doyle who owned the Marblehead, Massachusetts-based Doyle Sailmakers loft with which Joe had worked over many years. It was probably a much bigger task than anybody could have predicted. Not only did the material have to be specially woven, but a lot of specialized research was involved before Robbie could even get started. That achievement went down in company history.

Eventually the job was done, and *Mirabella V* – the world's biggest single-masted sailing yacht, biggest sloop, biggest just about everything – finally hit the water after her slow-motion descent along the slipway. As soon as I could get away, I went down to the water's edge to check whether she floated on her lines. To my relief, she was bang on.

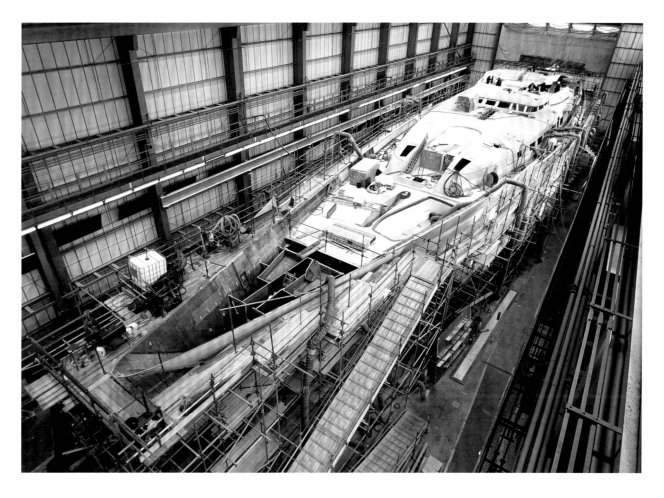

▲

A very big project. I never became
complacent about what we were
creating, and every time I visited
the VT shipyard I was taken aback,
to use a nautical expression.

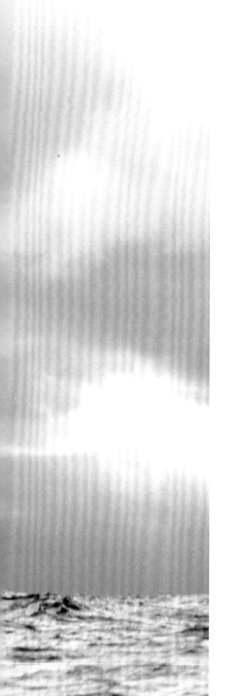

LEFT: *Rainbow Warrior II* in the South China Sea on passage from Hong Kong to Japan. I was invited to join her in Hong Kong during the Greenpeace Asia anti-toxic campaign. I welcome any opportunity to join any sailing vessel.

BELOW: Ron aboard *Rainbow Warrior II* off the south coast of Taiwan.

With Greenpeace aboard *Rainbow Warrior II*

I was very impressed by Westminster Abbey during the memorial service for Sir Edward Heath. He was my highest-profile racing yacht client.

I pass
an exam

I HAD SPENT ALL MY LIFE AROUND YACHTS, loving the banging and snapping of the sails and the rushing sound of the bow wave. But I also loved the whistling of the wind over the cockpit of a small aircraft, an emotion I probably owe to Johnny Mac. I'd owned a couple of aircraft but never been able to fly them – well, not officially – because I hadn't obtained the essential papers. So, in my forties I decided I wanted to get my hands on the controls and become a fully accredited pilot.

I started lessons with the local flying club at Cork airport, and continued with them whenever Joanna and I could get away together with the children and spend time at our holiday home in Ft. Myers, Florida. Because of my flying with Johnny Mac in the Beagle and with Hugh Woodsend in my own aircraft, I had a good working knowledge of what to do. Not one to shirk a challenge, Joanna decided to learn too, picking up the skills quickly from scratch. I was seriously impressed. After about 30 hours of instruction at Page Field Airport in Ft. Myers, Florida, we both flew solo and got through it with flying colors.

So far so good. But of course you can't fly around America just because you've proven you can take off and land. Next up was the private pilot's exam. As the written test loomed, I started to get stressed because it reminded me too much of my abortive schooldays. When I had to sit down with pen and paper, all those memories came flooding back and I just couldn't think straight. The inevitable happened – I flunked the private

▲

If you love aeroplanes and flying you have to visit the Reno Air Races in Nevada. At the invitation of Rod Lewis and Lewis Air Legends I got to hang out with the Texas team, which operates several modified World War II aircraft, including the world's fastest propeller plane. At the 2014 races Lewis Air Legends' Grumman Bearcat "Rear Bare" took the record at 528.3 MPH. L TO R: pilot Stuart Dawson, Ron Holland.

pilot's exam by a single point. Now what? I thought. Do I just quit or do I sit the test again? Oh, how I wanted to fly!

After a few days I decided to sign up for a crash course in Tampa, and after three days of solid instruction that left me mentally exhausted, I showed up for the test once again. And passed. By a single mark, one miserable mark. But I didn't care – I'd passed an exam and it felt like a triumph. Although she would certainly have aced the exam, Joanna opted not to sit it because she felt that the mother of two little girls shouldn't be flying around the skies in a light plane. As she pointed out, at least she knew enough to be able to get us home if there was an emergency of some sort, like me falling ill.

So, armed with my PPL License I took off. I flew all over Florida, stopping to visit yachting friends and clients, and often returning to Ft. Myers in the dark. I particularly enjoyed flying at night and accumulated almost as many night as day hours.

Then one night it very nearly all went wrong. When I was returning from Palm Beach, this time with Joanna and the girls on board, for the first and only time in my life I experienced spatial disorientation, the phenomenon that is thought to lie behind the deaths of John Kennedy Jr., his wife Carolyn and his sister-in-law Lauren Bessette when they crashed into the Atlantic off Martha's Vineyard one evening. Without warning, I experienced an overpowering sense that the plane was turning left. It wasn't, but I was fighting an irrational and dangerous urge to correct it by turning right.

"I'm in trouble here," I yelled to Joanna. "Tell the girls to shut up. I've gotta concentrate."

It took a little while but I was able to overcome the sensation, one of the most frightening I've experienced. Just calm down and fly the plane, I kept on telling myself, until a sense of normality returned, and shaken but alive we landed back at Page Field. At least, as we discussed later, Joanna could have taken over the controls.

I fell in love with light planes and owned several of them, a Piper Twin Apache, a Cessna Twin 402B and a Piper Twin Comanche. But I never forgot that small planes can be dangerous. As Johnny Mac used to say, "There's old pilots and bold pilots but there's no old bold pilots."

Along the way there were a few narrow squeaks, like the time I landed in a paddock in Ireland. I wasn't at the controls this time. The pilot was the remarkable J.J. Ebaugh. Universally known as J.J., she was one of those women who seemingly effortlessly collected accomplishments. A skilled racing car driver, sailor and commercial pilot who used to fly Ted Turner around, she was very capable at the controls. But one day she was flying

> "Because of strong headwinds we were taking longer than expected to reach Ireland, and as conditions worsened, J.J. dropped low to avoid ominous-looking clouds that would have prevented her from maintaining visual contact with the ground."

me and her boyfriend Kent from London back to Cork in a chartered single-engined aircraft in deteriorating weather. Because of strong headwinds we were taking longer than expected to reach Ireland, and as conditions worsened, J.J. dropped low to avoid ominous-looking clouds that would have prevented her from maintaining visual contact with the ground. Then we lost radio contact with Cork airport, and as night approached and the clouds grew more and more dense, J.J. made a professional decision instead of flying into danger.

"I don't want to take a chance landing in Cork," she announced. "I noticed a good field a few minutes back. I'm going to turn around and land there."

"OK," I replied, trying not to sound nervous, and thinking, that sounds like a good idea.

Turning the aircraft 180 degrees, J.J. zeroed in on a small headland she'd spotted that was projecting into the Irish Sea, known as Hook Head. First, she made a trial approach, swooping low over the hedges as she studied the terrain. Reasonably satisfied, she took the aircraft around again, this time to attempt a landing into the wind exactly as you're supposed to do. With night approaching, visibility had deteriorated further and she was straining to see through the windshield as we headed for the field, surrounded by stone walls and hedges.

Expertly fingering the controls, J.J. dropped the aircraft onto the grass, narrowly clearing a wall, and braked as hard as she dared. A hedge

▲
Johnny Mac flew his Piper Cub
from a field near his sail loft,
across the river behind the Royal
Cork Yacht Club. Here he is getting ready for another flight.

▶
Influenced by sailmaker and
pilot John McWilliam I caught
the flying bug! Here Johnny Mac
lands his Piper Cub in the field
next to our Strand Farmhouse
design studio. He skimmed the
trees on his final approach, but
anyway it was a good landing
and following take off.

was coming up fast as we bounced up and down on the uneven surface. This is going to be touch and go, I thought.

J.J. pulled up just short of the hedge and gave us a triumphant smile. Relieved, Kent and I looked at each other. We all clambered out and found our way to a nearby house, and knocked on a well-weathered green door. A farmer wearing a tweed jacket and cheese-cutter cap opened up.

"I hope its OK – we just landed in your field. We need to call Cork airport," explained J.J., pointing to our plane.

"Sure, would you like a cup of tea first?" the farmer said. Dry in the mouth, we accepted instantly and followed him inside. "The last plane to land in that field was during the war," our host told us. "The pilot was German and my father invited him in for a cup of tea." (Ireland was a neutral country throughout the Second World War.) So, we thought as we drained our tea, here's history repeating itself.

We were lucky. After we'd been picked up by my assistant Helen and driven home, J.J. returned to the field alone the next day and tried to take off. Expert though she was, she was unable to get the aircraft off the ground because the field was too wet and rough, and too short. This time not even her skills could save the day and she crashed into the hedge, wrecking the plane and suffering a deep cut to her forehead. Shaken, she got back into the car and drove back to Carrigaline where she found us at Finbar Coogan's. A tough customer, J.J. soon recovered her composure after a few drinks.

Around this time I started visiting the Option Institute, a place for personal development studies in Sheffield, Massachusetts. I was still unhappy. I often thought of Mr. Takeda and how right he'd been. "Why he unhappy?" he had asked all those years ago. I never really knew why at that time, but I certainly had good reason in the new millennium. After twelve years with Joanna, the marriage was breaking up and I couldn't really figure out why. I was coming to the painful conclusion it was something in me and I felt an obligation to find out what it was.

I'd never much thought about death and dying before Rob James had drowned, but I was increasingly being confronted with the inevitability of our mortality. Since the death of my mother and father, other people who were important in my life were dying and I found myself attending funerals, pretty much for the first time in my life. I had always avoided them because I found them depressing and upsetting. I had missed my mother's and father's funerals. I was traveling and preferred to think of them as they'd been when I – and they – were younger. But here I was in Westminster Abbey for a memorial service, sitting in the front row.

▲

After we safely landed in an Irish field the locals came to visit, with the recollection that the last plane to land here was a German during World War II!

The light poured through the stained glass windows of the awe-inspiring church as the organist played a Bach prelude, one of Mr. Heath's favorite pieces of music. Wearing red and white gowns, the choir rose to sing a chorale that the former prime minister had once conducted for the London Proms season. Seated with others who had shared my late client's life in sailing, I was stunned by the majesty and beauty of it all.

It was July 2005 and Sir Edward Heath – Mr. Heath, as I had always called him – had died a few weeks earlier, and, as befits a former prime minister, he was being given a grand and formal send-off. Not only was the magnificent building filled with the people you would expect to be invited – political colleagues, former prime ministers and foreign heads of state both current and past, royalty and dignitaries of all kinds – also in attendance were the musicians and yachties who had meant so much to him. We had all come to pay our respects to a fine individual whom I had gotten to know so well over the years.

About 50 seats had been reserved for the sailing fraternity. Arriving early, I was able to pick my place between Peter Nicholson and Olin Stephens, who had designed the first few *Morning Clouds* for Mr. Heath before he honored me with the privilege of taking over from the New York maestro. Leaning across, Olin whispered in my ear that he had come with one of his nephews all the way from his nursing home in Hanover, New Hampshire. Not bad for a 95-year-old, I thought. Every now and again, when I found myself in his neighborhood I would stop by to see Olin, and I was always amazed by how well he had aged. Once, with a twinkle in his eye, he'd introduced me to his girlfriend who lived across the hall from his apartment. Very convenient. A lovely lady, well into her eighties, who often drove Olin to lunch at my Irish friend Simon Pearce's restaurant in Quechee, Vermont.

Sitting nearby was sailing aficionado Anthony Churchill, a stalwart of Mr. Heath's crew over most of his yachting career. It was Anthony, a publisher as well as a yachtie, who had made sure that I received an invitation. Also, Owen Parker, who had sailed with Mr. Heath from the very beginning, was in the front row with Peter Nicholson.

As music filled the Abbey my mind wandered back to my relationship with Ted Heath. It had begun when he commissioned me to design his fifth *Morning Cloud*. Mr. Heath loved his sailing. Mentally disciplined, he had a lightning-quick mind and somehow managed to shoehorn his yachting life into a lot of other activities. Although he'd lost office by the time he asked me to design the yacht, he was always in demand for a multitude of things, most of them politically related, but he derived great

I will never forget the grand majesty of Westminster Abbey during the memorial service for Sir Edward Heath. I felt that for a Kiwi boy from the beach at Torbay, it was a privilege to be there.

"I left Westminster Abbey feeling uplifted by the occasion, understanding how lucky I was, but also reflective. Why wasn't I happier and more satisfied? I had achieved more than I could ever have dreamed. I had dreamed big, but I had achieved far more than I dreamed."

pleasure from everything to do with sailing including talking about it. Highly focused, he made sure to surround himself with people who had expertise that he didn't possess himself.

He was not nearly as reserved as most people seemed to think, or as he could sometimes appear in public. He had a quick sense of humor and a sudden chuckle. I think he enjoyed the fact that I had no apparent interest in politics, although I avoided telling him that I had never exercised my democratic right to vote, somewhat to my embarrassment when in his company. I never wore a suit, much preferring slacks with an open-necked shirt and cowboy boots. And I never had a tie during my visits with him in London, a sartorial weakness that seemed to amuse Mr. Heath. He'd often ask one of his bodyguards to loan me a tie if we had to go to some upscale restaurant where neckwear was obligatory. I ended up with an interesting collection of neckties.

During the development stage for *Morning Cloud* we sometimes met in the parliament buildings. He would often have to excuse himself and hurry downstairs for a vote in the Commons when we were in the middle of a discussion about sail plans or keel design, subjects about which he grew very knowledgeable. At other times we'd schedule a discussion in his London apartment on Wilton Street. His Italian housekeeper, a charming woman who got to know me over the years, would usher me into the study with its grand piano, piles of sheet music, breathtakingly lovely art, model yachts and scores of gifts of every kind – "the sort of things you have to be prime minister to get!" Mr. Heath once joked. And once or twice we met at The Ritz or The Savoy, favorite places of his.

Ever the alert politician, he never missed a face: on one occasion at The Savoy he grabbed my arm and said: "See that person over there?" indicating a man sitting alone at a table. "That's Tennessee Williams." I wouldn't have known the great playwright if I'd bumped right into him, but Mr. Heath invited him over, and over the next surreal half-hour or so I found myself discussing sailing with the author of *A Streetcar Named Desire* and the ex-prime minister of England. A special experience for a kid from Torbay. Later, after he'd retired from politics, I would drive down to his beautiful house in Hampshire, practically next door to Winchester Cathedral, and sometimes we'd walk around the garden with a stream running past.

As the music filled the great London abbey, I also thought back to the times I went sailing aboard *Morning Cloud*, usually during trials and warm-up races. By then Mr. Heath was already an accomplished sailor with a thorough overall grasp of the required skills. After all, before he got into bigger yachts he had gained his initial experience in the extremely skittish, two-man Fireball dinghy that could be a real handful in a breeze. Despite his fame and reputation, I admired the way he would defer to others if he thought they knew more than him. For instance, he would not hesitate to throw over the wheel the instant Owen Parker yelled, "Tack now, skipper."

Mr. Heath had lived the fullest possible life – politician and Europhile, musician, sailor, author – and I'd never detected any melancholy in him. I'm sure he ended his days with a deep sense of satisfaction of what he'd done, though I don't believe he could ever bring himself to develop a friendship with Margaret Thatcher.

I left Westminster Abbey feeling uplifted by the occasion, understanding how lucky I was, but also reflective. Why wasn't I happier and more satisfied?

I had achieved more than I could ever have dreamed. I had dreamed big, but I had achieved far more than I dreamed. The yachts I had designed were sailing the world's oceans, and production versions of my creations were being built in a dozen countries. A few years later English couple John and Carolyn Charnley commissioned a 55-footer I designed for them to go world cruising, developing it into a production series to be known as the Discovery 55 whose sales would top the 50 mark. Their owners would voyage to the far corners of the globe: to the South Island of New Zealand, to Australia's Great Barrier Reef, across the Indian Ocean, north to Alaska and the icebergs of Greenland.

▲

During the 1980s most of my clients were based in New York. We were fortunate to often commute to New York City by Ventura Air float plane or Thomson Industries helicopter.

My design work for Discovery Yachts in England was created to allow yachts with small crews to voyage the world. Discovery Yacht owners have sailed everywhere, from the ice-choked waters of the northern latitudes to the shiny blue Pacific and Indian Oceans.

Hundreds of my smaller designs had come off production lines too. In Britain, Camper and Nicholson had sold many 33-footers. For years Nautor in Finland, builders of Swan yachts, had enjoyed a steady stream of orders for my mid-sized yachts, from 37 feet up to 44 feet in length, and these boats were sailing just about everywhere. In Sweden, Omega Yachts was building production versions of my smaller boats. In France, at one point Jeanneau was building a Rush 30 performance cruiser, also developed from one of my winning designs, at a rate of almost one a week. Jeanneau would go on to sell hundreds of them. In Italy, Perini Navi and I would soon start collaborating on customized semi-production superyachts, the first over 180 feet in length, and soon we would work again with Perini on a sailing yacht over 200 feet long.

And good old *Eygthene*, now known in the USA as the Kiwi 24, was under construction in Florida, the Channel Islands, Japan, South Africa and Australia.

I never really added the numbers up but hundreds of my designs were afloat somewhere in the world. It was immensely gratifying to know that my sailboats were giving so much pleasure. Wherever I went in the world, owners and crew would corner me and ask for tips, generally about how to make my boats go faster. Hardly a day went by when somebody didn't call the studio from Oslo or San Francisco or Hamble or elsewhere, and put a question to me or one of my team.

So, I could honestly say I hadn't failed in my professional life.

That left my family life: two marriages and four wonderful daughters of whom I was extremely proud. While I hadn't been at home with them nearly as much as would have been expected of a good father, they were the light of my life and I believed they knew that. And yet my second great relationship was falling apart. Oh no, not again! I kept on thinking, I've got to try and understand this.

One of my early self-inquiry efforts took me to Esalen institute in Big Sur, California. Then, later, at the suggestion of one of Joanna's friends, a teacher in yoga and psychotherapy, I enrolled at the Option Institute in Massachusetts and braced myself for a serious bout of soul seeking. I just hoped it wasn't going to be too searing.

I had looked up the Institute on the internet and learned that it had been established in 1983 by Barry (Bears) Neil Kaufman and his wife Samahria Lyte. They had a severely autistic son, and against conventional advice pursued a very personal route to make contact with their little boy. It worked, and they found themselves successfully responding to many parents looking for help with their autistic kids. Bears also realized that

▲

The pond at Option. A wonderful environment for self inquiry.

the parents needed as much help as their autistic children, so an important aspect of their work was helping people like me: adults looking for answers to their personal questions.

I flew from Shannon in Ireland to Boston, where I picked up a rental car and drove west to the Option property, near the intersecting borders of Massachusetts, Connecticut and New York in the beautiful Berkshires. I had signed up for what was described as a "Happiness Weekend" – more accurately, an introductory program of the Option Institute for self-exploration and discovery.

Option and Esalen weren't the first times I had embarked on an internal discovery voyage of this kind. My first experience was in London in the early '70s with a class led by Robert D'Aubigny called Exegesis. I had also attended mindfulness training in Buddhism at Plum village, near Bordeaux in France, following Buddhist teacher Thich Nhat Hanh. These all proved helpful on my quest to understand Mr. Takeda's observation. I left my first visit to the Option Institute feeling I'd touched on something important, something very helpful, but it was too late to save my marriage. I saw when I looked deeply with these self-inquiry studies, that my marriage was not meant to be saved. However, I wanted to get to the bottom of what I thought at the time were relationship failures and I duly signed up for another course at the Institute. I felt I learned so much that I would keep attending annual classes there for the next 20 years, and continue to do so.

▲

From the Lewis Air Legends collection's B25 Mitchell WWII bomber, I photographed an F7F P3 Tigercat over the island of St. Barths in the Caribbean.

...World's Fastest
Qualifying Sea Fury
480.249 Mph
Reno 2013

◄ I had to say yes to an invitation to board this beautiful WWII B25 bomber for a flight over the St. Barths Bucket racing yachts.

▲ Thumbs up for the start of the Reno Air Races. The Lewis Air Legends' Sea Fury will go again – at this time the fastest propeller plane in the world, at 480.2 mph. In Reno I'm surrounded by fast planes: it's a bit like the Admiral's Cup but more life and death!

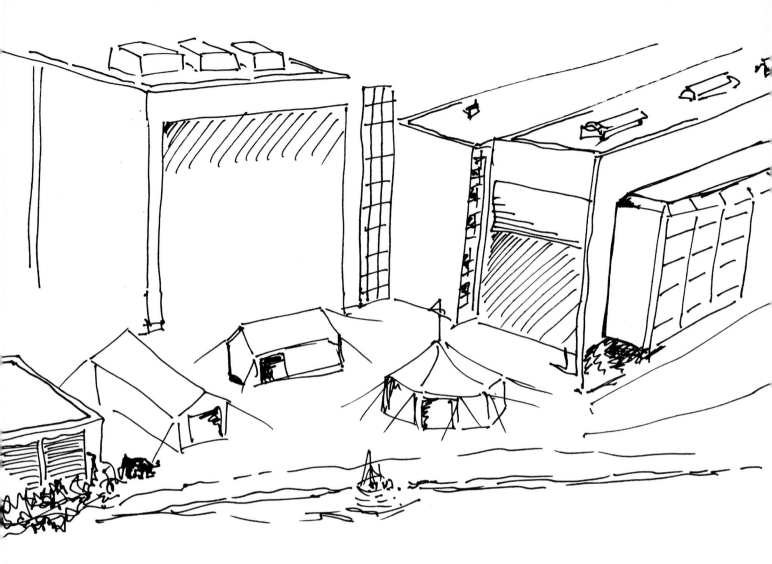

Before we created the sailing design concept for *Ethereal*, our clients Bill Joy and Shannon O'Leary insisted all involved were exposed to a unique research program. The Rocky Mountain Institute created a tent campus at Royal Huisman Shipyard, and all were exposed to new thinking before "putting pen to paper" or "cutting any metal."

An ethereal experience

IN ALL MY YEARS OF DESIGNING YACHTS I had never heard of something called a charrette. And here I was involved in exactly that in Vollenhove, a small town in the Netherlands, at the request of American software pioneer Bill Joy. One of the most stimulating clients I have ever worked with – Bill was once dubbed the "Edison of the Internet" – he'd flown in a high-powered team of very experienced colleagues to float ideas, no matter how radical, that might be incorporated into my second-biggest design commission to that date, a 182-foot, globe-girdling ketch. She wouldn't be as big as *Mirabella*, but she promised to be even more radical.

A charrette, I was learning, is a kind of think tank in which just about anything and everything is on the table for discussion. And here I was moving between tents, yes, actual tents specially erected next to the ship-yard, in which separate and earnest discussions were taking place among Bill's invited friends.

Wow! I was thinking as I jotted down notes. Some of these guys are crazy, smart but crazy! But I was also learning that this just might be the whole point. In a charrette, you throw an idea into the pot and it gets kicked around until it's discarded because it doesn't work, or until something new and startling emerges from it. It's a fascinating and creative process. These guys didn't mind ripping tradition to shreds and starting from scratch. Few of them had any knowledge of the tradition and history of yacht design, and they didn't care a jot. They liked nothing better than questioning everything, which was why they were there. I was amused and stimulated at the same time, as many of the most basic assumptions about big sail-powered yachts were being put under the microscope. And the microscope started at the top of the mast and went all the way to the bottom of the keel, including everything else in between.

According to the organizer of the charrette, the Rocky Mountain Institute, a specialist in advanced energy research, the dictionary definition of a charrette is as follows: "An intensive, transdisciplinary, round-table design workshop." As the institute's Will Clift, a Masters graduate in management science and engineering from Stanford University, put it in a subsequent article, a charrette's purpose is, by throwing a lot of very bright people together, "to achieve many months of normal conceptual design in typically a few days." In other words, adds Clift, it's "an accelerated process of discovery."

I wasn't quite sure what I was discovering but the ideas were certainly coming thick and fast. Co-founder and former chief scientist of Sun Microsystems, Bill helped design the UNIX code while still a graduate student at Berkeley. Unsurprisingly, he's highly focused when in pursuit of an exciting goal, and he wanted the greenest, most energy-efficient sailing yacht ever built. Bill and his wife Shannon had already given their yacht a name, *Ethereal*, which pretty much summed up the couple's philosophy.

In the room, actually a hotel lobby near the Royal Huisman yard, were gathered eleven world authorities in fields ranging from the design and manufacture of high-strength glass, the latest lighting systems, the biological treatment of wastewater, storage of electricity in lithium batteries and – a subject that really caught my attention – biomimicry.

This last is defined – brace yourself! – as the imitation of the models, systems and elements of nature for the purpose of solving complex human problems. I could immediately see its relevance to design and engineering of water-borne craft. Also present were some naval architects, including Pieter Beeldsnijder who would design the interior and styling of this new yacht, plus a handful of yacht builders with firm ideas of their own. I'm sure they were as nonplussed as I was by what was going on. It had already been made clear to me that the Joys were not interested in just another superyacht, but desired a beautiful sailboat whose technology would be relevant to the kind of life they believed would be the future. As I had seen during the years I'd attended the Monaco Grand Prix to pick up ideas for my racing yachts, some of the technological advances achieved in Formula One racing trickled down to your average street vehicle, and Bill wanted *Ethereal* to achieve much the same result.

A self-made man, he certainly had the budget to get the job done. On the basis of my experience with European-built superyachts of this size, and allowing for the cost of developing and installing these custom-made advanced systems, I estimated *Ethereal* could not be done for much under $60 million. My other big yachts, not including the giant *Mirabella V,* had not gone over a €50 million cost.

At one point I got so concerned about the high costs that I expressed my worries to Bill over dinner one night in the Amstel Hotel in Amsterdam. "Don't worry," he said. "We're creating something special." And no doubt about it, that was true.

Bill and Shannon have serious ecological consciences. As Will Clift summarized in crystal-clear words: "During the charrette Bill frequently reiterated that *Ethereal* should be thought of as self-contained, as though she were an isolated island that could travel the seas. The boat must keep her passengers (crew and guests) safe, regardless of location and weather. She must have redundant critical systems, be resilient to breakdown, be easily fixed with spare parts on hand, and – in an emergency – provide life support for an extended period of time. Secondly, all systems must be easy to run with the least possible upkeep, as crew time is precious. Thirdly, *Ethereal* must provide her passengers with high-quality food and water without relying on frequent shipments from distant sources; she must be able to store or produce several weeks' worth of nourishment. Also, like a

The Rocky Mountain Institute charrette encouraged all involved to look at designing and building Bill Joy's new yacht with a fresh approach. I was involved in a similar study with myself. While ongoing inquiry at the Option Institute was my principal method, I also found very helpful, closer to home, the teachings of Sogyal Rinpoche, at the Dzogchen Beara retreat center on the dramatic southwest coast of Ireland. In fact, if I had to choose just one book to read for the rest of my life, I would without hesitation choose Sogyal Rinpoche's manual for life and death, *The Tibetan Book Of Living and Dying.*

OVERLEAF: After launching, *Ethereal* sailing fast, on her way to sail all the oceans.

▲

An important design collaboration with Dutch designers PB
Design and the Royal Huisman
Shipyard. When Bruce Katz described his vision for the new
yacht, I was thinking he wanted
a sister to *Whirlwind XII* at 103
feet in length. Unable to contain
his creative vision at that size,
Juliet grew to over 143 feet and
became a new benchmark for high
quality custom sailing yachts.

modern community of people, a yacht produces wastes, organic and non-organic, that must be treated and disposed of responsibly. On a yacht the issue of trash is much harder to ignore than on land – there is no "away" to throw it; all trash must be kept on board until it can be unloaded ashore. Finally, *Ethereal* must minimize or, ideally, design out the emissions of odors, gases, and noises, which not only reduce enjoyment of a voyage, but can also pose health threats to passengers and those living near areas in which she docks. *Ethereal* must provide all of these services in a relatively tiny envelope."

None of my other clients had ever expressed a vision remotely similar to this one. And I fully understood this wasn't so much a wish list as a firm set of specifications. Although it wasn't my job to solve the challenges of designing plants for wastewater treatment, desalination and power, plus the equivalent of a landfill, in a relatively small space, it was my job to deliver the sailing experience that the Joys so much desired. So I had to be involved in all the detail of where these things would be installed. If this weight wasn't distributed properly, *Ethereal* would sail disappointingly, and I couldn't have that.

I had been invited to Vollenhove because of *Juliet*, a 143-footer that I had designed for Bruce Katz, the founder of the Rockport Shoe Company, and more recently the Samuel Hubbard Shoe Company. We had collaborated with Pieter Beeldsnijder, the talented Dutch yacht designer and interior design specialist whose studio, PB Design, we had worked with on several other projects before creating *Juliet*.

A giant step forward from *Whirlwind XII* in both size and complexity, *Juliet* had also been built at the Huisman yard (it was granted its Royal status later) and gone on to win several design awards. She even had a book devoted to her under the title of *Juliet, Creation of a Masterpiece*. The Joys were friends of Bruce, had sailed aboard *Juliet*, and so much enjoyed the experience that they decided they wanted a similar yacht of their own. Following Bruce's suggestion, they had signed up Huisman, Pieter and myself to fulfill their dream. Extremely well connected, Bill had also engaged another friend of his, the Rocky Mountain Institute's chairman and chief scientist Amory Lovins, a distinguished physicist among other things, to run the charrette.

After the first day I was in despair. I couldn't see anything useful emerging from this forum. As far as I could tell, some of the ideas that had been debated bore little or no relation to the normal disciplines of yachting or marine design. This is all a waste of time, I'd decided.

But by the end of the second day I began to feel more hopeful. The

▲

Directly after launching in England *Christopher* crossed the Atlantic Ocean to race in the St. Barths Bucket. Here she is off St. Barths racing towards the finish line. *Christopher*'s design is a development of *Juliet* and *Ethereal* with more classic exterior styling. A fast comfortable yacht for crossing all the oceans.

benefits of thinking outside the box were starting to appear as the discussions covered examples from other industries less traditional than boatbuilding, and the lessons we can learn from nature.

I might learn something here, I thought.

And, just maybe, so could the wider yachting industry which at that time often betrayed an unnecessarily cautious mentality. While I fully understood this caution originated mainly from the dangers inherent in offshore sailing that had engendered a tried-and-tested approach rather than an innovative one, I had long believed that yacht builders were often too conservative for their own good. This was – and is – particularly the case in big custom yachts. In my hundreds of visits to boatyards I had come to see that bespoke designs could be built faster, better and less expensively if new methods were developed. By the third day, I was sold. Yes, I am learning lots.

I returned to Ireland, my head buzzing with ideas from the charrette. I briefed my team, their eyes widening as I described some of the ideas that had come up for discussion, and we got down to work. Everything that the studio and I knew about sailing and yacht design in all its aspects went into what I finally presented to the Joys. My best shot. I had every confidence she would be fast and comfortable in every kind of weather they would encounter in their long-distance voyaging.

That wasn't good enough for Bill.

He urged me to subject the design to yet more research, so I suggested we go to the Wolfson Unit in Southampton for a scale-model tank test. I had often visited the unit to test my assumptions and I greatly valued their science. Also, working with me at the suggestion of Wolter Huisman was Dutch marine engineer and naval architect Dr. Peter van Oossanen, who was engaged in refining the hydrodynamics of the propellers and providing his views on the all-important underwater engineering. Simultaneously other researchers were developing models based on computational fluid dynamics, the latest tool that aimed to provide a more accurate prediction of how a yacht will perform in her natural environment of the sea. At Bill's urging, we also developed several variations of my design that incorporated some of the ideas that emerged during the charrette, just to see if they might or might not work.

After the tests at the Wolfson Unit to check my original design and all the variations, we sat down and asked ourselves the big question, Which design is the best? By general agreement it was decided to build my original design. I had learned a lot from the charrette, but it was gratifying to see that a lifetime of experience – if you like, the instinctive sense that

▲
Ethereal racing in light trade winds during the St. Barths Bucket.

▲

My last Royal Huisman-built
yacht, *Ethereal*, cruising in New
Zealand waters: doing what she
was designed to do.

"As Bill later told *Fortune* magazine, 'Ron drew it (the hull and the keel) and we tried longer and shorter and other things. In the end we came back to what he had done in the beginning – in other words his intuitive feeling for what was going to work turned out to be correct. We did a lot of computer simulations and tank testing to go in a big circle.'"

you get from thousands of hours on the water and at the drawing board – is hard to beat.

As Bill later told *Fortune* magazine, "Ron drew it (the hull and the keel) and we tried longer and shorter and other things. In the end we came back to what he had done in the beginning – in other words his intuitive feeling for what was going to work turned out to be correct. We did a lot of computer simulations and tank testing to go in a big circle."

I was pleased that Bill had not pursued some offbeat idea that would have spoiled the yacht's performance. I had designed *Ethereal* to sail at speeds of up to 18 knots, which is roughly as fast as the old tea clippers, but with modern comfort and safety. The clippers needed a crew of 25 to 50 brave, hard-bitten men who sailed them pretty much permanently on the brink of disaster, with green waves thundering across the decks.

Yet I could still see the benefit of the rip-it-up-and-start-again approach of the charrette because it's amazing what you discover in the process. It had also been an eye-opener to work with such impeccably credentialed people. Naturally, it was Bill who signed everything off. It was his way to listen and learn, and then decide. He discarded two important technical issues that I proposed. One was for a single propeller; twin propellers, I argued, would create too much drag when the yacht was under sail. At the time there was a marked swing to single propellers and today all modern commercial ships use single props.

The other issue was a so-called drop keel, technically known as a variable geometry keel, a system I favor for big sailing yachts. This is because the giant centerboard, as it really is, can be wound up so the boat can enter shallower waters than it could with a deep fixed keel. Although drop keels improve sailing performance, in big yachts they require some complex engineering. Anyway, Bill decided on the simplicity of a shallower fixed keel and I was fine with it. I've always believed it's a mistake to try and impose your own ideas on an owner, unless it's an issue of safety or some other matter of overriding importance.

But how to get the best possible sailing performance with a shallow fixed keel? After a lot of thought I designed it with wings located on the bottom. Keel wings, as the world saw in the America's Cup races in 1983 when *Australia II* beat the Americans, help "lift" a shallow-keeled yacht to windward – that is, they assist her in sailing closer to the wind. Thus, the wings would compensate in some measure for the shallow fixed keel. Designed and manufactured by a process known as computer numerical controlled machining, or CNC milling, the wings were masterpieces of functionality that I modeled on the wings of supersonic jet fighters.

Bill's willingness to push the envelope was also reflected in the rig. Instead of the aluminum masts and booms installed on *Juliet*, he opted for carbon fiber. I had already specified carbon fiber spars on some of my latest designs, most notably on *Mirabella V*, and knew how effective they were, but I was impressed that he was willing to take the chance on his new yacht. Made by New Zealand-based Southern Spars, *Ethereal*'s carbon fiber mast and boom were lighter, easier to maintain and, above all, they improved the yacht's sailing performance.

Always looking to do things better, Southern Spars had also devised a much more efficient way of furling these giant sails. Instead of them being rolled into the mast, as with *Juliet*, which requires a stick with fatter dimensions, the mainsail and mizzen sail for *Ethereal* were to be lowered into the boom. Although it means the boom needs a bigger cross section to accommodate the sail when furled, it's better to have that amount of size and weight low down instead of high up because it makes the yacht more stable. Once again reflecting Bill's ecological ambitions, the sails would be raised and lowered by a hybrid-powered Caterpillar engine using diesel and – a breakthrough in yachts at this time – lithium batteries.

But if the outside appearance of the yacht wasn't much changed by the intense debates that went on in the tents, the inside certainly was. As the participants "tunneled through the cost barrier," in one of Amory Lovins's favorite expressions, they came up with deeply practical, useful and trans-

▲

The August 2006 issue of *Fortune* highlighted a story of building *Ethereal* at Royal Huisman Shipyard in Holland. The article presented a photograph of me with Bill Joy relaxing on the yacht's unfinished bulb keel. The story also described The Rocky Mountain Institute research project, which influenced energy-efficient solutions that my clients insisted on incorporating during the design and building program.

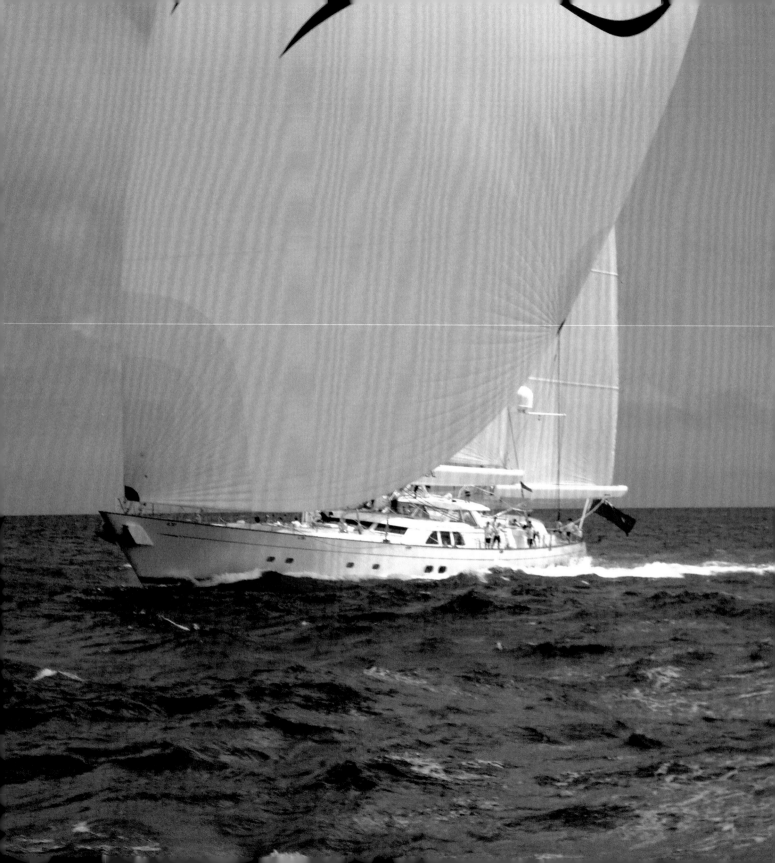

LEFT: When the 182-foot ketch *Ethereal* was launched in 2009 many of her engineering and operating systems were of a pioneering nature. Our clients Bill Joy and Shannon O'Leary insisted that their new yacht was designed and built taking into account forward-thinking solutions that had not yet been incorporated in any existing ocean-going vessel. Ron Holland Design and PB Design as collaborating designers, with the builder Royal Huisman Shipyard and many contractors, were exposed to fresh territory. These new ideas originated from our clients' relationship with the Rocky Mountain Institute, their members presenting us with unconventional design possibilities to ensure that *Ethereal* would be the most efficient yacht afloat.

ABOVE: Here I'm at the helm of *Ethereal* on passage between Palma de Majorca and Barcelona. We must be going fast – I look happy!

formational ideas that, one by one, would show up in the finished yacht.

Take the interior lighting, for example. The incandescent lights, mainly tungsten-halogen, that were then standard on yachts were replaced with light-emitting diodes that we know today as LEDs. They cost more but, as Will Clift noted, the extra expense would be quickly recouped. For a start, LEDs last many times longer than conventional lighting, and because they release less heat that meant the air conditioning system could be turned down. "This in turn would not only save energy but would also allow a smaller air conditioning system to be installed, again saving cost and space," Clift wrote. One good thing was leading to another. And, probably to the consternation of the traditionally-minded Huisman people sitting in on the charrette, the participants also mounted an assault on water use. Although this wasn't my main area of concern, I was more than interested because I had to know how this would affect the weight. I needed to ensure this yacht floated to her lines.

On any superyacht water is a huge item. A boat like *Ethereal* would normally consume around 2,000 gallons of water a day in cooking, drinking, showering, laundry, washing the salt off the decks and a host of other activities. But no yacht was able to store this much H_2O: it had to come from the ocean, pumped through a highly effective but energy-devouring desalination system.

"Let's see what we can do here," the participants said in effect. It didn't take them long to come up with something. They proposed tapping existing technologies for showers, laundry and the other uses, and by recycling some of the used water for washing the deck, a routine exercise for already hard-working crews, they estimated savings of nearly 50 percent in water use. In a superyacht that's enormous. Just as exciting, because of their acquaintance with emerging technologies, the scientists were able to build in assumptions about the future that could be incorporated into the interior design when, or if, the technologies became available. Thus, incredibly, they estimated that within a few years of *Ethereal*'s launch she would need just four percent of the water normally used by such a yacht, with correspondingly reduced needs for storage, purification and the various energy systems.

Another big issue that came up was "waste streams." When they're not actually sailing, superyachts use engines to drive them through the sea and generators to run everything else. These massive engines discharge nearly all their pollutants into the sea or air, a stream of waste that contributes nothing to the boat and clogs up the atmosphere. As Will Clift recorded: "Yachts use engine-generated electricity to provide thermal

Fulfilling one of the original goals for the creation of *Ethereal*, a voyage into the South Pacific Ocean, Shannon O'Leary Joy gets to talk to whales off the Friendly Islands.

services such as water heating, space heating, and clothes drying. It is far more fuel-efficient to capture, store, and use the waste heat freely available from the engines."

That's where it got really interesting. As I already knew, the U.S. Navy was using electric motors to drive the propellers but the charrette took the technology a step or two further. Why not use the prop as a tool for generating electricity when it's not being employed for its primary purpose? All you had to do was trail it in the water, spinning round and round, when the yacht was under sail, and the batteries would store the resulting energy. The underwater drag created by the turning of the prop, that I had expressed concern about, would be more than compensated for by the extra available energy. "With such a system, a substantial amount of energy can be generated with only a very slight decrease in wind-provided speed, and the energy can be stored and re-used later, often eliminating the need to run the diesel generators," explained Clift.

Basically, all of this meant that *Ethereal*'s propulsion would come from a proposal for three renewable sources – obviously, the sails, but also from solar cells and from wind-turned turbines fixed to the mast. These sources would be boosted by a series of identical, small diesel generators. At the heart of the system lay the lithium-ion batteries, an already available technology that was making rapid advances. But the charrette was looking ahead to the next generation of power in the form of fuel cells producing electricity from stored hydrogen. Bill was very interested in this approach.

We also got a further glimpse into a head-spinning future. One of the participants in the charrette was Janine Benyus, a Rocky Mountain Institute board member and the author of *Biomimicry: Innovation Inspired by Nature*, a groundbreaking book about what the world of design can learn from nature. Her fundamental question was: "How has nature solved our design problem?"

Janine had some formidable backup in the form of Jayden Harman, founder and chief executive of San Raphael, USA-based research and design firm PAX Scientific, specializing in fluid dynamics, and Dr. John Todd, a pioneer in ecological design who had done life-improving work in communities around the world, especially in water and waste projects. The ideas they proposed really got me thinking. How about, for example, an anti-fouling paint that mimics the uneven surface of the lotus leaf to repel the myriad creatures that like to attach themselves to the hull? As Clift pointed out: "This could save significant crew and haul-out time, water, cleaning agents used for daily maintenance, overhaul cost, and marine toxicity." Yes, I thought, and it could also make the yacht slip faster through the water.

Next up, the biomimicry experts wondered, could the sails be configured in some way that would enable them to capture water from moist air, as do the wings of the Namibian desert beetle? Wow! And, a really far out notion, could the vapor-absorbing ability of other desert-dwelling insects be developed into a system that, as Clift put it, "not only passively dries the air for comfort, but also captures and collects pure water?"

The amazing thing was that, based on profound knowledge and experience, the scientists had no doubt that these things would happen, not necessarily in the immediate future, but at some time not too far distant. It was a Jules Verne-like approach and *Ethereal* would become, in Bill's words, a "continuing instrumented laboratory."

Around this period I joined the devil. For the first time in my career I was asked to contribute to the design of a motor yacht – and I willingly accepted. This commission came from John Thomson Jr., an industrialist and pillar of the New York sailing community, and his wife Adrienne, who had owned a sister ship of *Imp* and thoroughly enjoyed the experience of a fast, wet 40-footer, then had a new 47-foot ocean racing yacht built to my design. But now they wanted to go a whole three times bigger and build a 150-foot ocean-going motor yacht, without sails of any kind.

As far as I was concerned, this fitted my evolving design criteria – an ocean-going motor vessel that gave me creative freedom in a new direction.

▲

Under the red Golden Gate Bridge *Thalia* sets her red spinnaker. From San Francisco *Thalia* sailed across the Pacific Ocean to New Zealand.

▲

Marco Polo afloat in Hong Kong
harbor: an inspiring yacht in an
inspiring location – and an inspiring photograph by Neil Rabinowitz.
Next stop anywhere in the world!

▲

I designed the General Arrangement of *Marco Polo* to fulfill my
client's ocean exploring goals.
He invited award-winning KCA
International to detail the look
and feel of the interior. A very
successful design collaboration.

◄

Ocean explorer yachts don't have
to look like commercial vessels.
Building *Marco Polo*'s superstructure
in fiberglass composite materials
allowed me the design freedom
to create aesthetic solutions that
enhanced life aboard.

"In a purely design sense I felt I had something to say. I was convinced that I could use my ocean racing design experience to good purpose and make a worthwhile contribution to the performance of motor yachts."

Some of the purists, including some of my yacht racing friends, thought I'd abandoned my principles, but the truth is that motor yachts were starting to make sense to me, the lifelong sailing fanatic. Like the Thomsons, some of my sailboat clients, having reached a certain age, were beginning to move on to purely engine-powered vessels, and I could see an interesting new line of design work developing. Also, belatedly, I realized that I'd spent my whole career to date catering to just ten percent of the pleasure boat market. Motorboats account for over 90 percent of that market.

In a purely design sense I felt I had something to say. I was convinced that I could use my ocean racing design experience to good purpose and make a worthwhile contribution to the performance of motor yachts. I was not able to approach this new 150-footer with a clean sheet of paper: John and Adrienne asked me to help them with the overall above-the-waterline look of their new yacht. In collaboration with Seattle-based Delta Yachts, who were contracted to build the yacht of composite materials, which in itself was a daring initiative, I worked with the Thomsons and the Delta engineers on the new yacht's exterior styling. Named *Affinity,* her first major voyage took her across the Pacific Ocean to New Zealand. After years of crisscrossing the world's oceans, *Affinity* was sold to the Boeing Corporation and based in the Pacific Northwest.

In the process of working with Delta Yachts on designing *Affinity,* I'd become more aware that most motor yachts spend nearly all their life moored at the dock and are used as glorified beach houses. But that wasn't the case with my clients. Most of them were true adventurers who loved to voyage the world, and none more so than Roland Sturm, a German real estate and hotel developer for whom I'd once designed a 118-foot ketch named *Globana*. Beautifully built by the German shipyard of Abeking & Rasmussen, *Globana* had more than fulfilled Roland's love of worldwide exploration. From her European base he'd taken her just about everywhere including Alaska, British Columbia and California. If not all the oceans, he'd covered many of them. But then he too decided it was time to retire from sailing and go motor yachting, so he asked me to design a 150-foot explorer-type vessel that would carry on where *Globana* had left off, and push into extreme latitudes. He was even thinking of Canada's Hudson Bay, challenging waters for any kind of yacht. Roland already had a name for the yacht, *Marco Polo*. This was my first "clean sheet of paper" motor yacht design opportunity.

Based on my years of ocean crossings and on observing developments with commercial ship design, I was convinced that the way to go for any long-distance explorer-type motor yacht was a single engine linked to one large-diameter propeller. Not only does this more efficient configuration save on building costs, it greatly reduces fuel consumption, which of course has the effect of increasing the vessel's cruising range. This wasn't wild speculation by any means: it was the way that many of the latest commercial vessels were being built.

More radically, because it contradicted the conventional view, I also believed in big rudders. A rudder with a small area might be acceptable for a passage along the coast or on inland waters, but I knew from experience that rudders of large surface area would make *Marco Polo* much easier to control in an ocean storm. The only thing more terrifying than a broach in a sailboat in dangerous conditions is the same thing happening in a motorboat, which doesn't have a deep keel to bring her back upright. I also believed in using skegs, fixed extensions of the hull on which rudders are mounted. This improves the efficiency of a rudder. But it has another significant benefit: skegs like those I was planning for *Marco Polo*'s twin rudders would provide an extra measure of safety because they would protect the rudders from collision with solid objects. If *Marco Polo* were to hit a rock, or a hefty piece of flotsam such as a log or one of the containers that occasionally fall off ships and float dangerously to and fro, the rudders and propeller would probably survive intact.

As an experienced ocean yachtsman, Roland liked the efficiency of the single engine. However, we designed in a safety margin using a special

▲

My clients John and Adrienne Thomson invited me to contribute to the exterior styling of their first big motor yacht, here nearing completion at Delta Yachts in Seattle. Let's paint her green!

▲

A fine model of *Scout* by
Richard Outram: my last
motor yacht design.

bow thruster forward. Powered by its own Caterpillar engine in its self-contained engine room, this German-made Schottel bow thruster could power the motor yacht at a speed of five knots in calm water, in the event of a failure in the main engine's belt-and-braces systems.

But where would *Marco Polo* be built? I fully expected Roland to commission one of the established German shipyards, but after he visited the China-based builder Cheoy Lee at my suggestion, he was sufficiently impressed with their quality and production facilities to hand the job to them.

By any measure *Marco Polo*, my first "clean sheet of paper" motor yacht design, was a roaring success, making several transatlantic crossings. Today, renamed *Dorothea* III under new ownership, she's keeping up the tradition, having traversed the Pacific Ocean to Australia. And so has *Qing*, a sister ship of *Marco Polo* that has cruised through the Panama Canal to the Galapagos Islands, among other exotic anchorages. In the wake of *Affinity, Marco Polo*, and *Qing* I received more commissions for motor yachts, which soon became half of our total design work.

There was one five-star motor yacht commission that slipped through my fingers. I was sailing aboard *Mirabella* with Irish racing yachtsman and property developer Ken Rohan and his wife Brenda, the first people to charter Joe Vittoria's elegant giant for a Caribbean cruise, when I received an email from a high level in the United Arab Emirates. Would I please come to Abu Dhabi to discuss the design of a big motor yacht for the royal family?

"Yes," I replied, "I certainly would."

After a long and wearying series of flights that took me from the nearest local airport to Antigua aboard a single-engine Cessna 172, then to London via British Airways, and finally to Dubai with Emirates, I was picked up by a limousine at the airport. Dog-tired, I was looking forward to an early night so I could present myself sharp and ready to go the next day – but no way. The ruling family's agent was impatiently waiting for me at the hotel, where he informed me Their Highnesses were expecting me. After a quick shower I arrived at the Palace at 11:30 PM, an ungodly hour to do business, and was ushered into a small room where the four ruling brothers were wide awake and eager to discuss yachts. Having been tipped off along the way by the agent that the new yacht must have a capacity for over 50 guests, I had done some quick thinking and presented my concept for a multi-hulled vessel of 250 feet in length with a vast interior and even more vast deck space. You would practically be able to play football and land two choppers on this yacht.

As I explained to Their Highnesses, the multihull design not only made for a lot of free space that they unquestionably needed, but also greatly

"Having delivered my spiel and hardly able to hold my head up, I was allowed to return to the hotel at around 1:30 AM and immediately collapsed into a deep sleep. At 6:30 AM I was rudely awoken by a phone call: it was the agent again, advising me the brothers required my attendance once more to clarify some design points."

reduced underwater resistance because this yacht would have slim, very efficient hulls. As a result, that meant the new royal yacht would need relatively small engines to drive her. It wasn't that small engines would be cheaper to buy and run – I'm sure that didn't worry them in a kingdom awash with crude – but that they would be lighter, thus allowing me to design the world's most efficient royal yacht.

Having delivered my spiel and hardly able to hold my head up, I was allowed to return to the hotel at around 1:30 AM and immediately collapsed into a deep sleep. At 6:30 AM I was rudely awoken by a phone call: it was the agent again, advising me the brothers required my attendance once more to clarify some design points. Apparently, they'd been discussing my design throughout the night. Racing back to the palace, I found this next meeting was held in the presence of the Admiral of the United Arab Emirates Navy, whom I was made to understand would run the project, and I was plied with a whole lot more impressively informed questions.

Not long after the sun had come up, I was thanked for my visit (which I noted lasted a lot less time than the accompanying travel) and told that I could leave.

"There will be no more meetings for now," I was informed. Within hours I was on my way back to Cork via London, my Caribbean cruise cut short.

Regrettably, because I would have enjoyed such an interesting project, the big multihull yacht never happened.

▲

Designed for long-distance ocean voyaging, *Scout* was created for a very experienced client. Built in Turkey by RMK Marine, this yacht has crossed both the Atlantic and Pacific Oceans.

Over the next two years *Ethereal* took shape in the Vollenhove shipyard. Without a doubt it was one of the most challenging and exciting projects the Huisman family had ever dealt with. Sadly, it wasn't Wolter who was guiding it at the end but his highly capable daughter Alice, who had taken over the running of the yard. Wolter had fallen ill and was spending much of the time resting at home near by his shipyard, so I could see him during my visits to this important new project.

As *Ethereal* developed, I could see some of the charrette-sparked ideas turning into reality. The fuel tanks were 30 percent smaller than they would have otherwise been. Water consumption was reduced by nearly half, and so was the use of electricity. Most of the stuff that a standard superyacht uses or produces was also pretty much halved – diesel, trash, even noise.

Regarding just the last, I knew this would be a big hit. There's something magical about being aboard a yacht in a quiet anchorage when you can't hear the generators. The beauty of the quiet anchorage was something Bill and Shannon fully understood. "Nothing beats the motion of a sailboat, the feel of the wind, or the rocking at anchor with the sound of the sea outside," Bill told *Fortune*.

Less had become more.

That was exactly what Bill, Amory Lovins and his colleagues had aimed for, a kind of aesthetic and practical simplicity that reflected the words of the French writer Antoine de Saint-Exupéry when he'd been writing about the shape of an airplane. As Lovins paraphrased it, this ultimate simplicity comes "not when there's nothing left to add, but when there's nothing left to take away." I loved that.

Ethereal was launched in 2009 – the world's first hybrid-powered sailing superyacht – and the Joys set sail on the first of many voyages. Sadly, Wolter never saw his last masterpiece hit the water. One of the hardest-working men I have ever met, and one of the most dedicated and painstaking, he died at the age of 73 before *Ethereal* was finished. Although the Dutch are supposed to be conservative in their attitudes, I'm sure that Wolter, as well as Alice and her team, learned a lot from the charrette. I certainly did.

While we've not yet seen sails that can do what the Namibian beetle can, I wouldn't be at all surprised if it happened one day soon.

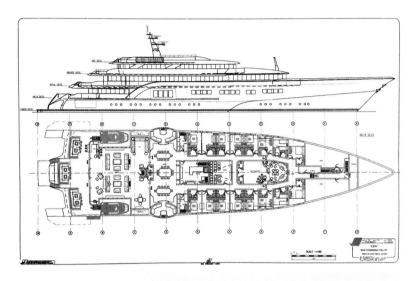

I responded to an inquiry from the royal family in Abu Dhabi for a big yacht. It would need to sleep 50 guests and service people: the owners would arrive by very big helicopters.

I immediately thought the best way to achieve this would be to follow the multihull concept of the Incat vessels built in Hobart, Tasmania. Big deck and internal volume areas, and a very efficient, easily-driven, multihull design.

This was one of the most interesting design projects I have been involved with. This yacht has not been built, but I believe this multihull design approach has many benefits for the recent trend towards very big private motor yachts – especially if fast cruising is a priority.

EPILOGUE

Seat of the pants

WITH CATHERINE WALSH, whom I met in Kinsale via an introduction from Johnny Mac's wife Diana – ironically considering the McWilliams had originally invited me to Ireland all those years ago – I moved to Vancouver. I decided I needed a change of location. Catherine had joined me in Kinsale for ten years and wanted to return to Canada. I was ready for a change. Back to the Pacific, but only just back. On the edge of the Pacific Ocean, so to speak. Following the emotional and physical upheaval of leaving Ireland after more than 40 years with all the accumulated personal effects, mostly papers, drawings and books, it was a relief to finally get settled in Canada. My new office overlooked Coal Harbour, the downtown marina near Vancouver's main commercial port: through the window I had a clear view of boats moored at the Royal Vancouver Yacht Club marina, and beyond, of the snow-capped peaks of Cypress Mountain. It's a dramatic but calming location, and I was looking forward to another phase of my life.

One morning I was working on the design of a new motor yacht for a Canadian client when I suddenly felt lightheaded and faint, almost as though I was going to pass out. I slid out of my chair and lay down with my head on the carpet, hoping this might provide some relief. It had worked before when, as a kid, I used to swoon at the sight of blood or a hypodermic needle.

I'd been pretty much headache-free for years, hangovers excepted. However, in my late fifties my blood pressure started creeping up and the doctors had put me on low-level medication when, unexpectedly, at the age of 62 I had a succession of migraines for a few months. My mother having suffered from them, I put this down to hereditary factors and I didn't worry too much, unpleasant though they were.

Then one day a blinding headache hit me when I was in London. Catherine and I were making our way with friends to the Royal Albert Hall for a concert by Eric Clapton, one of my favorite musicians, when the pain became so severe that I had to abandon the concert, to my extreme disappointment. We took a taxi back to the Royal Thames Yacht Club in nearby Knightsbridge, where we often stayed when in London. By the time we arrived there I couldn't see straight, and I began to wonder whether this marked the onset of something more serious.

A series of visits to specialists ensued. I saw top medics in London and Cork, and had various MRI scans, all while suffering frequent headaches. To my relief and Catherine's the results didn't raise any red flags, and after a few weeks the headaches gradually disappeared all by themselves.

But now, in Vancouver, they'd come back with a vengeance.

I lay on the office floor for a while – I can't remember exactly how long – but eventually I realized it wasn't working. Soon the office was swirling around me. This is different, I thought, I need help.

David Campbell, a successful yacht broker, was downstairs in the Freedom Marine office. As loudly as I could, making my head pound even more, I called out, "David, I'm in trouble." In an instant David leaped into action, calling the paramedics and Catherine in that order. Within less than ten minutes I found myself being carried outside to an ambulance just as Catherine, in a shocked state, arrived to join me. Sirens screaming, lights flashing, we were transported to the emergency ward of Vancouver General Hospital.

"You're bleeding in the cerebral cavity," the specialist told me.

Oh, great! I didn't know exactly what it meant but it sounded serious.

The next few days are engrained on my memory. For one of the few times in my life, I was completely helpless. I'd completely lost my sense of balance and couldn't sit up, let alone get out of bed. Every time I turned over, or even moved my head from side to side, I started to vomit violently. The sensation was that of a crippling bout of seasickness combined with being dead drunk, sensations with which I'm very familiar. Had to keep my sense of humor.

As I lay there, all I could draw on was my years of meditation practice, so I forced myself to lie quietly in bed and focus on my breathing. I tried to tune out all the disturbing noise of the hospital – the groans of the other patients, the hiss and hum of the machines, the chatter of the nurses and attendants. I thanked my lucky stars I'd learned how to do this process at various retreats. Otherwise, I think I might have gone crazy.

Towards the end of the week I began to improve slightly and I was able to get to the toilet, albeit courtesy of the nurses' supporting shoulders. As my brain began to clear, I reflected on presentations I had often given to various Chambers of Commerce, yacht clubs and other organizations around the world. I'd even made presentations at the House of Commons in London, the New York Yacht Club in Manhattan and NASA's own sailing club in South San Francisco. After I spend some time on these occasions reflecting on my yachting experiences, my design work and my life in general, I usually end up saying something personal that goes more or less along these lines: "I'm confident that on my deathbed I won't have any regrets. My life has been bigger than anything I could have possibly dreamed about." And I dreamed big. Here in hospital, with doctors telling me I'd had a full-blown stroke, and for good measure, that I could have another one within a year, I had an opportunity to reflect on the validity of my deathbed views. I clearly remember lying between the sheets and asking myself, "OK, Ron, how do you feel about this now? Is it still true you'll have no regrets?"

The answer came with astonishing clarity. "Yes," I told myself. "It's true. I'm OK with it." I thought about people close to me who'd died. There were my parents of course, Phil and Gwen, who'd done so much for me. Hugh Coveney who had brought me to Ireland so long ago. Brilliant, inventive Lars Bergstrom who had been killed in a glider crash. Rob James, almost like a brother to me, who had drowned in the cold sea. Of course, most of the people who'd crossed my path were still alive and well. Ever the athlete, Jim Kilroy had turned a hale 90 years old.

And the smart-as-paint Sandy Stosz who had kept an eye on me on the U.S. Coast Guard's square-rigger, *Eagle,* all those years ago was now Rear Admiral Sandra Stosz, one of the top brass in one of the world's most admired nautical organizations, based in Washington D.C. Not long before, I'd completed another voyage on the *Eagle* at her invitation, sailing from Portland, Maine, to Newport, Rhode Island via Cape Cod and the entrance to New York Harbor with a young cadet crew, many of them around the same age as Sandy when I'd taken the ship from Cork to Lisbon. Philip was selling boats in New Zealand and Butch now was happily running a classic boat yard in France. So, I reflected, most of the people I knew were doing OK.

As I lay there, trying to shut out the sounds of illness, flashbacks entered my mind. I remembered the beach at Torbay with all the kids rigging

▲

With Catherine's encouragement I agreed to have a serious 60th birthday party, and with military precision she set the wheels in motion. I created a list of friends to invite, never thinking many would attend. We chose to do it in May so the weather would be more conducive than on my actual birthday in January. Everyone invited said yes and came to Ireland! The Old Head Golf Links, not far from my Kinsale design studio, are a spectacular, world class location and everyone had a wonderful time. A once-in-a-lifetime and totally memorable birthday celebration.
L TO R: my daughters Nicola, Aisli, Kelly and Benna.

Following the success of the Perini Navi 56-meter sailing yachts – 10 of these Perini/Ron Holland Design collaborations were launched – we developed a new 60-meter design, the first launched being *Seahawk*. This, the second, *Perseus^3*, was developed for higher sailing performance at the request of Mark Byrne, her experienced owner. I designed a single-mast rig with a long bowsprit to maximize her downwind performance, and included twin rudders, a first design feature for a Perini Navi sailing yacht.

▲

I was invited to make a presentation at the 2017 Australian Wooden Boat Festival in Hobart, and Charlie Bishop met me with a welcoming sign. I was on the same flight as the Beach Boys from California: they approached Charlie to comment about her sign, and asked her about the yacht on display. They normally expect airport arrival signs to be for the Beach Boys!

their boats. I saw myself with Brian Holgate on *Happy Daze*. I heard people talking about the Sydney Hobart Race. I sat in the Auckland Town Hall with Mum, listening to the Modern Jazz Quartet. The years passing, I was attending rock concerts in the Haight-Ashbury district. I could still picture Jimi Hendrix playing one of his last gigs at the Berkeley Community Centre… one by one, the events of my life vividly returned to me.

Yet even though I was happy enough with what I'd achieved, that didn't mean I wanted to die. Not just yet, thank you!

For a start, I had my daughters and a growing number of grandkids to live for. Three of my four daughters, Kelly, Nikki and Aisli, came to visit me in Vancouver General, the first two from Los Angeles and the third all the way from Australia. They probably thought it would be the last time they would see their father alive.

Then, to my joy, after twelve days I was allowed to go home. Catherine bundled me into a taxi and we headed back to our apartment overlooking English Bay and Stanley Park. Sitting in the back seat, I was aghast at the speed of the taxi and the noise of the traffic flying by. Everything was hurtling past. Why was everybody in such a hurry? This was ridiculous!

Relieved to get back home, I began to relax. Suddenly, as I sat in an armchair looking out over English Bay and the mountains, another revelation dawned. I'm not in a hurry anymore!

After a lifetime of hurtling around the world in aircraft and yachts, steering sailboats through storms, and squeezing in those extra meetings, I began to realize I'd changed. If I never got on another plane, or tried to fit in a couple more meetings, I wouldn't complain. All my scheduled visits to shipyards, boat shows and client meetings were canceled. None of them seemed urgent to me anymore.

I decided to take time for some self-reflection and the revelations came thick and fast. I'd never thought of myself as having a philosophical bent, but my thoughts surprised me. If I've done all I want in life, what am I going to do now? I asked myself. If the doctors are wrong and I live longer than a year, what's left for me?

The answer was a perverse one – If the doctors' predictions are right, another stroke within a year, what's the point of getting out of bed? While I thought about these questions, I experienced a bout of mild depression. I couldn't see the point of starting something that I couldn't finish.

Organized by a concerned Catherine, my post-stroke regime was highly detailed. I took pills, I attended speech therapy lessons (I'd been slurring my words), I received physiotherapy and kinesiology treatment to get the muscles moving again.

As my thoughts began to take a more concrete form, the way forward slowly became clearer. This all started, I reflected, because I loved sailing and drawing yachts. Then it became a serious business with ever-mounting pressures and imperatives, posing demands and stress that I never really understood; partly because I prided myself on being able to handle them with ease, so I ignored them.

Bit by bit, I thought about the next phase of my life. During my recovery period, I thought, Why don't I go back to the work I love, the way it all began?

One day, a year after the stroke, it suddenly seemed so simple, and I finally made up my mind. I had closed down Ron Holland Design before leaving Kinsale, while handing some aspects of current projects to my colleagues but still maintaining those with existing clients who had become friends. I decided I would do it differently. I would go sailing again and racing for fun. It would be more like the good old days, designing boats for mates. Suddenly I felt a weight fall from my shoulders, a weight I had not realized was there. No wonder I had a stroke! I told myself. That was a stressful life.

Thinking it through further, I would do other things with my life, fulfilling long-buried desires. I would read more. I would teach. I would take piano lessons, as I had in my teens with my mother's encouragement. I would do more drumming, which would also have the bonus of restoring some of the dexterity in my left hand.

In short, I would start a new life in Vancouver – and I did.

In mid-2016, four years after the stroke, I stepped aboard *M5*, one of my most headlined designs, the former *Mirabella V*, in the safe Pacific anchorage of Espiritu Santo, biggest of the Vanuatu islands. We were waiting impatiently for Cyclone Nelson to stop wreaking havoc on the nearby Fiji islands that I had come to love. I was revisiting my old sailing playground of the South Pacific which I had first seen when I was still a teenager, and revisited a few years earlier aboard my *Golden Opus*. We were island-hopping towards the active volcano on Tana Island that had scared the life out of me and my girls one evening during our visit to the edge of the crater, when it sounded like the volcano was about to blow! As soon as the cyclone moved on, we planned to sail across the Western Pacific to my old hometown of Auckland.

During the crossing, with time on my hands, I could reflect on how much things had changed during my 50 years of Pacific sailing. In the old days we might have unknowingly sailed into 200-mph winds and yacht-breaking seas, but now we could accurately track the path of the cyclone

▲

I'm aboard *Wavelength* for the St. Barths Bucket. Crew member Emily Leeming shows off her cap which I've modified with my signature after crossing the finish line.

▲

The 2017 6-Meter world championship was held in Vancouver, so I decided to enter. I never imagined I would be racing a world championship at 70 years of age. Just keep saying yes.

in real time on our electronics. An extensive but highly concentrated depression, Cyclone Nelson was raging right across our rhumbline, the yacht's direct route to Auckland.

After four days of destruction, Nelson finally weakened and drifted off towards the Queensland coast. "We're safe to go," skipper Don Andersen announced. And so we threw off the mooring lines and headed south for New Zealand.

I had made a good recovery from the stroke, and I jumped at the chance to sail aboard my biggest design. As *M5*, the former *Mirabella V* had undergone an extensive redesign, and had been stretched in length and fitted with new engines and a new interior.

Her new American owner, Rod Lewis, has made his money in oil and gas. Low-key in manner, Rod is a man who believes wealth is to be enjoyed rather than hoarded. As well as owning *M5*, he's a very experienced pilot who owns and flies a fleet of aircraft including his very own bomber, a reconditioned B25 Mitchell, and he likes nothing better than to take people up in it so they can experience what flying in World War II was like. A year earlier at the St. Barths Bucket, the annual premier gathering of big sailing yachts, he'd invited me to join him on the B25. Although I was flying a lot less, as I'd also promised myself, this was different and I felt I couldn't turn the offer down.

I was installed in a simple seat behind Rod, who was at the controls with another B25-trained pilot alongside. There was a thunderous roar as the twin engines burst into life – the bomber has rudimentary insulation, well – none – to protect the eardrums, just like during the war. He finished his checks, taxied down the runway and pushed the power control fully forward. He pulled back the control stick, and the massive aircraft rumbled down the tarmac and slowly lifted into the air. Hardly were we aloft when two more of Rod Lewis's aircraft legends, Tiger Cats, joined us, so close that I could practically wave at their pilots.

In the pre-flight safety briefing Rod had explained that, if I wanted, I could move after takeoff into the forward gun turret where I would get a clear view of the yachts racing below us. The gun turret! Great!

I was strapped in tight, but curiosity got the better of me so I unbuckled my safety belt, slipped down below the cockpit and crawled forward into the narrow opening of the turret. It was all glass with a clear view all around and below. Scary. Later I moved into the upper gun turret with my head and shoulders sticking above the fuselage protected by the Perspex dome. It struck me as the most vulnerable place anybody could imagine. With the hammering of the engines filling my ears, I thought about those young pilots, many hardly into their twenties, flying combat missions over Germany in the Second World War, while the gunners maintained a lookout for fighter planes intent on blowing them out of the sky. What courage!

I was still adjusting to what seemed a precarious position when, without warning, Rod put down the nose and dived towards the notoriously tricky St. Barths runway. I hung on grimly as the ground approached at high speed. Still Rod held the dive until, at what seemed like the last minute, he flattened out the trajectory and did a low-level pass of the short runway and the Bay of St. Jean, before pulling the monster into a steep left bank climb that cleared the beach. I suddenly realized I was yelling my head off.

Rod loves the sea as much as he does the sky, and he spends as much time as he can on his fishing boats and on *M5*, sailing her to remote Pacific island anchorages and dropping anchor. Lying a thousand miles east of the tip of Northern Australia, Espiritu Santo certainly qualifies as remote. For a superyacht like *M5* though, distance isn't a problem.

I recalled the first time I sailed on the southern edge of the Pacific, aboard *Aloha* in 1962, when it was considered an achievement to clock a hundred miles in one day. 40 years later, on a good day my *Golden Opus* could cover over 200 miles, a speed of around nine nautical miles an hour. By comparison, *M5* can not only motor across the ocean at 13 to 14 knots if the wind drops and the skipper chooses to switch on the Caterpillar engines, on a good sailing day she can burn up the ocean under sail alone at over 15 knots, and I have been sailing aboard her at 19 knots. How much faster can this yacht go? I told Rod one day he will see *M5* sail at over 20 knots. No problem!

During the last few years, back in Auckland, I'd delivered a lecture to the yacht engineering students on Master of Engineering courses at the University of Auckland, and I liked to tell them that, really, sailboats still aren't that fast. Centuries ago, while Captain Cook was working his way at a painfully slow five or six knots around the Pacific in an old coal barque, the Pacific Island natives were hurtling along at four times that pace in outrigger sailing canoes, skillfully navigating from island to island. And now just recently we've had America's Cup catamarans literally flying on foils at speeds up to 40 knots. But these speed increases don't match car or aircraft performance development.

Fortunately, today there's a decent breeze and the crew decide to break out some of the sails. Soon *M5* is motor-sailing along at 14 knots, close to 340 miles a day. At this rate we'll be off North Cape, the landfall for New Zealand, in five days.

▲

H.M. King Juan Carlos is happy: he won his division in the 2017 International Six Meter Class World Championship. We gained second place in our division.

I'm up before dawn, feeling the wind on my face. I don't want to miss a minute of the experience. It's 20 years since I sailed out of sight of land in the Pacific. Far too long for my liking. We pass the latitude of North Cape and raise Cape Brett lighthouse, the entrance to the beautiful Bay of Islands, on our starboard beam. Next morning, after swooping down the North Island coast, we reach the Hauraki Gulf.

The recollections are starting to pile up. We pass Torbay where my old sailing club is still active and where I first jumped aboard Brian Holgate's *Happy Daze*, then we pass Browns Bay where I did my boatbuilding apprenticeship at the Keith Atkinson yard. Off Rangitoto Island we are met by the Auckland Harbour pilot boat at pretty much the same spot where I was becalmed in my 10-foot Flying Ant, *Tempo*, nearly 60 years earlier; then finally we are past North Head and into Auckland Harbour.

After the pilot steps back aboard the pilot boat, *M5* ties up at the Westhaven Silo dock where I shipped aboard little *Aloha* so many years ago and in a state of high excitement began my first ocean crossing to Lord Howe Island and Sydney.

Before I disembark *M5*, her vast and graceful hull dwarfing all the other yachts tied up at the dock, her mast towering above the nearby office blocks, I spend some time alone, standing on her foredeck just thinking about things.

The Masters of Engineering students at the University of Auckland often ask me, "How did you do it?" meaning how did I make an international career in yacht design from what wasn't exactly the most auspicious of beginnings. I always say something like, "Say yes to every opportunity that comes your way. And the opportunities are always coming. Look out for them. Believe in yourself. Don't let others tell you what to do because nobody can know you like you do."

"Be interested in everything. Just keep saying yes and never stop learning."

And, looking back, I think that's all it is really. You may be right; you may be wrong. But in the long run it's best to do it your way. Have a go and learn from it.

I believe that's how I went from *Eygthene* to *M5*. From Torbay Beach to dinner with British Prime Minister Edward Heath at the Savoy Hotel in London.

CREDITS

Every reasonable effort has been made to trace and contact all holders of copyright and to credit sources correctly. In the event of omission or error Ron Holland Design should be notified so that a full acknowledgment may be made in future editions.

Photography contributors

Anand, Paal: 319
Auckland Star: 140
Barker, David: 303
Barker, David (painting): 266, 271
Beken of Cowes: 110, 111, 170, 207
Bonnamy, Frank: 320
Bradley, Andrew: 126, 236, 237, 287, 288, 298
Copyright: Dean and Chapter of Westminster, 331
Cork Examiner: 151, 155
Discovery Yachts: 334
Dosil, Roberto: 76, 229
Enersen, Dick: 369
Forster, Daniel: 45, 100, 101, 106, 133, 147, 164, 171, 202
Fortune Magazine: 349
Gurney, Guy: 74-75, 132, 137, 152, 157, 175, 177, 188-189, 197, 211, 214, 220, 232-233, 252, 257, 259, 276a, 277, 283a, 318, 328a, 344, 382
Hames, Holly: 119
Hamlet, Leon: 59
Holland, Laurel: 81
Holland, Ron: 5, 8, 9, 30, 33, 42, 53, 62, 64, 65, 66, 92, 93, 115, 128, 167, 169, 190, 195, 219, 225, 279, 283B, 304A, 304B, 312, 322, 328, 329, 333, 341, 346, 350, 354, 359, 373, 335, 336

Horton, John (painting): 230
Johnson, Paul: 317
Jolley, Sheena: 210
Jornstedt, Bengt: 83, 85
Joy, Bill: 353
Kennedy, Kathy: 337
Levitt, Michael: 192, 193
Lusher, Kat: 313, 375, 377
Meyer, Elizabeth: 250
Outram, Richard: 360
Pace, Franco: 315, 342, 343
Rabinowitz, Neil: 0, 1, 311, 355, 356, 357, 364, 365, 374, 370, 371
Raycroft, Jim: 362
Ron Holland Design: 363
Sundelin, Peter: 265
Tomlinson, Rick: 242
Uhl, Phil: 268
VT: 321
Walsh, Catherine: Foreword, 345, 351
Walsh, Roger: 263A, 263B
Wellman, Ko: 253
Wilkins, Ivor: 299, 347
Wright, Andrew: Title page
Yachts and Yachting: 159

Copyright © 2018 Ron Holland

Published by
Ron Holland Design Canada Inc.
info@ronhollanddesign.com

All rights reserved. No part of this book may be stored in a retrieval system, reproduced or transmitted in any form or by any means, without written permission from the author. Critics and reviewers may quote brief passages in connection with a review or critical article in any media.

Distributed in the USA by:
Cardinal Publishers Group
2402 North Shadeland Av., Suite A
Indianapolis, IN, 46219
Customer Service:
800–296–0481
customerservice@cardinalpub.com
cardinalpub.com

For individual copy orders, bulk orders, or to request a review copy, outside of the USA, please contact:
Ron Holland Design
216 – 1650 Duranleau Street
Vancouver, BC, Canada, V6H 3S4
+1 604–566–9936
info@ronhollanddesign.com
alltheoceansbook.com

ISBN 978-1-7750968-0-1
First edition / Second printing

Gleam sailing downwind under full sail during the first St. Barths Bucket in 1995.

This book was inspired by
Selwyn Parker

Recollection & story:
Ron Holland

Book concept & text design by:
Roberto Dosil

Assistant to Ron Holland:
Holly Hames

Project coordinator:
Catherine Walsh

Edited by:
Guy Gurney, Senior editor
Jane Kristinsson, Laurie Ann Smith, Dick Enersen, Catherine Walsh, and **Naomi Pauls**

Indexed by:
Naomi Pauls

Cover designed by:
Nevil Swinchatt
www.nevils.co.uk

Printing & binding by:
C&C Offset, China

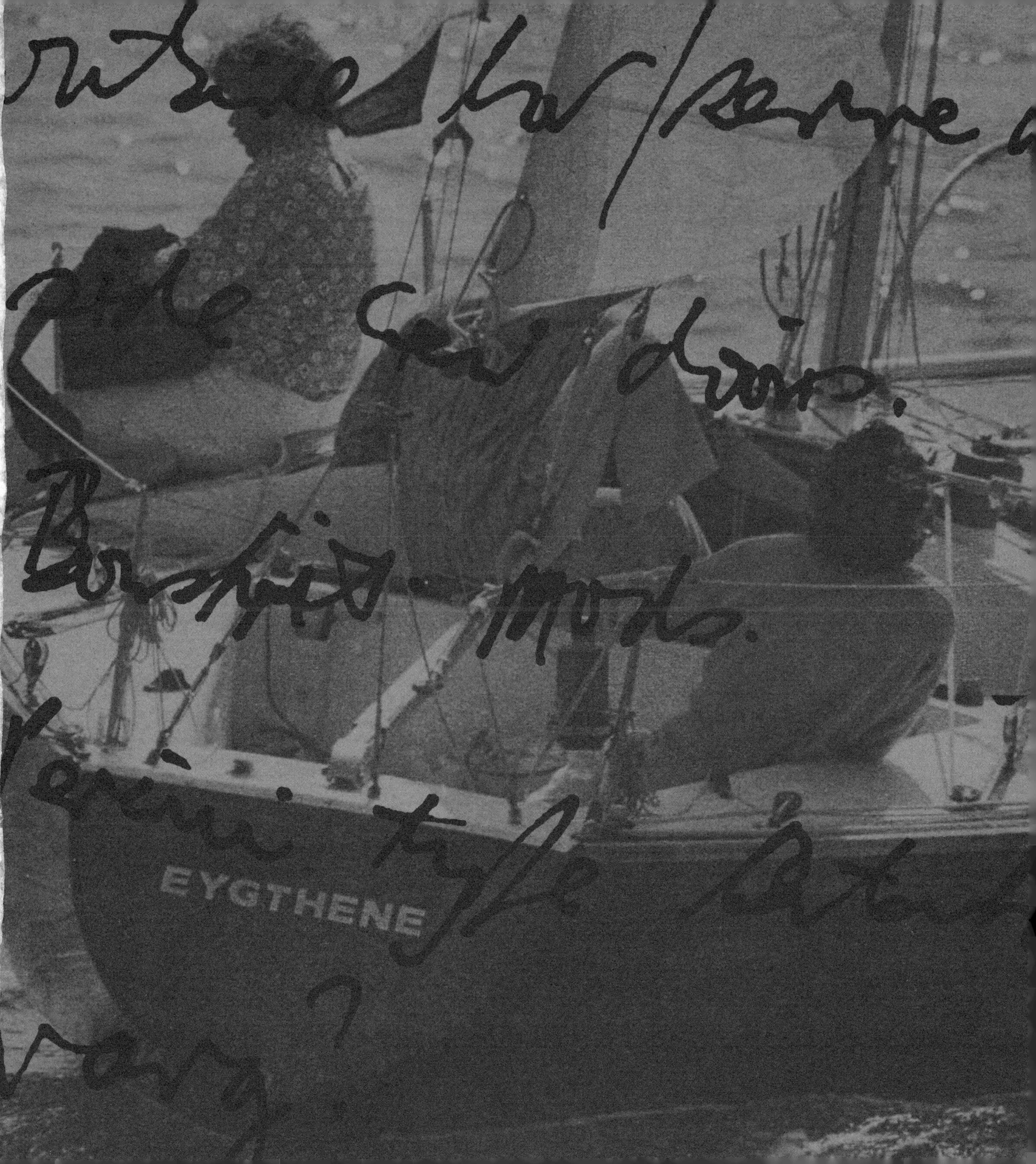
EYGTHENE

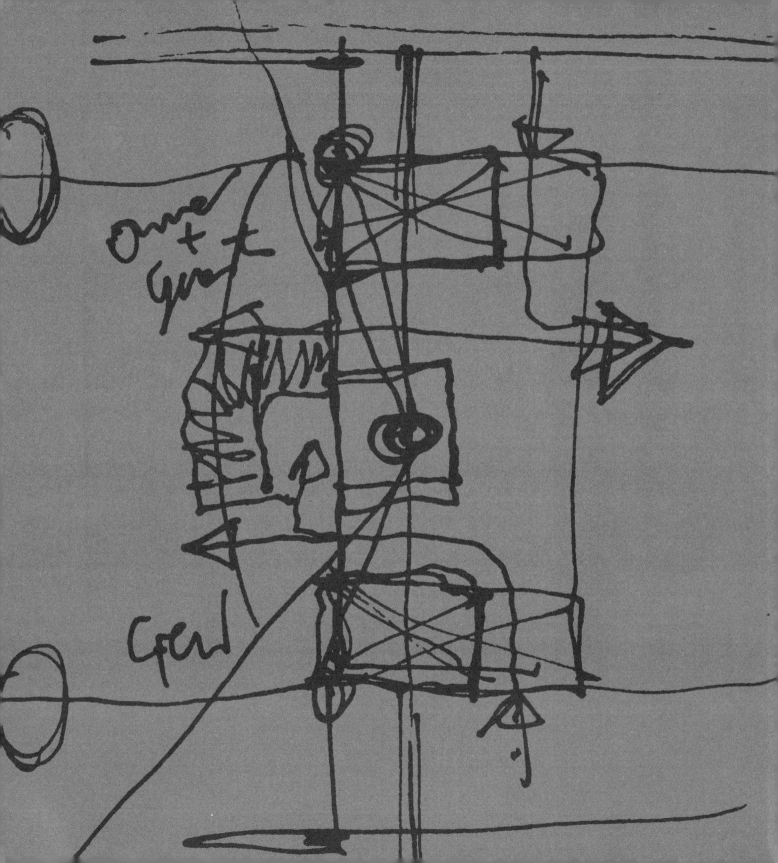